Essentials of
CAS2 Assessment

Essentials of Psychological Assessment Series

Series Editors, Alan S. Kaufman and Nadeen L. Kaufman

Essentials of 16PF® Assessment by Heather E. P. Cattell and James M. Schuerger

Essentials of ADHD Assessment for Children and Adolescents by Elizabeth P. Sparrow and Drew Erhardt

Essentials of Assessing, Preventing, and Overcoming Reading Difficulties by David A. Kilpatrick

Essentials of Assessment Report Writing by Elizabeth O. Lichtenberger, Nancy Mather, Nadeen L. Kaufman, and Alan S. Kaufman

Essentials of Assessment with Brief Intelligence Tests by Susan R. Homack and Cecil R. Reynolds

Essentials of Autism Spectrum Disorders Evaluation and Assessment by Celine A. Saulnier and Pamela E. Ventola

Essentials of Bayley Scales of Infant Development-II Assessment by Maureen M. Black and Kathleen Matula

Essentials of Behavioral Assessment by Michael C. Ramsay, Cecil R. Reynolds, and R. W. Kamphaus

Essentials of Career Interest Assessment by Jeffrey P. Prince and Lisa J. Heiser

Essentials of CAS Assessment by Jack A. Naglieri

Essentials of CAS2 Assessment by Jack A. Naglieri and Tulio M. Otero

Essentials of Child and Adolescent Psychopathology, Second Edition by Linda Wilmshurst

Essentials of Cognitive Assessment with KAIT and Other Kaufman Measures by Elizabeth O. Lichtenberger, Debra Y. Broadbooks, and Alan S. Kaufman

Essentials of Conners Behavior Assessments™ by Elizabeth P. Sparrow

Essentials of Creativity Assessment by James C. Kaufman, Jonathan A. Plucker, and John Baer

Essentials of Cross-Battery Assessment, Third Edition by Dawn P. Flanagan, Samuel O. Ortiz, and Vincent C. Alfonso

Essentials of DAS-II® Assessment by Ron Dumont, John O. Willis, and Colin D. Elliot

Essentials of Dyslexia Assessment and Intervention by Nancy Mather and Barbara J. Wendling

Essentials of Evidence-Based Academic Interventions by Barbara J. Wendling and Nancy Mather

Essentials of Executive Functions Assessment by George McCloskey and Lisa A. Perkins

Essentials of Forensic Psychological Assessment, Second Edition by Marc J. Ackerman

Essentials of Gifted Assessment by Steven I. Pfeiffer

Essentials of IDEA for Assessment Professionals by Guy McBride, Ron Dumont, and John O. Willis

Essentials of Individual Achievement Assessment by Douglas K. Smith

Essentials of Intellectual Disability Assessment and Identification Alan W. Brue and Linda Wilmshurst

Essentials of KABC-II Assessment by Alan S. Kaufman, Elizabeth O. Lichtenberger, Elaine Fletcher-Janzen, and Nadeen L. Kaufman

Essentials of KTEA™-3 and WIAT®-III Assessment by Kristina C. Breaux and Elizabeth O. Lichtenberger

Essentials of MCMI®-IV Assessment by Seth D. Grossman and Blaise Amendolace

Essentials of Millon™ Inventories Assessment, Third Edition by Stephen Strack

Essentials of MMPI-A™ Assessment by Robert P. Archer and Radhika Krishnamurthy

Essentials of MMPI-2® Assessment, Second Edition by David S. Nichols

Essentials of Myers-Briggs Type Indicator® Assessment, Second Edition by Naomi L. Quenk

Essentials of NEPSY®-II Assessment by Sally L. Kemp and Marit Korkman

Essentials of Neuropsychological Assessment, Second Edition by Nancy Hebben and William Milberg

Essentials of Nonverbal Assessment by Steve McCallum, Bruce Bracken, and John Wasserman

Essentials of PAI® Assessment by Leslie C. Morey

Essentials of Planning, Selecting, and Tailoring Interventions for Unique Learners by Jennifer T. Mascolo, Vincent C. Alfonso, and Dawn P. Flanagan

Essentials of Processing Assessment, Second Edition by Milton J. Dehn

Essentials of Psychological Testing, Second Edition by Susana Urbina

Essentials of Response to Intervention by Amanda M. VanDerHeyden and Matthew K. Burns

Essentials of Rorschach® Assessment by Tara Rose, Michael P. Maloney, and Nancy Kaser-Boyd

Essentials of Rorschach Assessment: Comprehensive System and R-PAS by Jessica R. Gurley

Essentials of School Neuropsychological Assessment, Second Edition by Daniel C. Miller

Essentials

of CAS2 Assessment

Jack A. Naglieri, PhD
Tulio M. Otero, PhD

WILEY

Library of Congress Cataloging-in-Publication Data is Available

9781118589274 (Paperback)
9781118705384 (ePDF)
9781118876640 (epub)

Cover design: Wiley
Cover image: © Greg Kuchik/Getty Images

Printed in the United States of America

FIRST EDITION

PB Printing   10 9 8 7 6 5 4 3 2 1

I would like to dedicate this book to my wife, Kathleen Kryza, who has greatly helped me take the PASS theory to teachers in a way I could never have achieved on my own. With much appreciation and love. I also dedicate this book to my friend and coauthor of the CAS and CAS2, J. P. Das. His contributions over these 30-plus years have had and continue to have a significant impact on the tests we have published and the many children who have been assessed. A final dedication to my parents and grandparents, especially my mother, who taught me the value of persistence and frequently reminded me that "you can be anything you want if you try hard enough."
—*J. A. N.*

There are several people I wish to dedicate this book to. First of all, my sincerest gratitude goes to my good friend and colleague Jack Naglieri for his friendship, continued encouragement, professional mentorship, and trust in my understanding of PASS theory as measured by the CAS2 and how to demonstrate its relevance in the trenches of clinical practice. To my friend and colleague Mary Moreno from the University of Puerto Rico, who throughout the years has worked closely with me in providing a variety of workshops on developing interventions based on PASS and demonstrating the use of the CAS and CAS2 with Hispanic/Latino populations. Mary Moreno, along with many of our colleagues and students, was instrumental in the development of the CAS2, Spanish Edition. To my wife, Bernadette, who understood the importance of this project and the time commitments it required. Her loving support helped me to remain on task in spite of our multiple family and social commitments and my tendency to become easily distracted. To my sons, Tulio and Willy, who even though they are adults, I feel the need to be a good example and a source of pride for them. Last, to my mother, who by example showed us never take no for an answer, to persevere patiently even when you think you can't anymore, and when you fall do your best to minimize any damage.
—*T. M. O.*

Never tell people how to do things. Tell them what to do and they will surprise you with their ingenuity.
—*George S. Patton*

CONTENTS

SERIES PREFACE

In the *Essentials of Psychological Assessment* series, we have attempted to provide the reader with books that will deliver key practical information in the most efficient and accessible style. Many books in the series feature specific instruments in a variety of domains, such as cognition, personality, education, and neuropsychology. Other books, like *Essentials of KABC-II Assessment* focus on crucial topics for professionals who conduct assessments—topics such as specific reading disabilities, evidence-based interventions, or ADHD assessment. For the experienced professional, books in the series offer a concise yet thorough review of a test instrument or a specific area of expertise, including numerous tips for best practices. Students can turn to series books for a clear and concise overview of the important assessment tools, and key topics, in which they must become proficient to practice skillfully, efficiently, and ethically in their chosen fields.

Wherever feasible, visual cues highlighting key points are utilized alongside systematic, step-by-step guidelines. Chapters are focused and succinct. Topics are organized for an easy understanding of the essential material related to a particular test or topic. Theory and research are continually woven into the fabric of each book, but always to enhance the practical application of the material, rather than to sidetrack or overwhelm readers. With this series, we aim to challenge and assist readers interested in psychological assessment to aspire to the highest level of competency by arming them with the tools they need for knowledgeable, informed practice. We have long been advocates of "intelligent" testing—the notion that numbers are meaningless unless they are brought to life by the clinical acumen and expertise of examiners. Assessment must be used to make a difference in the child's or adult's life, or why bother to test? All books in the series—whether devoted to specific tests or general topics—are consistent with this credo. We want this series to help our readers, novice and veteran alike, to benefit from the intelligent assessment approaches of the authors of each book.

We are delighted to include *Essentials of the CAS2* in our series. This book offers an innovative approach to understanding intelligence as a set of neurocognitive processes. The authors offer a succinct overview of the CAS2 suite of tests, administration and scoring guidelines, its use with Hispanic/Latino English Language Learners and the development of interventions based on PASS theory. The CAS2 is a valuable tool in the detection of specific learning disabilities, ADHD, TBI, intellectual disability, giftedness, and nondiscriminatory assessment of diverse populations.

Alan S. Kaufman, PhD, and Nadeen L. Kaufman, EdD, Series Editors
Yale University School of Medicine

PREFACE

I n a 2015 publication entitled, "One Hundred years of intelligence testing: Moving from traditional IQ to second-generation intelligence tests" (Naglieri, 2015), I suggested that it is time for the field of psychology to embrace a revolutionary step in the assessment of intelligence. This book is designed to help professionals understand *why* a substantially different approach to defining and measuring ability is so desperately needed and *how we can* achieve this goal. To illustrate the magnitude of the need we remind the reader that all traditional IQ tests with verbal, quantitative, and nonverbal content are based on the US Army and Beta Tests (Yoakum & Yerkes, 1920) which will be 100 years old in 2017! Cosmetic modifications, extraordinary efforts on the part of the publisher to modernize the test, and extensive methods to reinterpret subtests according to contemporary ideas of intelligence, do not change the fact that the "new" Wechsler (now in its fifth edition) is an antique.

Traditional IQ tests which were originally devised to "aid in segregating and eliminating the mentally incompetent, classify men according to their mental ability, and assist in selecting competent men for responsible positions" (Yoakum, 1921, p. 19) are insufficient for the demands of today for several reasons. First, these tests were not built on any theory of intelligence which is critical for test development and puts undue responsibility on the user to determine what the scores mean. Second, the use of verbal and quantitative tests as measures of *ability* is hard to justify because the test questions are often virtually indistinguishable from questions on tests of *achievement*. Third, the fact that these IQ tests demand knowledge of English creates considerable problems for the assessment of those with limited familiarity with English. Fourth, traditional IQ tests also are ineffective for non-discriminatory assessment and yield inaccurately large racial and ethnic differences. Fifth, these tests have failed to yield profiles for students with specific kinds of learning problems. Finally, IQ test scores continue to have no relevance to instruction. (The evidence for all these limitations is provided in

Chapter 1) For years, critics of IQ tests have noted these limitations and argued that measures of intelligence should not be used at all.

Rather than eliminating tests of intelligence in this book we advocate for a revolutionary step in how to conceptualize and measure human cognitive functioning. We will describe an approach that works *because* it departs considerably from traditional IQ, *and* rather than rely on a 100-year-old concepts, we take a brain-based approach to defining and measuring essential neurocognitive abilities.

Our neurocognitive approach begins with a theory called PASS, which stands for the following basic psychological processes: Planning, Attention, Simultaneous, and Successive (Chapters 1 & 2). These constructs were described by A. R. Luria and have been widely studied, especially within the field of neuropsychology. Instead of building upon the US Army Mental Tests, our conceptualization of intelligence is based on Luria's understanding of actual brain function. In this book, we will clearly define this four-dimensional theory and how it has been operationalized in the CAS2. We will also address the administration and scoring of the test, a theory based interpretation method, how to use the PASS scores for assessment of individuals with various kinds of learning problems, and finally how to build or select interventions based on a student's PASS profile (Chapter 7).

Having a theory of human cognitive processes provides a tremendous advantage over traditional IQ. First, starting with a well-grounded theory provides a clear vision of what needs to be measured. In our case, this means the four PASS constructs, which are easy to describe. Importantly, the definitions guided the development of subtests included in the first and second editions of the Cognitive Assessment System (see Chapters 5 & 6). This means that practitioners do *not* have the responsibility of figuring out what the test scores mean nor do they have to choose from a list of possible abilities measured by every subtest. The responsibility of the test author is to describe and validate what the test scores measure, not the practitioner. Most importantly, the PASS theory as operationalized by the CAS and CAS2 is well supported by empirical research. In this book, we will show how PASS scores (a) are more predictive of achievement test scores than any other ability test; (b) show distinctive profiles for different children with different disabilities; (c) can be used for SLD eligibility determination consistent with Federal Law; (d) offer the most equitable way to measure diverse populations; and (e) can be readily used for instructional planning and interventions. Thus, we start with a theory (PASS) which is operationalized by a test (CAS2) and has been well validated for the most important tasks that tests of ability should have—understanding the basic neurocognitive processes underlying learning and academic difficulties and providing solutions to maximize learning.

Our overarching goal for this book is to help practitioners better assess the neurocognitive abilities of the students they intend to help. For us, this means using the PASS theory as measured by the CAS2 (as part of a comprehensive assessment process). This also means that this book is a call for the field of cognitive assessment to embrace a revolution in the way we define and measure ability. This requires that practitioners embrace a new way of describing human cognitive functioning that is conceptualized as neurocognitive functions so that we can be instrumental in helping children achieve their greatest potential.

Change is not always easy, and in fact, it requires looking at what we have known and done with a fresh perspective. PASS is an innovative way of thinking about ability, and the CAS2 is a new way to measure neurocognitive abilities. This book provides the scientific evidence to support this approach. We suggest that practitioners manage this necessary transition with the assurance that an evolutionary step in our field is most definitely needed given all we have learned in the past 100 years. As one of our founding fathers, Thomas Jefferson, noted: "I am not an advocate for frequent changes in laws. But laws must go hand in hand with the progress of the human mind. As that becomes more developed, more enlightened, as new discoveries are made, new truths discovered and opinions change, institutions must advance also to keep pace with the times." Only though revolutionary change can we improve the evaluation of human cognitive function and better serve children and adolescents with learning needs.

Jack A. Naglieri
Tulio M. Otero

ACKNOWLEDGMENTS

We would like to acknowledge the support that Alan and Nadeen Kaufman showed when they supported the publication of the *Essentials of CAS Assessment*, and now the *Essentials of CAS2 Assessment* in the Essentials series. Their recognition of the value of PASS theory as measured by the CAS and CAS2 is a clear endorsement of our efforts to measure neurocognitive processes rather than IQ. We also recognize Andrea F. Lupton for her excellent work with the manuscript, development of the figures and tables, and management of all the other details needed to make this book. The final product was much improved by her expert assistance. We also thank Steve Feifer for his very valuable contribution to the intervention chapter. Special recognition goes to my coauthor Tulio Otero for his outstanding work, excellent insights, and friendship. Finally, we thank all the staff at Wiley for their support and guidance throughout the publication process.

One

OVERVIEW

I n 1905 Alfred Binet published the first edition of what would become, about 100 years later, the Stanford-Binet V (Roid, 2003). Fifteen years after the first Binet scale, Yoakum and Yerkes published the Army Mental Tests (1920), on which the Wechsler Intelligence scales (originally published in 1939) were largely based. These measures of IQ all contained test questions that have verbal, quantitative, and nonverbal (spatial) content. The view that an intelligence test should include measures that require knowledge of vocabulary and quantitative concepts has been the basis of both group as well as individually administered IQ tests for a century (Naglieri, 2015).

IQ tests took an important evoluationary step when Alan and Nadeen Kaufman published the K-ABC in 1983. Their approach was revolutionary: take verbal and quantitative measures out of the measurment of ability and use a conceptualization of intelligence to guide the inclusion of subtests. A second evolutionary step in the advancement of intelligence and its measurement was provided in 1997 when Naglieri and Das published the Cognitive Assessment System (CAS). That approach was simlar to the one taken by the Kaufmans in so far as subtests requiring knowledge of vocabulary and arithmetic were excluded. The CAS was unique in that it contained four scales following Luria's (1973) view of four brain-based abilities. The goal was to provide a new way of defining ability based on a cognitive and neuropsychological theory and develop a test to measure these basic psychological processing abilities. The K-ABC and the CAS departed from the traditional approach to IQ because of content differences and their strong conceptual basis.

There has been an evolution in thinking about what a test of ability should be. First, there are traditional IQ tests in which verbal and quantiative test questions are an intergral part of the scales. In these instruments, vocabulary, block building, and arithmetic are considered fundamental and important ways to measure ability. More recently these tests have been partitioned in more

DON'T FORGET 1.1

....

Psychology advanced considerably during the 20th century, especially in the knowledge of specific abilities and the essential cognitive processes that make up intelligence. Our tests of ability should reflect that evolution.

subscales based on combining subtests into new categories conceptualized from a variety of models. For example, although Wechsler originally had Verbal and Performance IQ scales, now the Wechsler Intelligence Scale for Children, Fifth Edition (Wechsler, 2014), has scales labeled Verbal Comprehension, Visual Spatial, Fluid Reasoning, Working Memory, and Processing Speed (see Naglieri, 2016a, for a review of the WISC-V). The content of the test, however, remains remarkably the same as what was in the Wechsler-Bellevue 1939 edition.

≡ *Rapid Reference 1.1*

....

Stanford-Binet Scales

1905	First Binet scale is published by Binet and Simon, subsequently revised in 1908.
1909	Goddard translates Binet-Simon from French to English.
1916	Terman publishes the Stanford revision and extension of the Binet-Simon scale that is normed on American children and adolescents and is widely used.
1937	Terman and Merrill publish a revision of the 1916 scale called the Stanford-Binet Intelligence Scale.
1960	Stanford-Binet, Form LM (Second Edition)
1972	Stanford-Binet, Form LM (Third Edition)
1986	Stanford-Binet, Fourth Edition (by Thorndike, Hagen, & Sattler)
2003	Stanford-Binet, Fifth Edition

There is a stark contrast between traditional IQ tests and the CAS (Naglieri & Das, 1997) and CAS2 as well as the K-ABC (Kaufman & Kaufman, 1983) and K-ABC-II. The essential difference between CAS (and CAS2) and traditional IQ tests relies on two main points. First, PASS (Planning, Attention, Simultaneous, and Successive) theory (see following discussion) was used to build the test and, second, CAS2 (similar to the CAS) does not have test questions that are better described as knowledge (i.e., information, similarities, vocabulary, comprehension, arithmetic) (see Naglieri & Bornstein, 2003). For these two reasons, CAS2 is not the same as a traditional IQ tests exemplified by the Binet and Wechsler scales. This raises the question: "Why use the CAS and CAS2?"

≡ *Rapid Reference 1.2*

Wechsler Scales

1939	Wechsler-Bellevue, Form I
1946	Wechsler-Bellevue, Form II
1949	Wechsler Intelligence Scale for Children (WISC)
1955	Wechsler Adult Intelligence Scale (WAIS)
1967	Wechsler Preschool and Primary Scale of Intelligence
1974	WISC-Revised
1981	WAIS-Revised
1989	WPPSI-Revised
1991	WISC-III
1997	WAIS-III
2003	WISC-IV
2008	WAIS-IV
2014	WISC-V

One of the most important services professionals in this field provide is a thorough assessment of a person's abilities to answer important questions such as, "Why is the student having trouble learning?" and "How can instruction be modified to improve the student's learning?" IQ tests have been used with varying degrees of effectiveness to determine, for example, if a learning disability exists and to explain poor performance in school. Researchers have found that traditional IQ tests have three main weaknesses. First, because the content of the verbal and quantitative questions is so similar to academic skills taught in the classroom, these tests unfairly penalize students or adults with limited educational opportunity, especially to acquire the English language (Naglieri, 2008a). Second, IQ tests have been shown to be insensitive to the cognitive problems experienced by those with, for example, specific learning disability (SLD), traumatic brain injury (TBI), and attention-deficit/hyperactivity disorder (ADHD) (Naglieri & Goldstein, 2009). Finally, attempts to use the information from IQ tests to design academic instruction have been disappointing. These limitations of traditional IQ tests provided the impetus to consider an alternative view of intelligence, which led us to the PASS theory as measured by CAS2.

DON'T FORGET 1.2

....

The test you select has a profound impact on what you learn about a student and what you can do to help that student.

When Naglieri and Das (1997) published the first edition of the CAS, they stated clearly that this test was based on *one* theory of ability. This was the first time a *test* of ability was built on a *specific theory*. That theory was chosen because of its relationship to neuropsychology as described by A. R. Luria (1973) (see Naglieri & Otero, 2011). The genius of Luria has been widely recognized and demonstrated by the considerable volume of his writings and the application of his ideas in numerous settings and places around the world.

In his book *The Working Brain: An Introduction to Neuropsychology* (1973), Luria described four neurocognitive processing abilities associated with three functional units of the brain. The first ability is Planning, which is a mental activity that provides cognitive control; use of processes, knowledge, and skills; intentionality; organization; and self-monitoring and self-regulation. This processing ability is closely aligned with frontal lobe functioning (third functional unit). Attention is the ability to demonstrate focused, selective, sustained, and effortful activity over time and resist distraction associated with the brain stem and other subcortical aspects (first functional unit). Simultaneous processing ability provides a person with the ability to integrate stimuli into interrelated groups or a whole usually found (but not limited to) on tasks with strong visual-spatial demands. Successive processing ability involves working with stimuli in a specific serial order, including the perception of stimuli in sequence and the linear execution of sounds and movements. It is clear from this brief explanation that PASS is *very* different from traditional IQ assessment, which is why researchers have found it to be more effective.

Since the publication of the first edition of the CAS there has been considerable research on the theory and the test. Naglieri (2012) and Naglieri and Otero (2011) suggested that the PASS theory has a very strong research foundation that continues to grow. For example, researchers have shown the following:

- Individuals with distinct disabilities such as SLD and ADHD have specific PASS profiles (Naglieri 2012; Naglieri & Goldstein, 2011).
- The CAS and CAS2 yield small differences between PASS scores across race (Naglieri, Rojahn, Matto, & Aquilino, 2005) and ethnicity (Naglieri, Rojahn, & Matto, 2007).
- Small differences between PASS scores have been found when the CAS is administered in English or Spanish (Naglieri, Otero, DeLauder, & Matto, 2007; Otero, Gonzales, & Naglieri, 2013).

- Small differences between PASS scores have been found when the Italian and English versions of the CAS were compared (Naglieri, Taddei, & Williams, 2013).
- PASS scores have shown to be strongly correlated with academic achievement scores (Naglieri & Rojahn, 2004).
- PASS scores have been successfully used for instructional planning and intervention (Naglieri & Conway, 2009).

These findings illustrate the value of the PASS theory as measured by the CAS. In this book we will provide a thorough examination of the CAS2 suite of tools, all of which are based on the PASS neurocognitive theory, and provide an update on the way in which the new versions extend the value of the orginal CAS.

≡ Rapid Reference 1.3

Cognitive Assessment System 2

Authors: Jack A. Naglieri, PhD, J. P. Das, PhD, and Goldstein, S.
Web Location: http://www.proedinc.com/customer/ProductView.aspx?ID=6768
Publication Date: 2014
What the Test Measures: PASS theory
Age Range: 5 years through 17 years 11 months
Administration Time: Core Battery = 40 minutes, Extended Battery = 60 minutes

Qualifications of Examiners:
The CAS2 is intended for individuals with credentials as psychologists (e.g., clinical, school, developmental, counseling, neuropsychological, rehabilitation); certified specialists (educational diagnosticians, psychometrists); and other professionals who are certified to use tests of this type. Users should be knowledgeable of best practices using comprehensive measures of ability, including specific procedures for administration, scoring, and interpreting test results, as well as the PASS theory that underlies this test.

Ordering Information:
CAS2: Cognitive Assessment System, Second Edition (with case) (product #14300), price $999.00.

Cognitive Assessment System 2: Brief

Authors: Jack A. Naglieri, PhD, J. P. Das, PhD, and Goldstein, S.
Web Location: http://www.proedinc.com/customer/ProductView.aspx?ID=6777

(continued)

Publication Date: 2014
What the Test Measures: PASS theory
Age Range: 4 years 0 months through 17 years 11 months
Administration Time: 20 minutes

Qualifications of Examiners:
The CAS2: Brief is intended for individuals who have backgrounds or credentials as educational diagnosticians, speech and language specialists, and professionals involved in identification of students for gifted and talented programs, as well as those who are qualified to give the CAS2. Users should be knowledgeable of best practices using brief measures, including specific procedures for administration, scoring, and interpreting test results, and the PASS theory that underlies the test.

Ordering Information:
CAS2: Brief Complete Kit (product #14285), price: $266.00

Cognitive Assessment System 2: Rating Scale

Authors: Jack A. Naglieri, PhD, J. P. Das, PhD, and Goldstein, S.
Web Location: http://www.proedinc.com/customer/ProductView.aspx?ID=6765
Publication Date: 2014
What the Rating Scale Measures: PASS theory
Age Range: 4 years 0 months through 17 years 11 months
Time to Complete: 10–15 minutes

Qualifications of Examiners:
This rating scale can be used by a wide variety of professionals including those with backgrounds or credentials as teachers and those qualified to give the CAS2 and CAS2: Brief. Users should be knowledgeable of rating scales and their use, including procedures related to using, scoring, and interpreting the scores from this rating scale, and the PASS theory that underlies the instrument.

Ordering Information:
CAS2: Rating Scale Complete Kit (product #14295), price: $127.00

Publisher:

PRO-ED, Inc.
8700 Shoal Creek Boulevard
Austin, Texas 78757-6897
E-mail: general@proedinc.com
Web: http://www.proedinc.com

Contact Customer Service:

Telephone: 800.897.3202
Local: 512.451.3246
Fax: 800.397.7633

Note: All prices as of December 2015.

⚏ *Rapid Reference 1.4*

Descriptions of the PASS Neurocognitive Abilities

Planning is a neurocognitive ability used to determine, apply, self-monitor and self-correct, and control thoughts and actions so that efficient solutions to problems can be attained.

Attention is a neurocognitive ability used to selectively focus on a particular stimulus while inhibiting responses to competing stimuli presented over time.

Simultaneous processing is a neurocognitive ability used to integrate separate stimuli into a single whole or group.

Successive processing is a neurocognitive ability used to integrate information into a specific serial order.

INTRODUCTION TO CAS2

Since the first edition of the Cognitive Assessment System (Naglieri & Das, 1997) was published there has been a substantial increase in interest in measuring abilities within a neuropsychological perspective as well as a growing recognition of the limitations of tradition IQ tests. The publication of a new suite of tests, which includes the Cognitive Assessment System, Second Edition (CAS2; Naglieri, Das, & Goldstein, 2014a); the CAS2: Brief (Naglieri, Das, & Goldstein, 2014b); the CAS2: Rating Scale (Naglieri, Das, & Goldstein, 2014c) and the CAS2: Spanish (Naglieri, Moreno & Otero, 2017) extend the approach used when the CAS was originally published to a new level by providing measures that can be used in a wide variety of settings by professionals of different qualification levels and for different purposes. These measures provide for multiple ways to evaluate the four neurocognitive processes we call Planning, Attention, Simultaneous, and Successive (PASS), which can be used to (1) help identify a disorder in basic psychological processing that is related to specific learning disabilities (and learning strengths); (2) prescribe academic instructions that best match the characteristics of the student; and (3) evaluate ability equitably across race and ethnicity.

The essential goal of the CAS and CAS2 suite of measures is to provide a way to evaluate neurocognitive abilities in a manner that is focused on basic psychological processes related to brain function. The use of a specific theory (PASS), which was used to define the abilities included in the CAS and CAS2, makes it very different than all the other test options. The most salient differences between CAS2 and traditional IQ is (1) the use of the PASS neurocognitive theory to define the constructs to be measured and their interpretation; (2) the wider range of abilities measured by PASS than traditional IQ tests; (3) and the exclusion of verbal and quantitative test questions that require the child to define words, describe similarities or differences between verbal concepts, and solve math word problems. These three key differences have considerable impact on the information the CAS2 yields.

In this book, we will show how the PASS theory as measured by the several different CAS2 measures provides information critical to understanding learning and learning problems. We believe that a strong theoretical perspective can also provide down-to-earth practical solutions to everyday problems. Real-life case studies as well as research reports will illustrate how PASS theory can be applied to help students be more successful. The topics include administration and scoring, interpretation, intervention, and use of the instruments in several different contexts. Points that are especially important are noted in "Don't Forget," "Rapid Reference," and "Caution" boxes and included as "Test Yourself" items at the end of the chapters.

> **DON'T FORGET 1.3**
>
> ....
>
> The purpose of the CAS2 is to measure specific PASS neurocognitive abilities in a way that will detect specific learning disabilities, will accurately evaluate a wide variety of students, and have relevance to instruction and intervention.

> **DON'T FORGET 1.4**
>
> ....
>
> **The Goals of PASS and CAS2**
>
> - Have a test of ability based on a specific theory of ability
> - Measure more abilities than traditional IQ
> - Measure neurocognitive processes
> - Replace IQ with cognitive processes

This book was developed to give professionals a way to quickly obtain knowledge of the CAS2 (English and Spanish), CAS2: Brief, and CAS2: Rating Scale in an easy-to-read format. Throughout the book emphasis will be given to the importance of the PASS theory and practical application of the CAS2 measures for effective evaluation of children's neurocognitive performance and consideration of this information for diagnosis and treatment. The overarching goal of this book is to provide you with all the information needed to use the three CAS2 measures with confidence. An initial description of each of the CAS2 measures is necessary in order to provide a general overview.

DESCRIPTION OF THE CAS2 MEASURES

The ultimate goal of the CAS2 (English and Spanish), CAS2: Brief, and CAS2: Rating Scale is to provide three ways to apply the PASS theory to better understand students' learning and learning problems. The CAS2 is intended to provide the most complete examination of the individual's ability to solve problems across the four PASS scales. This version will be most often used in comprehensive evaluations, typically in response to a referral, and especially for determining if a student has a disorder in basic psychological processing that is affecting academic or social performance. The CAS2: Brief is intended to be used in situations when a fast measure of PASS can be obtained for screening or reevaluation. The CAS2: Rating Scale provides a way for the user of the CAS2 or the CAS2: Brief to evaluate behaviors related to PASS theory that can be observed by the teacher in the classroom. Each of these three measures (illustrated in Figure 1.1) is described in the following sections.

CAS2

The CAS2 is an 8- or 12-subtest individually administered measure of PASS neurocognitive processing abilities for student ages 5 years 0 months through 18 years

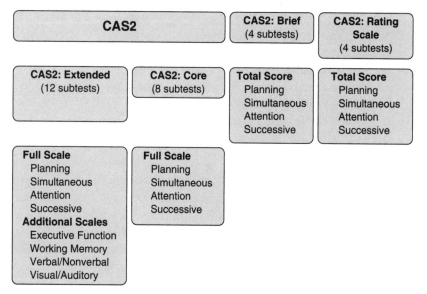

Figure 1.1 PASS Comprehensive System

11 months. It was normed on a sample of 1,342 cases representative of the US population on a number of essential demographic variables (see Naglieri, Das, & Goldstein, 2014a). *CAS2 Interpretive and Technical Manual* for more details). The CAS2 provides three levels of scores: the Full Scale score, the PASS cognitive processing scales (both set as a mean of 100 and standard deviation of 15), and the subtest scores (mean of 10 and standard deviation of 3). The test has seven components:

- The *administration and scoring manual* provides general information about testing, specific instructions for administering and scoring the subtests, norms tables, and interpretive tables.
- The *interpretive and technical manual* is a resource for information needed to use the test, including a description of the PASS theory; explanations of the test's organization and development; and information on standardization and norming, reliability, validity, and interpretation.
- There are three *stimulus books* that provide the items for the Matrices, Verbal-Spatial Relations, Figure Memory, Expressive Attention, and Visual Digit Span subtests.
- Two *student response forms* are provided, one for ages 5 through 7 years and one for ages 8 through 18 years. The forms are used for paper-and-pencil responses for the Planned Number Matching, Planned Codes, Planned Connections, Number Detection, and Receptive Attention subtests.
- A *Figure Memory response form* is used for the paper-and-pencil responses for the Figure Memory subtest.
- *Scoring templates* offer examiners a convenient aid for ease and accuracy in scoring student responses for Planned Number Matching, Number Detection, and Receptive Attention subtests.
- The *examiner record form* is used for recording responses for each subtest, as well as for a summary of the scoring and permanent documentation of test results.

Select CAS2 subtests are used to obtain the 8-subtest Core Battery which yields the Planning, Attention, Simultaneous, Successive, and Full Scale scores. The 12-subtest Extended Battery also yields these five scales as well as additional scales to measure working memory, executive function without working memory, executive function with working memory, verbal content, and nonverbal content. The subtest scores from two or more subtests are combined to form these various scales are shown in Table 1.1. Each of these scales is described more fully in Rapid Reference 1.5.

≡ Rapid Reference 1.5

Primary CAS2 Scales

Planning This scale describes a student's ability to create a plan of action, apply the plan, verify that an action taken conforms to the original goal, and modify the plan as needed. It is based on the Planned Codes, Planned Connections, and Planned Number Matching subtests.

Attention This scale describes a student's ability to focus cognitive activity and inhibit responding to irrelevant distracting stimuli. It is based on the Expressive Attention, Number Detection, and Receptive Attention subtests.

Simultaneous This scale describes a student's ability to organize separate elements into a coherent whole. It is formed by combining the Matrices, Verbal-Spatial Relations, and Figure Memory subtests.

Successive This scale describes a student's ability to recall or comprehend information arranged in a specific serial order. The scale is composed of the Word Series, Sentence Repetition (ages 5–7 years) or Sentence Questions (ages 8–18 years), and Visual Digit Span subtests.

Full Scale The Full Scale score provides an index of the overall level of an individual's cognitive functioning. It is formed by combining the scores of the Planning, Attention, Simultaneous, and Successive subtests.

Additional CAS2 Scales

Executive Function This scale provides a measure of the child's ability to achieve a goal by planning and organizing a task while paying careful attention to the stimuli and resisting distractions in the environment. It is formed by combining the Planned Connections and Expressive Attention subtests from the Planning and Attention scales, respectively.

Executive Function With Working Memory This scale evaluates the student's ability to achieve a goal by planning and organizing a task while paying careful attention to the stimuli, resisting distractions in the environment and keeping information in memory during problem-solving. It is formed by combining the Planned Connections, Expressive Attention, Verbal-Spatial Relations, and Sentence Repetition (ages 5–7 years) or Sentence Questions (ages 8–18 years) subtests, which are included in all four PASS scales.

Working Memory This score reflects the student's ability to mentally recall and manipulate information for a short period. It is formed by combining the following subtests from the Simultaneous and Successive scales: Verbal-Spatial Relations and Sentence Repetition (ages 5–7 years) or Sentence Questions (ages 8–18 years).

(continued)

Verbal Content This composite measures the child's ability to process information that requires recall and/or comprehension of verbal concepts or words across the Simultaneous, Successive, and Attention scales. It is formed by combining the Verbal-Spatial Relations, Receptive Attention, and Sentence Repetition (ages 5–7 years) or Sentence Questions (ages 8–18 years) subtests.

Nonverbal Content This composite measures the child's ability to process information with images across the Simultaneous and Planning scales. It is formed by combining the Matrices, Figure Memory, and Planned Codes subtests.

Visual-Auditory Comparison Scores on the Word Series and Visual Digit Span subtests are used to investigate the role visual or aural presentation of stimuli may have in the student's ability to remember information that is arranged in a specific order.

Description of the CAS2 Subtests

Planning Subtests

Planned Codes (PCd): Planned Codes items present the child or adolescent with a legend at the top of each page that shows a correspondence of letters to specific codes (e.g., A, B, C, D to OX, XX, OO, XO, respectively). Just below the legend are four rows and eight columns of letters without the codes. The student is required to write the corresponding codes in each empty box beneath each of the letters. Students have 60 seconds per item to complete as many empty code boxes as possible.

Planned Connections (PCn): The Planned Connections subtest requires the student to connect a series of stimuli (numbers and letters) in a specified order as quickly as possible. Students have between 60 and 180 seconds to complete each item.

Planned Number Matching (PNM): Each Planned Number Matching item presents the student with a page of eight rows with six numbers on each row. The student is required to find and underline the two numbers in each row that are the same. Students have 180 seconds per item to find as many matching numbers as possible.

Simultaneous Subtests

Matrices (MAT): The Matrices are a multiple-choice subtest that uses shapes and geometric placements that are interrelated through spatial or logical organization. Students are required to analyze the relationships among the parts of the item and solve for the missing part by choosing the six best options.

Table 1.1 CAS2 Subtests and Composite Scales

CAS2 Subtests	Core and Extended Battery Scales					Supplemental Scales					
	Planning	Simultaneous	Attention	Successive	Full Scale	Executive Function Without Working Memory	Executive Function With Working Memory	Working Memory	Verbal Content	Nonverbal Content	Speed/Fluency
Planned Codes	C				C					X	
Planned Connect	C				C	X	X				
Planned Number Matching	E				E						
Matrices		C			C					X	
Verbal-Spatial Relations		C			C		X	X	X		
Figure Memory		E			E					X	
Expressive Attention			C		C	X	X				X
Number Detection			C		C						
Receptive Attention			E		E						
Word Series				C	C						
Sentence Repetition/Sentence Questions				C	C		X	X	X		
Visual Digit Span				E	E						

Note: C = Core Battery subtest; E = Extended Battery subtest. Speed/Fluency is composed only of the first two pages of the Expressive Attention subtest.

Verbal-Spatial Relations (VSR): Verbal-Spatial Relations is a multiple-choice subtest in which each item consists of six drawings and a printed question at the bottom of each page. The examiner reads the question aloud, and the child is required to select the option that matches the verbal description.

Figure Memory (FM): For each Figure Memory item, the examiner presents the student with a two- or three-dimensional geometric figure for 5 seconds. The stimulus is then removed, and the student is presented with a response page that contains the original figure embedded in a larger, more complex geometric pattern. The student is required to identify the original figure with a red pencil on the Figure Memory Response form.

Attention Subtests

Expressive Attention (EA): The Expressive Attention subtest consists of two sets of three items. Students ages 5–7 years are given three pages consisting of seven rows that each contain six pictures of common animals, with each picture depicted as either big (1 inch × 1 inch) or small (1/2 inch × 1/2 inch). In each of three pages, the student is required to identify whether the animal depicted is big or small in real life, ignoring the relative size of the picture on the page. In item set 1, the pictures are all the same size. In item set 2, big animals are depicted with big pictures, and small animals are depicted with small pictures. In item 3, the realistic size of the animal often differs from its printed size.

Students ages 8 to 18 years are presented with three Expressive Attention pages consisting of eight rows of five words each. On page 1, students are asked to read the words *blue, yellow, green,* and *red* printed in black ink. On page 2, students are asked to name the colors of four colored rectangles (printed in blue, yellow, green, and red). On page 3, the four color words from page 1 are printed in the color from page 2 and the word name and the color do not match. In this item, students are required to name the color of the ink in which the word is printed rather than read the word.

Number Detection (ND): Each Number Detection item presents the student with a page of approximately 200 numbers. Students are required to underline specific numbers (ages 5–7 years) or specific numbers in a particular font (ages 8–18 years) on a page with many distractors.

Receptive Attention (RA): The Receptive Attention subtest consists of four item sets, each containing 60 picture pairs (ages 5–7 years) or 180 letter pairs (8–18 years). Both versions require the child or adolescent to underline pairs of objects or letters that either are identical in appearance or are the same from a lexical perspective (i.e., they have the same name).

Successive Subtests

Word Series (WS): The Word Series subtest uses nine single-syllable, high-frequency words: *book, car, cow, dog, girl, key, man, shoe,* and *wall.* The examiner reads aloud a series of two to nine of these words at the rate of one word per second. The student is required to repeat the words in the same order as stated by the examiner.

Sentence Repetition (SR): The Sentence Repetition subtest (administered only to ages 5–7 years) requires the child to repeat syntactically correct sentences containing little meaning, such as "The blue is yellowing."

Sentence Questions (SQ): The Sentence Questions subtest (administered only to ages 8–18 years) requires the child or adolescent to listen to sentences that are syntactically correct but contain little meaning and answer questions about the sentences. For example, the student is read the sentence "The blue is yellowing" and then asked the following question: "Who is yellowing?"

Visual Digit Span (VDS): The Visual Digit Span subtest requires the student to recall a series of numbers in the order in which they were shown using the Stimulus Book. Each item that is two to five digits in length is exposed for the same number of seconds as there are digits. Items with six digits or more are all exposed for a maximum of 5 seconds.

Table 1.2 Structure of the CAS Scales and Subtests in Order of Administration

Scale	Subtests
Planning	
	Matching Numbers (MN)
	Planned Codes (PCd)
	Planned Connections (PCn)
Simultaneous	
	Nonverbal Matrices (NvM)
	Verbal-Spatial Relations (VSR)
	Figure Memory (FM)
Attention	
	Expressive Attention (EA)
	Number Detection (ND)
	Receptive Attention (RA)
Successive	
	Word Series (WS) and or Sentence Repetition (SR)
	Speech Rate (SpR, ages 5–7 years) or Sentence Questions (SQ, ages 8–17 years)

CAS2: Brief

The CAS2: Brief is 4 subtest individually administered measure of PASS neurocognitive processing abilities students ages 4 years 0 months through 18 years 11 months. It was normed on a sample of 1,417 students who are representative of the US population on a number of important demographic variables (see the examiner's manual for more details). The CAS2: Brief yields standard scores (mean of 100 and standard deviation of 15) for PASS and a total scale.

This test has the following five components:

1. *Examiner's manual.* This manual provides general information, general information for administering and scoring the subtests, norms tables, and interpretive tables.
2. *Examiner record form.* The administration and scoring instructions are provided on the examiner record form. In addition, the form provides space for recording responses for each subtest as well as a summary of the scoring and permanent documentation of test results.
3. *Stimulus book.* The stimulus book provides the items for the Simultaneous Matrices and Expressive Attention subtests.
4. *Student response booklet.* The student response booklet is used for the Planned Codes subtest.
5. *Scoring templates.* A spiral-bound booklet with six scoring templates provides an efficient way for scoring the Planned Codes subtest.

The CAS2: Brief yields scores (mean of 100 and standard deviation of 15) for the four PASS scores and a Total Score. The subtests used in the CAS2: Brief are similar to, but not the same as, those used in the CAS2. Each PASS scale is assessed using one subtest described in the following.

≋ *Rapid Reference 1.6*

Description of the CAS2: Brief Subtests in Each PASS Scale in Order of Administration

Planning

Planned Codes The Planned Codes subtest presents the child or adolescent with a legend at the top of each page that shows a correspondence of numbers to specific codes (e.g., 1, 2, 3, 4 to OX, XX, OO, XO, respectively). Just below the legend are four rows and eight columns of numbers without the codes. The student is required to write the corresponding codes in the empty box beneath each number. Students have 60 seconds per item to complete as many empty code boxes as possible on each of the six items. Success on Planned

Codes requires that the student develop a plan of action, evaluate the value of the method, monitor its effectiveness, revise or reject an old plan as the task demands change, and control the impulse to act without careful consideration.

Simultaneous

Simultaneous Matrices The Simultaneous Matrices subtest requires that the student understand how shapes are interrelated through spatial or logical organization. Students are required to analyze the relationships among the parts of the item and solve for the missing part by choosing the best of six options. Simultaneous Matrices requires comprehension of how many geometric parts are organized into a larger, sometimes multidimensional, pattern. All of the items on this subtest are different from those used in the CAS2 as is the color pallet (blue, yellow, teal, and black).

Attention

Expressive Attention The Expressive Attention subtest presents a task that requires focus on one stimulus and resistance to responding to distractions over time. The subtest consists of two age-related sets of three items. Students ages 4 through 7 years are presented with seven rows containing six pictures of common animals that are depicted as either big (1 inch × 1 inch) or small (1/2 inch × 1/2 inch). In each of the three items, the student is required to identify whether the animal depicted is big or small in real life, ignoring the relative size of the picture on the page. In item set 1, the pictures are all the same size. In item set 2, the pictures are sized appropriately (i.e., big animals are depicted with big pictures, and small animals are depicted with small pictures). In item set 3, the realistic size of the animal often differs from its printed size.

Students ages 8–18 years are presented with three item sets, each consisting of eight rows of five randomly ordered stimuli. In item set 4, students read color words (*blue, yellow,* and *red*) printed in black-and-white ink. In item set 5, students name the colors of four rectangles (printed in blue, yellow, green, and red) that are presented in a quasi-random order. In item set 6, the four color words are printed in a different color ink than the color name. In this set, students name the color of the ink in which the word is printed rather than read the word.

The items on both versions of the Expressive Attention subtests are different from those used in the CAS2. The CAS2: Brief version does not include the color green used in the CAS2.

Successive

Successive Digits In the Successive Digits subtest, the examiner orally reads sets of numbers between 1 and 9 to the student. Each set of numbers ranges in length from two to nine numbers, read at the rate of one number per second. The student is required to repeat the numbers in the same order as the examiner. This Successive subtest requires reproduction of the serial order of numbers, whereas words are used in the CAS2.

CAS2: Rating Scale

The CAS2: Rating Scale is a measure of behaviors associated with the four PASS abilities for students ages 4 years 0 months through 18 years 11 months. It was normed on a representative sample of 1,383 students that represent the US population on a number of key variables (see the Examiner's Manual for more details). Similar to the CAS2 and the CAS2: Brief, the CAS2: Rating Scale yields standard scores for the four PASS scales and a Total Score (mean of 100 and standard deviation of 15), each of which is described in Rapid Reference 1.7. The rating scale has two components: an examiner's manual and a record form.

The examiner's manual provides specific instructions for administering, scoring, and interpreting the scale. In addition, it includes information needed to use the scale, a discussion of the PASS theory; explanations of the CAS2: Rating Scale's organization and development; and information on standardization and norming, reliability, validity, and interpretation. The rating form provides instructions to the rater, space for the rater to record ratings of behaviors observed by the teacher, and a section for the examiner to record the scores. The scale contains 40 items that are rated by the teacher.

≡ Rapid Reference 1.7

Description of the CAS2: Rating Scale Items in Each PASS Scale in Order of Administration

Planning

This scale is composed of items that ask about how well the student makes decisions about how to do things. This includes items to assess if the student thinks before acting, evaluates his or her actions, controls impulses, devises new solutions, and reflects on the extent to which actions matched intentions. In general, the Planning score provides a measure of how and what a student decides to do. An example of a Planning Scale item would be "During the past month, how often did the child or adolescent have a good idea about how to complete a task?"

Simultaneous

This scale addresses how well the student understands interrelationships among ideas and objects. The questions determine if a child can understand relationships among physical objects as well as verbal concepts. An example of a Simultaneous scale item would be "During the past month, how often did the child or adolescent figure out how parts of a design go together?"

Attention

This scale evaluates how well a student can focus attention and resist distractions, sustain attention over time, and concentrate in noisy settings. An example of an Attention scale item would be "During the past month, how often did the child or adolescent work without getting distracted?"

Successive

This scale evaluates the student's ability to work with information that is in a specific order, including remembering numbers, letters, and words in order and blending sounds of words in the correct sequence. An example of a Successive scale item would be "During the past month, how often did the child or adolescent follow three to four directions given in order?"

Total Score

The PASS scale standard scores can be combined to create a composite score called the *Total Score*. The Total Score, however, should be used with the understanding that when there is considerable variability in PASS scores, the Total Score may be different from any of the four part scores used to create it. See Chapter 2 of this book for more information.

USES OF THE CAS2

The CAS2 (English and Spanish versions), CAS2: Brief, and CAS2: Rating Scale can be used to assess children and adolescents ages 4 (or 5) through 18 years. The CAS2: Rating Scale can be used whenever an evaluation of classroom behaviors related to PASS as reported by a teacher is desired. The information can be used for instructional planning as well as screening for strengths and weaknesses. The CAS2: Brief is intended to be used as a short measure of PASS to be obtained when an initial concern is raised as well as during reevaluation of a student already receiving educational services. The CAS2: Brief is also intended to be used whenever a short evaluation of a student's ability is desired as part of a larger testing program, for example, gifted screening. The CAS2: Brief is particularly useful for gifted assessment because the test measures neurocognitive abilities that go beyond a typical IQ test. These three versions of the CAS2 are appropriate when initial instructional planning (Rating Scale) or screening (CAS2: Brief) as well as comprehensive psychological, clinical, psychoeducational, or neuropsychological evaluation (CAS2) is indicated. The results from all these measures of PASS can be used at different points of the process of making clinical diagnoses, educational eligibility determination, treatment planning, and for fair and equitable assessment of diverse populations.

THEORETICAL FOUNDATION

Roots of PASS

The PASS theory is based on the neuropsychological, information-processing, and cognitive psychological research of A. R. Luria (1966, 1973, 1980a, 1980b, 1982), who is the "most frequently cited Soviet scholar in American, British, and Canadian psychology periodicals" (Solso & Hoffman, 1991, p. 251). Luria's view of the brain function was partially based on his own research and the integration of his findings with those of other researchers. He gives ample credit to those on whom he drew information about the specific functions of the brain in his 1973 book, *The Working Brain: An Introduction to Neuropsychology*. Luria described the basic building blocks of intelligence as functional systems, which means that there are basic cognitive processes that provide the ability to perform certain acts, each of which is distinctive in character and associated with different areas of the brain. Luria understood the brain as an extremely complex organ, and he viewed the PASS cognitive processes to be dynamic. Each functional system was characterized by a specific aim and carried out by several participating subprocesses. Indeed, Luria's conceptualizations of how the brain worked was revolutionary, and many of his contributions to the understanding of brain-behavior relationships were derived without the benefit of modern imaging and other methods now available in the field of neuroscience.

Luria associated each of the three functional units with specific regions of the brain. The first functional unit is associated with the brain stem, diencephalon, and medial regions of the hemispheres. The occipital, parietal, and temporal lobes posterior to the central sulcus regulate the second unit's functions. The third unit's functions are regulated by the frontal lobes, especially the prefrontal region. These functional units, illustrated in Figure 1.2, will be described in the following section.

PASS Theory

In this section each of the four PASS processes are described. Luria's three functional units include the four PASS processes as follows: Attention is in the first functional unit, Simultaneous and Successive are in the second, and Planning is in the third. To illustrate each process, one subtest from each of the four scales of the CAS2, CAS2: Brief, and CAS2: Rating Scale is discussed and examples of children's classwork that involve the process are illustrated. Rather than follow the first, second, and third functional unit sequence, this section will be organized by the PASS acronym; beginning with Planning, then covering Attention, and concluding with Simultaneous and Successive processes.

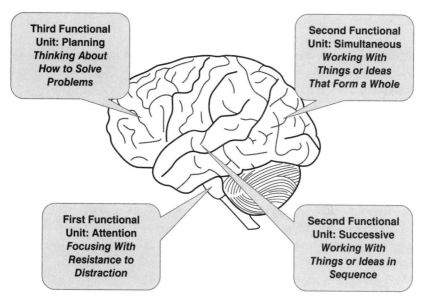

Figure 1.2 Three Functional Units and Associated Brain Structures

The PASS theory provides a conceptualization of four basic psychological processes that can be described as the basic building blocks of human functioning. The four PASS constructs are defined by Naglieri et al. (2014a) in the CAS2 interpretive manual as described in the following sections.

Planning

Planning is a neurocognitive ability used to determine, apply, self-monitor, self-correct, and control thoughts and actions so that efficient solutions to problems can be attained (Naglieri et al., 2014a). This includes control of actions and thoughts so that efficient solutions to problems can be achieved. Planning provides the means to solve problems for which no method or solution is immediately apparent and may involve retrieval of information as well as use of the other PASS abilities to process the information. Planning ability is also important when individuals reflect on events following a problem that was completed, recognizing what worked, what did not work, and considering other possible solutions in the future. The frontal lobes of the brain are directly involved in Planning processing (Naglieri & Otero, 2011).

Planning is a process essential to all activities in which there is intentionality and a need for some method to solve a problem. This includes an awareness of what is a good course of action, how well things are going, evaluation of alternative activities as they might become appropriate from moment to moment, and consideration of the relative value between continuing with a behavior or changing to a different one (Shadmehr, Smith, & Krakauer, 2010). These ongoing aspects can be either explicit or implicit and may be automatic or demand considerable cognitive control (Blais, Harris, Guerrero, & Bunge, 2010; Koziol, Budding, & Chidekel, 2010).

The essence of subtests that measure Planning is that the examinee must solve novel problems for which there is no previously acquired strategy and there should be minimal constraints placed on the way the student completes the task. All of the Planning subtests on the CAS2 and CAS2: Brief are best solved using strategies for efficient performance. In addition, the instructions were designed to fully inform the student to complete the task using whatever method seems best. This instruction provides the opportunity to apply strategies to the novel test questions that are designed to be relatively easy to complete. This enables the score to reflect efficiency, measured by how long it takes to complete the task with the most number correct. For example, the Planned Codes subtest on the CAS2 or CAS2: Brief is best completed using a strategy. Recall that Planned Codes requires the child to write a specific letter code under the corresponding letter (e.g., XO for A, OX for B, etc.) as shown in Figure 1.3. Children can use different strategies to complete the test in an efficient and timely manner. Importantly, children who use a strategy on Planned Codes obtain a significantly higher scaled score mean score than those who do not (Naglieri et al., 2014a). The CAS2: Rating Scale provides information about the student's behavior in school settings.

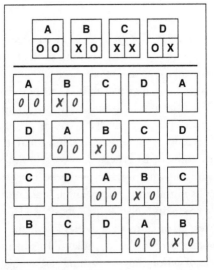

Figure 1.3 Example of a Planning Test

Classroom behaviors can provide insight into a student's neurocognitive concept of planning in school. To calibrate such observations, the Planning scale items on the CAS2: Rating Scale focus on topics such as how well the student can solve new problems and especially how well a student can think of several ways to solve the same

> **DON'T FORGET 1.5**
>
> The more novel a task is, the more Planning it requires. As a solution becomes well learned, the role of Planning decreases and the role of knowledge and skills increases.

problem. This includes having a good goal in mind when various strategies are being considered, applying a strategy, and deciding if the result is consistent with the intention. These kinds of observable classroom behaviors inform us about how well the student is meeting the demands of tasks within the context of the instructional approach. That is, if instruction allows for multiple ways to solve problems, then observation of these behaviors can be helpful in gauging a student's Planning processing. Note, however, if the classroom instruction is very structured and each student is taught to use the same method of solving problems, then the behavior in the class will reflect how well the student is meeting those requirements rather than how well the student could develop a variety of solutions.

Classroom performance on *academic tasks* can also provide insights into a child or adolescent's Planning ability. Most any task can involve Planning processing regardless of the content *if* the student has to make decisions about *how* to complete the task. For example, a student may memorize the sequence of letters to spell the name *Jacqueline* or think of a way to remember the sequence by chunking the letters into groups. Chunking letters into more manageable units such as *Jac-que-line* is an excellent plan for remembering the spelling of this complicated name. If the student decides to put the letters into groups, that behavior can be deemed a reflection of his or her Planning ability. If, however, the student was taught a chunking strategy by a parent, then the student's selection of the strategy from memory represents good planning. Both behavioral outcomes are valuable, the former representing a more optimal level of Planning because it involves problem identification, generation of a possible solution, execution of the solution, and monitoring effectiveness of the strategy. The latter solution demands less Planning but still involves problem identification, selection of a strategy, execution of the solution, and monitoring the effectiveness of the plan.

Attention

Attention is a neurocognitive ability used to selectively focus on a particular stimulus while inhibiting responses to competing stimuli presented over time (Naglieri et al., 2014a), as shown in Figure 1.4. Attention is a basic component of intelligent

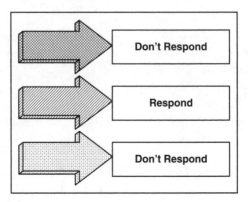

Figure 1.4 Cognitive Processing Structure of a Task That Requires Attention

behavior because it provides cortical arousal and higher forms of attention. Luria stated that optimal conditions of arousal are needed for the more complex forms of attention involving "selective recognition of a particular stimulus and inhibition of responses to irrelevant stimuli" (Luria, 1973, p. 271). Higher forms of attention are conceptualized as a mental activity that provides focused, selective cognitive activity over time and resistance to distraction. The process is involved when a person must demonstrate focused, selective, sustained, and effortful activity. The longer attention is needed, the more the activity necessitates vigilance. Intentions and goals managed by the ability to plan, control attention, and knowledge and skills also play an integral part. Brain structures such as the reticular formation enable people to focus selective attention toward a stimulus over a period of time without the loss of attention to other competing stimuli.

The *subtests* used in the CA2 and CAS2: Brief Attention scales were constructed so that each stimulus is multidimensional and the tendency is to respond to the most salient part that is incorrect. For example, the student is instructed to identify one aspect of the target (e.g., the color blue) and resist responding to distractions (e.g., the word *red* written in blue ink) as in the Stoop test (Lezak, 1995). This kind of a task requires selective focus of attention over time and resistance to distraction. Attentional processing assessed using CAS2 subtests demands focused, selective, sustained, and effortful activity. Focused attention involves directed concentration toward a particular activity, selective attention provides the inhibition of responses to distracting stimuli, and sustained attention refers to the variation of performance over time, which can be influenced by the different amount of effort required to solve the test.

Classroom behaviors can reflect a student's ability to attend and resist distractions over time. For example, behavioral evidence of good attention would be suggested when the teacher sees a student stay focused on his or her work despite distractions in the class and maintain effort over time despite continued noises. By contrast, poor attention can be inferred when a student can work only for a short period of time, has problems listening and following directions, and cannot concentrate except when distractions are minimal.

There are many *academic tasks* that are particularly dependent on the neurocognitive concept of Attention. Clearly, all academic tasks (as well as everything a person does in and outside of school) require attention and resistance to distractions (in the environment as well as distracting thoughts). Some tasks require more attention than others, particularly because as the complexity of a task increases, so too will the attentional demands. For example, reading a single word requires much less attention than reading and understanding a paragraph. Solving a math problem such as $2 + 4 - 1 = ?$ involves attending to the numbers and the signs in addition to knowing the math facts. Answering a multiple-choice test can be particularly demanding on attention when the problem requires deciding what part of the information given is important and what is not and when the options are very similar. For example, Figure 1.5 illustrates a math word problem that requires attention to the details to determine the exact question (what is 6×5.25).

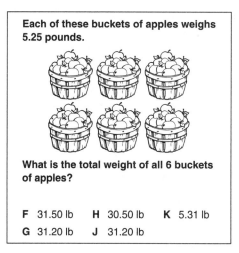

Each of these buckets of apples weighs 5.25 pounds.

What is the total weight of all 6 buckets of apples?

F   31.50 lb   H   30.50 lb   K   5.31 lb
G   31.20 lb   J   31.20 lb

Figure 1.5 Example of a Task That Requires Attention and Resistance to Distraction

The reader has to decide what is important (the number of buckets and the amount each weighs) and what is not (e.g., what is being weighed). Then the options need to be carefully examined to determine which one is correct. In this example, two of the options are the same to the left of the decimal and two are the same to the right of the decimal. There is a lot of information to examine for this relatively simple math word problem, making it challenging from an attentional perspective.

Simultaneous

Simultaneous is a neurocognitive ability used to integrate separate stimuli into a single whole or interrelated group (Naglieri et al., 2014a). The essence of Simultaneous processing is that separate elements must be combined into a conceptual whole. This ability is involved in visual-spatial tasks as well as those language activities that require comprehensive grammatical structures. The spatial aspect of Simultaneous ability involves the perception of stimuli as a group or whole and the formation of visual images. The grammatical dimension of Simultaneous processing allows for the integration of words into ideas through the comprehension of word relationships, prepositions, and inflections so the person can obtain meaning. Thus, Simultaneous processes involve nonverbal-spatial as well as verbal content. This ability is associated with the parietal-occipital-temporal brain regions.

The distinguishing characteristic of CAS2 *subtests* designed to measure Simultaneous processing is the requirement that information must be organized into a coherent whole. One example is the Matrices subtest on the CAS2 and the Simultaneous Matrices subtest on the CAS2: Brief. The Verbal-Spatial Relations subtest also measures Simultaneous processing, but it requires verbal comprehension of the grammatical components of language such as word relationships and understanding of prepositions and inflections (Naglieri, 1999). Although the Matrices and Verbal-Spatial Relations subtests differ in their content (nonverbal and verbal, respectively) they demand the same Simultaneous neurocognitive ability because both subtests require an understanding of the interrelationships of information. The information in the Matrices subtest is represented by the graphic representation of shapes on the page, and the information in Verbal-Spatial Relations subtest is presented in the written statement at the bottom of the page, in the oral reading of the statement by the examiner, and in the way images are arranged on the page. In both subtests the student has to understand these relationships to arrive at the correct response.

Classroom behaviors can provide insight into a student's Simultaneous processing ability. To measure this ability, the CAS2: Rating Scale items focus on topics such as if the student likes hands-on materials and visual-spatial tasks. Children who like to draw designs, especially three-dimensional ones, and those who are good at patterns and complex shapes are usually good in Simultaneous processing. But Simultaneous neurocognitive ability is also the foundation of understanding the reading of a whole word; understanding grammar, patterns in language, verbal concepts, reading comprehension; following a discussion; and getting the big-picture. Figure 1.6 provides an example of an item similar to those found in the CAS Verbal Spatial Relations subtest. In this item the child must decide which of the six options shows "the arrow pointing to the square in the circle." In order to solve this problem, the child must understand the relationships among each of the objects (in this case an arrow, circle, and square) to determine which option matches the written statement. This test demands simultaneous processing because the child must organize the three objects into a whole to solve the problem. The important thing to remember is that any task that demands that someone pull many parts of information together into an organized whole requires a lot of Simultaneous neurocognitive ability.

Successive
Successive is a neurocognitive ability used to work with information that is arranged in a specific serial order in which each part follows the other in a strictly defined order (Naglieri et al., 2014a). Successive processing is involved

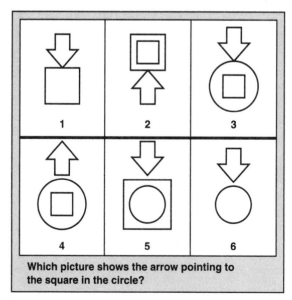

Figure 1.6 Example of a Simultaneous Processing Test

in the perception of stimuli in sequence as well as the formation of sounds and movements into a specific order. This type of ability is necessary for the recall of information in order as well as phonological analysis and the syntax of language (Das, Naglieri, & Kirby, 1994). Deficits with successive processing are also associated with early reading problems in young children, because it requires a child to learn sounds in a sequential order. This ability is associated with the temporal brain regions.

Successive processing is also involved in subtests like Digit Span Forward (as well as the recall of numbers, words, or movements), which is found on many tests of ability. These tests are sometimes described as measures of working memory or sequential processing (a concept very close to Successive processing in PASS theory). Sometimes a backward version is included that involves Successive as well as Planning processing abilities. The Successive tasks included in the CAS and CAS2 provide a way to measure this ability using tests that demand repeating a sentence using the correct series of words (Sentence Repetition) as well as comprehension of sentences that are understood only by appreciating the sequence of words (Sentence Questions; see Figure 1.7). Additionally, CAS2 has a Visual Digit Span test, allowing for measurement of successive processing across auditory and visual modalities. It is important to note that Successive neurocognitive tests all demand working with information in order, and they do involve remembering information, but it is the sequencing of information that is most critical to success on these subtests.

Classroom behaviors can inform us about a student's ability to work with information in order. For example, the examination of a successive series of events is also involved in reading, especially initial reading to decode unfamiliar words and spelling. Successive processing is critical when a student is presented with very confusable words and must focus carefully on the pronunciation of sounds in order. In addition, the child must learn the association of the sounds, in order, with the letters of the words, and this demands Successive processing.

Based on Sequence of Information
1. The blue is yellow. Who is yellow?
2. The red greened the blue with a yellow. Who used the yellow?
   The red blues a yellow green of pinks that are brown in the purple, and then grays the tan. What does the red do first?

Figure 1.7 Example of a Successive Processing Subtest That Demands Comprehension

STANDARDIZATION, RELIABILITY, AND VALIDITY

In this section we provide an overview of standardization of the CAS2 suite of tests, and their reliability, and brief summary of validity. For more information about these psychometric issues see each of the three manuals as well as sources such as Naglieri (2015) and Naglieri and Otero (2012, 2014).

Standardization

The CAS2 scales were standardized, and norming was based on a total sample of 4,142 children and adolescents ages 4 to 18 years. The CAS2 ($N = 1,342$), CAS2: Brief ($N = 1,417$), and CAS2: Rating Scale ($N = 1,383$) samples were chosen carefully to match closely the 2013 US Census data on the variables of age, gender, geographic region, and ethnicity. Procedures used for data collection and norming as well as a description with regard to geographic region, gender, race, ethnicity, family income, educational level of parents, and educational classification of the three samples are fully described in the respective manuals. Some important psychometric qualities are summarized in the sections that follow.

Reliability

The average reliability coefficients by age for the three CAS2 measures are summarized in Rapid Reference 1.8. The CAS2 subtest reliabilities range from .80 (Planned Connections) to .91 (Verbal-Spatial Relations) and overall illustrate that these subtests have good reliability. Importantly, when these subtests were combined into PASS scales, the reliability coefficients were very high, ranging from .84 (Attention) to .93 (Simultaneous) for the 8-subtest Core Battery and ranging from .90 (Attention) to .94 (Simultaneous) for the 12-subtest Extended Battery. The Full Scale reliabilities were .95 and .97 for the CAS2 Core and Extended Batteries, respectively. The PASS scale and Total Score reliability coefficients for the CAS2: Brief were high, ranging from .88 (Simultaneous Matrices) to .93 (Planning) with a .94 on the Total Score. The CAS2: Rating Scale reliability coefficients were also high, ranging from .93 (Simultaneous Matrices) to .96 (Attention) with a .98 on the Total Score. These reliability results were also similar across gender, race, ethnicity, and special education categories (see respective manuals and Rapid Reference 1.9).

≡ Rapid Reference 1.8

Coefficient Alpha Reliabilities for the CAS2

Subtests/Scales	CAS2
Planned Codes	.88
Planned Connections	.80
Planned Number Matching	.82
Matrices	.88
Verbal-Spatial Relations	.91
Figure Memory	.85
Expressive Attention	.82
Number Detection	.80
Receptive Attention	.83
Word Series	.83
Sentence Repetition	.83
Sentence Questions	.85
Visual Digit Span	.86
Core Battery (8 Subtests)	
Planning	.90
Simultaneous	.93
Attention	.86
Successive	.89
Full Scale	.95
Extended Battery (12 Subtests)	
Planning	.92
Simultaneous	.94
Attention	.90
Successive	.92
Full Scale	.97
Supplemental Composites	
Executive Function Without Working Memory	.86
Executive Function With Working Memory	.91
Working Memory	.92
Verbal Content	.91
Nonverbal Content	.92

≡ Rapid Reference 1.9

Coefficient Alpha Reliabilities for the CAS2: Brief and CAS2: Rating Scale

Scales	CAS2: Brief	CAS2: Rating Scale
Extended Battery (12 Subtests)		
Planning	.93	.95
Simultaneous	.88	.93
Attention	.89	.96
Successive	.86	.94
Total Score	.94	.98

Stability of scores is an important statistic, especially to determine if there are practice effects on the CAS2, CAS2: Brief, and CAS2: Rating Scale. Each of the manuals for these measures contains information about the similarities or differences between first and second test administrations. Table 1.3 shows CAS2 mean scores for the first and second administrations and the difference in standard score units (mean of 100 and standard deviation of 15). The differences between the mean scores are very small, illustrating that the CAS2 scores show little practice effects over time. The Extended Battery PASS score differences ranged from less than 1 (Planning) to 2.8 (Successive), and similar differences for the Core Battery. Practice effects for the CAS2: Brief and the CAS2: Rating Scale were also small, as shown in Table 1.4.

Validity

The validity of PASS constructs measured by the CAS2, CAS2: Brief, and CAS2: Rating Scale rests as much on the considerable amount of research already published (see Naglieri, 2012; Naglieri & Otero, 2011) as it does with the evidence for the second edition. In this section, previous research on CAS will be merged with the research conducted as part of the development of the three CAS2 tools for measuring PASS theory. More details about these topics will be summarized in the sections that follow. Interested readers may find other evidence of validity more fully presented in the respective CAS2 manuals. This discussion of validity will begin with the correspondence of the PASS theory to the subtests and behavioral items included across the three CAS2 measures designed to evaluate this neurocognitive conceptualization of ability.

Table 1.3 Practice Effects for the CAS2 PASS, Full Scale, and Supplemental Scale Standard Scores (N = 144)

	First	Second	Difference
Core Battery (8 Subtests)			
Planning	99.0	100.2	1.2
Simultaneous	98.5	99.7	1.2
Attention	100.6	100.8	0.2
Successive	97.8	102.5	4.7
Full Scale	98.5	100.8	2.3
Extended Battery (12 Subtests)			
Planning	99.2	100.1	0.9
Simultaneous	98.6	100.9	2.3
Attention	100.2	101.7	1.5
Successive	98.6	101.4	2.8
Full Scale/Total	99.0	101.2	2.2
Supplemental Scales			
Executive Function Without Working Memory	99.5	102.7	3.2
Executive Function With Working Memory	98.2	101.7	3.5
Working Memory	97.9	100.7	2.8
Verbal Content	98.1	101.7	3.6
Nonverbal Content	98.9	102.1	3.2

Note: CAS2 was administered to students ages 5 through 18 years over an average interval of 19 days. See CAS2 manual for more details.

Table 1.4 Practice Effects for the CAS2: Brief and CAS2: Rating Scale

Subtests/Scales	CAS2 Pre	Post	Difference
CAS2: Brief			
Planning	98.8	104.2	5.4
Simultaneous	102.4	102.7	0.3
Attention	101.9	108.1	6.2
Successive	98.9	100.9	2.0
Total Scale	100.2	105.5	5.3
CAS2: Rating Scale			
Planning	98.8	98.3	−0.5
Simultaneous	98.2	98.2	0.0
Attention	99.9	100.1	0.2
Successive	98.9	99.4	0.5
Total Scale	99.1	99.1	0.0

Note: CAS2: Brief $N = 168$ (interval was approximately 3 to 4 weeks). CAS2: Rating Scale $N = 136$ (mean interval was 21 days).

OPERATIONALIZATION OF PASS THEORY IN THE THREE CAS2 MEASURES

The construct validity of the CAS2, CAS2: Brief, and CAS2: Rating Scale is supported by the factor-analytic studies described in the respective manuals. Results of the confirmatory factor analyses across the three measures supported the operationalization of the PASS scales. Confirmatory factor analysis is appropriate because (1) previous research has been published showing that PASS scales were successfully operationalized with the first edition of the CAS, (2) PASS is a well-supported theory and the second edition provides an opportunity to further confirm if test and the theory are consistent, and (3) the three CAS2 measures can be examined as a group to test the construct validity of PASS across direct testing and teacher observations. The results of the confirmatory factor analyses of the three CAS2 measures yield a remarkably consistent picture. Three confirmatory factor analytic studies were conducted, one each for the CAS2, CAS2: Brief, and CAS2: Rating Scale. This gives the opportunity to determine if the four PASS scales are supported using analysis of subtest scores (CAS2), groups of items within each subtest (CAS2: Brief), and behavioral item–level analysis (CAS2: Rating Scale). For each measure a one-factor (no PASS scales); two-factor (Planning and Attention as one factor and Simultaneous and Successive as a second); three-factor (Planning and Attention as one factor, Simultaneous as a second, and Successive as the third); and four-factor PASS structure was tested. In every instance the best fit to the three different standardization samples was PASS (see respective manuals for more details).

These three independent factor analyses confirmed that the best fit to the data was the arrangement of subtests to PASS scales for the CAS2 as well as items to PASS scales (CAS2: Rating Scale and CAS2: Brief) was the four dimensional PASS theory. These findings support the interpretation of the four PASS scales and provide confidence in the use of the CAS2 suite of measures. What follows are important findings about the PASS constructs as measured by the CAS and the CAS2, CAS2: Brief, and the CAS2: Rating Scale. These research findings illustrate that PASS (1) is strongly related to academic achievement, (2) is the most appropriate measure of ability for diverse populations, and (3) effectively identifies disorders in basic psychological processes that underlie specific learning disabilities, ADHD, and autism.

PASS RELATIONSHIP TO ACHIEVEMENT

Intelligence tests can play critically important roles in explaining academic performance and predicting future achievement. Studying the relationship between IQ and achievement is complicated by the fact that IQ test questions measure very similar content to achievement tests (e.g., vocabulary, arithmetic word problems, etc.). The similarity in content gives IQ tests an advantage over those measures that do not include verbal and quantitative test items (see Naglieri & Bornstein, 2003). Despite that advantage, Naglieri (1999) reported that the correlations between achievement test scores with the CAS and K-ABC were as high or higher than those found for the WISC-III and WJ-R. The results for the CAS were later reported by Naglieri and Rojahn (2004), who examined the relationships between the Planning, Attention, Simultaneous, and Successive scores as operationalized by the CAS, and achievement as measured by the Woodcock-Johnson Tests of Achievement–Revised (WJ-R; Woodcock & Johnson, 1989), using a nationally representative sample of 1,559 students. The correlation between the CAS Full Scale with the WJ-R was .71 and Naglieri et al. (2014a) reported an average correlation between the CAS2 and achievement of .70.

Naglieri (2016a) summarized the strength of the correlation between the WISC-V and WIAT-III using data from the WISC-V manual (Wechsler, 2015, Table 5.13). In order to look at the relationship with and without the influence of those portions of the WISC-V that clearly require verbal knowledge two procedures were used. First, the average correlation among all five WISC-V scales with the WIAT-III total was computed. Second, the average of the WISC-V scales when the Verbal Comprehension Index was excluded was obtained. This enables understanding how correlated the Wechsler is when the most achievement-like scale (Verbal Comprehension, which includes questions that require knowledge—Similarities and Vocabulary) is excluded. The same approach was taken with data from the WJ-IV test of cognitive abilities (McGrew, LaForte & Shrank, 2014, Table 5.7) and the K-ABC-II (Kaufman & Kaufman, 2004). The findings are provided in Table 1.5.

What is most revealing about the results in Table 1.5 is the clear pattern across the WISC-V, WJ-IV, and the KABC-II. The correlation between each of these tests and achievement was higher when the scales that demand verbal knowledge were included. The best explanation for why, for example, the Verbal Comprehension scale and the WIAT-III were so highly correlated is the similarity in content across the two tests. Some (e.g., Lohman & Hagen, 2001) argue that this is evidence of validity; we suggest, however, that correlations of achievement test scores with ability tests that demand knowledge of words and arithmetic are artificially inflated because of the shared content. The correlations between the scales that do not require knowledge are a more accurate estimate of the relationship between ability and achievement. In this summary, what is found is that the correlations of ability tests with achievement when controlling for overlap in content ranged

Table 1.5 Average Correlations Between Ability Tests and Achievement Including and Excluding Scales That Require Knowledge

| | Correlations | | Average Correlations | |
			All Scales	Scales Without Achievement
WISC-V	Verbal Comprehension	.74		
WIAT-III	Visual Spatial	.46		
$N = 201$	Fluid Reasoning	.40		
	Working Memory	.63		
	Processing Speed	.34	.53	.47
WJ-IV COG	Comprehension Knowledge	.50		
WJ-IV ACH	Fluid Reasoning	.71		
$N = 825$	Auditory Processing	.52		
	Short-Term Working Memory	.55		
	Cognitive Processing Speed	.55		
	Long-Term Retrieval	.43		
	Visual Processing	.45	.54	.50
KABC-II	Sequential/Gsm	.43		
WJ-III ACH	Simultaneous/Gv	.41		
$N = 167$	Learning/Glr	.50		
	Planning/Gf	.59		.48
	Knowledge/GC	.70	.53	
CAS	Planning	.57		
WJ-III ACH	Simultaneous	.67		
$N = 1,600$	Attention	.50		
	Successive	.60	.59	.59

Note: WJ-IV Scales Comprehension-Knowledge = Vocabulary and General Information; Fluid Reasoning = Number Series and Concept Formation; Auditory Processing = Phonological processing.

from .47 to .50. When including the knowledge-based scales the correlations were higher, ranging from .53 to .54. Most important, the correlation for the CAS, which does not include these achievement-laden subtests, was .59, higher than all the others.

These findings, as well as others (Naglieri & Bornstein, 2003; Naglieri & Rojahn, 2004; Naglieri, Goldstein, DeLauder, & Schwebach, 2006), of the PASS theory as measured by the CAS and CAS2 illustrate that this neurocognitive approach to understanding intelligence is strongly correlated with achievement test scores. Interestingly, these studies show that cognitive processes are as effective for prediction of academic performance as traditional IQ tests even though the CAS and CAS2 do not include academically laden measures such as vocabulary and arithmetic. This provides an advantage for understanding achievement strengths and weaknesses for children who come from disadvantaged environments as well as those who have had a history of academic failure.

RACE AND ETHNIC DIFFERENCES

The need for tests of ability to be appropriate for diverse populations has become progressively more important as the characteristics of the US population have changed. Recent federal law (e.g., IDEA 2004) stipulates that assessments must be selected and administered so as to be nondiscriminatory on a racial or cultural basis. It is, therefore, critical that any measures used for evaluation of ability be evaluated for test bias. The psychometric analysis should include internal evidence such as reliability, item difficulty, factor structure, as well as mean score differences; but the theoretical perspective taken by the test authors plays a critical role in making a test more or less appropriate for diverse populations.

Some researchers have suggested that conceptualizing intelligence on the basis of neuropsychological abilities would make tests more appropriate for diverse populations (Fagan, 2000; Naglieri, 2005). Fagan (2000) and Suzuki and Valencia (1997) argued that measures of cognitive processes that do not rely on tests with language and quantitative content are more appropriate for assessment of culturally and linguistically diverse populations. Although there is considerable evidence for the validity of general intelligence as measured by traditional IQ tests (see Jensen, 1980), researchers have traditionally found a mean difference of about 12 to 15 points between African Americans and Whites on measures of IQ that include verbal, quantitative, and nonverbal tests (Kaufman & Lichtenberger, 2006). Results for newer intelligence tests have been different.

The first evidence of smaller race differences for a different kind of ability test was reported in the original K-ABC manual. For children ages 2.5 to 12.5, without controlling for background variables, Whites ($N = 1,569$) scored 7 points higher than African Americans ($N = 807$) and 3 points higher than Hispanics ($N = 160$) on the global measure of mental processing (i.e., the total test score). These differences are considerably smaller than the differences of 16 points and 11 points, respectively, reported for the WISC-R Full Scale IQ (Kaufman & Kaufman, 1983, Tables 4.36 and 4.37; Kaufman, Lichtenberger, Fletcher-Janzen, & Kaufman, 2005, Table 6.7). Similar findings were reported by Naglieri (1986) in a study of 172 fifth-grade students (86 Whites and 86 African Americans matched on basic demographic variables) who were administered the K-ABC and the WISC-R. The difference between the groups on WISC-R Full Scale was 9.1, but the difference for the K-ABC was 6.0. Results for the KABC-II

(Kaufman & Kaufman, 2004) showed a similar reduction in race or ethnic differences. When controlling for gender and mother's education, African American children ages 3 to 18 years earned mean MPIs that were only 5 points lower than the means for White children (Kaufman & Kaufman, 2004, Tables 8.7 and 8.8; Kaufman et al., 2005, Table 6.7). Similar findings have been reported for the CAS.

Naglieri et al. (2005) compared PASS scores on the CAS for 298 African American children and 1,691 White children. Controlling for key demographic variables using regression analyses, they found a CAS Full Scale mean score difference of 4.8 points in favor of White children. Similarly, Naglieri, Rojahn, et al. (2007) studied the use of the PASS scores as measured by the CAS with Hispanic children by comparing Hispanic and White children. The study showed that the two groups differed by 6.1 points using unmatched samples, 5.1 with samples matched on basic demographic variables, and 4.8 points when demographics differences were statistically controlled. Researchers have also examined children with limited English language skills.

Naglieri, Otero, et al. (2007) compared scores obtained on the CAS when administered in English and Spanish to bilingual children ($N = 40$) referred for reading difficulties. They found a 3.0 point difference between the CAS Full Scale scores, and these scores were highly correlated (.96). Otero, Gonzalez, and Naglieri (2012) replicated that study with another group of students referred for reading problems and found CAS Full Scale scores that differed by less than 1 point and had a high correlation between the scores (.94). Results for the CAS2 Full Scale scores were reported in the test manual (Naglieri et al., 2014a). For children and adolescents ages 5 to 18 years without controlling for demographic variables, African Americans and non–African Americans differed by 6.3 standard scores, and with controls for demographic characteristics, the difference was 4.5. Similarly, without controlling for demographic differences, Hispanics and non-Hispanics differed on the CAS Full Scale scores by 4.5 points, and with controls for demographic characteristics, the difference was 1.8. Similar findings are reported for the CAS2: Brief (Naglieri, et al., 2014b).

These findings for race differences are best understood within the context of differences found on traditional intelligence tests. Table 1.6 provides a summary of standard score differences by race for the Stanford-Binet-IV (SB-IV; Roid, 2003); Woodcock-Johnson Tests of Cognitive Abilities, Third Edition (WJ-III; Woodcock, McGrew, & Mather, 2001); the WISC-IV (Wechsler, 2003); K-ABC and KABC-II (Kaufman & Kaufman, 1983, 2004); and the CAS (Naglieri & Das, 1997) and CAS2 (Naglieri et al., 2014a). The results for the WISC-IV are reported by O'Donnell (2009), for the SB-IV by Wasserman and Becker (2000),

Table 1.6 Standard Score Mean Differences by Race on Traditional and Nontraditional Intelligence Tests

Test	Difference
Traditional IQ Tests	
SB-IV (matched samples)	12.6
WISC-IV (normative sample)	11.5
WJ-III (normative sample)	10.9
WISC-IV (matched samples)	10.0
Nontraditional Tests	
K-ABC (normative sample)	7.0
K-ABC (matched samples)	6.1
KABC-II (matched samples)	5.0
CAS2 (normative sample)	6.3
CAS (demographic controls of normative sample)	4.8
CAS2 (demographic controls of normative sample)	4.3

Note: The data for these results are reported for the Stanford-Binet IV from Wasserman (2000); Woodcock-Johnson III from Edwards and Oakland (2006); Kaufman Assessment Battery for Children from Naglieri (1986); Kaufman Assessment Battery for Children II from Lichenberger, Sotelo-Dynega, and Kaufman (2009); CAS from Naglieri, Rojahn, Matto, and Aquilino (2005); CAS2 from Naglieri, Das, and Goldstein (2014a); and Wechsler Intelligence Scale for Children IV (WISC-IV) from O'Donnell (2009).

and the WJ-III results are from Edwards and Oakland (2006). The race differences for the K-ABC normative sample was reported in that test's manual (Kaufman & Kaufman, 1983) and the findings for the KABC-II were summarized by Lichtenberger, Sotelo-Dynega, and Kaufman (2009). Differences for the CAS were reported by Naglieri et al. (2005) and in the test manual for the CAS2 by Naglieri et al. (2014a). The results of this analysis of race differences illustrate that measuring ability as a cognitive process, in contrast to traditional concepts of IQ, provides a more equitable way to assess diverse populations of children. The findings suggest that as a group, traditional IQ tests showed differences in ability scores between the races that are about twice as large as that found for cognitive processing tests such as the CAS, CAS2, and K-ABC. All of the traditional tests included in Table 1.6 have verbal, quantitative, and nonverbal content, and two of these three types of questions demand knowledge that is very similar to that required by standardized achievement tests (see Naglieri & Bornstein, 2003). It is clear that conceptualizing and measuring ability using a cognitive processing approach results in smaller race differences without a loss of prediction to achievement or in the case of the CAS sensitivity to learning problems, both of which are critical components of validity.

DETECTING LEARNING PROBLEMS

All intelligence tests give a Full Scale score that is composed of scales that in turn are composed of subtests. The analysis of subtest and scale variation on ability tests is a method called *profile analysis,* which has been advocated by Kaufman (1994) and others (e.g., Sattler, 1988) to identify strengths and weaknesses that may underlie a learning disability. Information about strengths and weaknesses has been used to generate hypotheses that are integrated with other information so that decisions can be made regarding eligibility, diagnosis, and treatment. Despite the widespread use of this method, some have argued that subtest profile analysis does not provide useful information beyond that which is obtained from the IQ scores (e.g., Dombrowski & Watkins, 2013; McDermott, Fantuzzo, & Glutting, 1990). Naglieri (1999) proposed that subtest analysis is problematic because of limitations in subtest reliability and validity and suggested that profile analysis of scales could be more effective. Theoretically derived scales could be helpful if the ability test shows a specific pattern for a specific group of exceptional students, which in turn could have implications for understanding the cognitive character-istics of the group, allow for guidance during the eligibility process (see Naglieri, 2011a, 2012) and guide interventions (Naglieri & Pickering, 2010).

Naglieri (2011a) summarized research about students with reading decoding failure and ADHD reported in the technical manual for the Wechsler Intelligence Scale for Children, Fourth Edition (WISC-IV; Wechsler, 2003) technical manual; for the Woodcock-Johnson III Tests of Cognitive Abilities (WJ-III; Woodcock et al., 2001) from Wendling, Mather, and Shrank (2009), and CAS data from the technical manual and Naglieri, Otero, et al. (2007). For students with autism spectrum disorders (ASD) data were obtained for the WISC-IV (Wechsler, 2003), CAS (from Goldstein & Naglieri, 2011), WJ-III (from Wendling et al., 2009), and the K-ABC II (technical manual). The findings should be considered with recognition that the samples were not matched on demographic variables across the various studies, the accuracy of the diagnosis may not have been verified, and some of the sample sizes were small. Notwithstanding these limitations, the findings provide important insights into the extent to which these various tests are likely to yield scale-level profiles that are distinctive, theoretically logical, and ultimately relevant to instruction.

The results of the summary of scale profiles for the measures provided in Figure 1.8 suggest that some of these tests yield profiles that are more distinct than others across the three groups of exceptional children. The scores across all scales on the WJ-III for students with specific reading decoding difficulties were all within the average range, and all of the KABC-II scores were in the 80s. The

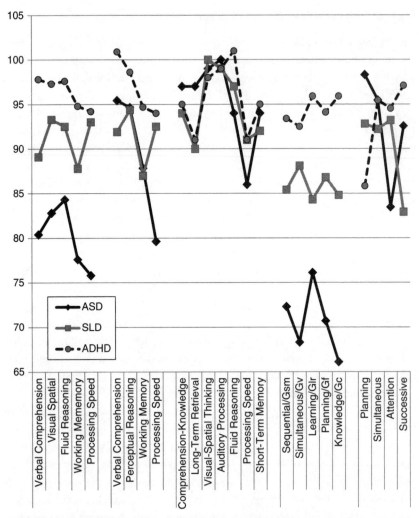

Figure 1.8 Scale Profiles Across Ability Tests for Special Populations

Note: Gc = Comprehension-Knowledge; Glr = Long-Term Retrieval; Gv = Visual-Spatial Thinking;
Ga = Auditory Processing; Gf = Fluid Reasoning: Gs = Processing Speed;
Gsm = Short-Term Memory; GIA = General Intellectual Ability.

WISC-IV profile was lowest for the Working Memory scale. The CAS profile showed variability across the four PASS scales with a very low score of 82.9 on the Successive scale. These findings are consistent with the view that students with specific reading decoding failure also have considerable difficulty with tasks that involve sequencing of information (Das, Janzen, & Georgiou, 2007).

The test profiles for students with ADHD showed that all scores for the scales on the WISC-IV, WJ-III, and KABC-II were within the average range. None of these tests provided evidence of a cognitive problem related to ADHD, except for a low score on the Planning scale of the CAS. Difficulty with Planning (e.g., executive function) for children with ADHD is consistent with Barkley's view that ADHD is a failure of self-control (Barkley, 1997), which has been described as frontal lobe functioning (Goldberg, 2009). Finally, the results for individuals with ASD show that processing speed on scores for the WISC-IV and the WJ-III were very low. This is similar to the findings for these two tests for individuals with ADHD. The low processing speed scores provide little insight into the cognitive characteristics of students with ASD and ADHD. Importantly, the low Attention score on the CAS is consistent with the conceptualization that individuals with ASD have "difficulties in disengaging and shifting attention" (Klinger, O'Kelley, & Mussey, 2009, p. 214). The findings for those with ASD, similar to the results for those with SLD and ADHD, show that the PASS scores indicated distinctive profiles for students with different diagnoses.

This summary of research on PASS as measured by the CAS, CAS2, CAS2: Brief, and CAS2: Rating Scale provides a brief examination of the information about the utility of this approach. Such a summary is, by definition, limited in details, and therefore interested readers should consult the CAS2 manuals as well as ongoing research on PASS theory. Additional information may also be obtained from one of the authors' website: www.jacknaglieri.com.

PASS AND ACADEMIC INTERVENTIONS

One of the most important goals for the assessment of PASS neurocognitive abilities is to help decide how a student learns best, what obstacles to learning exist, and how this information informs instruction. Knowing the PASS profile of an individual student can help determine instruction. Once we know how the student thinks and learns, then coordinating the information about the PASS profile from the CAS2 with the cognitive processing demands of the instruction (see the Chapter 5, "Intervention") will provide ways to maximize learning. The relationship between PASS neurocognitive processes and academic instruction has been examined in a series of research studies that will be briefly described.

There are several resources for applying the PASS theory to academic instruction and remediation. The PASS Remedial Program (PREP; Das, 1999) and COGENT (Das, 2004) are instructional methods that have been studied by Das and his colleagues. Naglieri and colleagues have studied a method known as the *planning facilitation* (see Naglieri & Pickering, 2010). This method draws heavily on cognitively based instructional methods described, for example, in Kirby and Williams (1991), *Learning Problems: A Cognitive Approach*; Pressley and Woloshyn (1995), *Cognitive Strategy Instruction That Really Improves Children's Academic Performance* (2nd ed.); Scheid (1993), *Helping Students Become Strategic Learners*; and Naglieri and Pickering (2010), *Helping Children Learn: Intervention Handouts for Use in School and Home* (2nd ed.). These two areas of research will be summarized in the next section.

PLANNING FACILITATION

The connection between planning and intervention has been examined in several studies involving math and reading. These intervention studies focused on the concept that children can be encouraged to be more strategic (use good Planning) when they complete academic tasks and that the facilitation of plans positively affects academic performance. The initial concept for planning facilitation was based on the work of Cormier, Carlson, and Das (1990) and Kar, Dash, Das, and Carlson (1992). These authors taught children to discover the value of strategy use without being specifically instructed to do so. The children were encouraged to examine the demands of the task in a strategic and organized manner. They demonstrated that students differentially benefited from the technique that encouraged the use of strategies. That is, students who performed poorly on Planning as measured by the CAS2 demonstrated significantly greater gains than those with higher planning scores or those with low scores on the Attention, Simultaneous, or Successive scales. These results indicated that a relationship between PASS and instruction was found.

Naglieri and Gottling (1995, 1997) demonstrated that planning facilitation could improve children's performance in math calculation. All children in these studies attended a special school for those with learning disabilities. In the investigations students completed mathematics work sheets in sessions over about a 2-month period. The method designed to indirectly teach planning was applied in individual one-on-one tutoring sessions (Naglieri & Gottling, 1995) or in the classroom by the teacher (Naglieri & Gottling, 1997) about two to three times per week in half-hour blocks of time. In the intervention phase, the students were given a 10-minute period for completing a mathematics page, a 10-minute period was used for facilitating planning, and another 10-minute period was devoted to mathematics. All students were exposed to the intervention sessions that involved the three 10-minute segments of mathematics-discussion-mathematics in 30-minute instructional periods. Students were encouraged to recognize the need to plan to use strategies when completing mathematic problems during the intervention periods. The teachers provided probes that facilitated discussion and encouraged the children to consider various ways to be more successful. A student's response often became the beginning point for discussion and further development of the strategy. More details about the method are provided by Naglieri and Gottling (1995, 1997) and by Naglieri and Pickering (2010).

Naglieri and Johnson (2000) further studied the relationship between planning facilitation and PASS profiles for a class of children with learning disabilities and mild mental impairments. The purpose of their study was to determine if children with cognitive weaknesses in each of the four PASS processes showed different rates of improvement when given the same group planning facilitation instruction. Students with a cognitive weakness (an individual PASS score significantly lower than the child's mean and below 85) in Planning, Attention, Simultaneous, and Successive scales were used to form contrast groups after all the classroom work was completed. A no-cognitive-weakness group was also identified. Naglieri and Johnson (2000) found that children with a cognitive weakness in Planning improved considerably over baseline rates, and those with no cognitive weakness improved only marginally. Similarly, children with cognitive weaknesses in Simultaneous, Successive, and Attention showed substantially lower rates of improvement. The importance of this study was that the five groups of children responded very differently to the same intervention. Thus, PASS processing scores were predictive of the children's response to this math intervention.

The effects facilitating planning had on reading comprehension were reported by Haddad, Garcia, Naglieri, Grimditch, McAndrews, and Eubanks (2003). Their study examined whether an instruction designed to facilitate Planning would have differential benefits on reading comprehension, and if improvement was related to the PASS processing scores of each child. The researchers used a sample of general education children sorted into groups based their PASS scale profiles. Even though the groups did not differ by CAS Full Scale scores or pretest reading comprehension scores, children with a Planning weakness benefited substantially (effect size of 1.4) from the instruction designed to encourage the use of strategies and plans. By contrast, children with no PASS weakness or a Successive weakness did not benefit as much (effect sizes of .52 and .06, respectively). These results further support previous research suggesting that the PASS profiles are relevant to instruction.

Iseman and Naglieri (2011) examined the effectiveness of the strategy instruction for 10- to 15-year-old students with LD and ADHD randomly assigned to an experimental group or a control group that received standard math instruction. They found large pre-post effect sizes for students in the experimental group (0.85) but not the control group (0.26) on classroom math worksheets as well as standardized test score differences in math fluency (1.17 and .09, respectively) and numerical operations (.40 and −.14, respectively). One year later, the experimental group continued to outperform the control group. These findings strongly suggested that students with LD and ADHD in the experimental group evidenced greater improvement in math work sheets, transfer to standardized tests of math, and at follow-up 1 year later than the control group. The findings also illustrate the effectiveness of strategy instruction, especially for those with low Planning scores on the CAS.

The results of these Planning strategy instruction studies using academic tasks suggest that changing the way aptitude is conceptualized (e.g., as the PASS rather than traditional IQ) and measured (using the CAS2) increases the probability that an aptitude-by-treatment interaction (ATI) is detected. Past ATI research suffered from conceptualizations of aptitudes based on the general intelligence model, which did not adequately assess basic psychological processes that are related to instruction. The traditional IQ approach is very different from the PASS theory as measured by the CAS2. The summaries of studies provided here are especially different from previous ATI research that found students with low general ability improve little, whereas those with high general ability respond more to instruction. By contrast, children with a weakness in one of the PASS processes (Planning) benefited more from instruction compared to children who had no weakness or a weakness in a different PASS process. The results of these studies also suggest that the PASS profiles can help identify which academic instruction will most likely be successful. The application of these results is further elaborated in Chapter 5 in this book and by Naglieri and Pickering (2010).

PREP AND COGENT

PASS Reading Enhancement Program (PREP), and Cognition Enhancement Training (COGENT) (Das, 2009) was developed as a cognitively grounded remedial program based on the PASS theory of cognitive functioning (Das et al., 1994). It aims at improving the processing strategies—specifically, Simultaneous and Successive processing—that underlie reading, while at the same time avoiding the direct teaching of word-reading skills such as phoneme segmentation or blending. PREP is also founded on the premise that the transfer of principles is best facilitated through inductive, rather than deductive, inference (see Das, 2009, for details). The program is, therefore, structured so that indirectly acquired strategies are likely to be used in appropriate ways.

PREP is appropriate for poor readers in grades 2 through 5 who are experiencing reading problems. Each of the 10 tasks in PREP involves a cognitive

processing–focused emphasis component and a curriculum-related component. The cognitive-processing components, which require the application of
Simultaneous or Successive strategies, include structured nonreading tasks.
These tasks also facilitate transfer by providing the opportunity for children
to develop and internalize strategies in their own way (Das, Mishra, & Pool,
1995). The curriculum-related components involve the same cognitive demands
as their matched cognitive-processing components (e.g., Simultaneous and
Successive processing). These cognitive processes have been closely linked to
reading and spelling (Das et al., 1994). Several studies attest to the efficacy of
PREP for enhancement of reading and comprehension (Boden & Kirby, 1995;
Carlson & Das, 1997; Das et al., 1995; Parrila, Das, Kendrick, Papadopoulos, &
Kirby 1999).

The utility of PASS Reading Enhancement Program (PREP) was examined
(Das, Hayward, Georgiou, Janzen, & Boora, 2008) on Canadian First Nations
children. Effectiveness of two reading intervention programs (phonics-based and
PREP) was investigated in Study 1 with 63 First Nations children identified as
poor readers in grades 3 and 4. In Study 2, the efficacy of additional sessions for
inductive learning was compared to PREP. Results of Study 1 showed a significant
improvement for word reading and pseudo-word decoding reading tasks following PREP. The phonics-based program resulted in similar improvement in only
one of the reading tasks, word decoding. In Study 2, the important dependent
variables were word reading and word decoding as well as passage comprehension. Results showed that PREP participants evidenced continued improvements
in their reading decoding and comprehension. The next study on PREP (Mahapatra, Das, Stack-Cutler, & Parrila, 2010) involved two groups of children selected
from two English schools in India. One group consisted of 15 poor readers in
grade 4 who experienced difficulty in comprehension and a comparison group of
15 normal readers in grade 4 who did not receive PREP. Performance on word
reading and reading comprehension scores (Woodcock's Reading Mastery Test)
and performance on tests of PASS cognitive processes were recorded pre- and
posttest. Results showed a significant improvement in comprehension as well as in
Simultaneous processing scores in the PREP group, suggesting that this approach
is effective even in children whose first language is not English. This has obvious
application possibilities for all children who learn English as a second language.

COGENT is a program designed to improve the cognitive development of
children ages 4 to 7 or those who are beginning readers. The COGENT program is designed for the enhancement of cognition especially linked to literacy
and school learning. The main objective is to supplement children's literacy skills,
and the program should benefit cognitive development of normal children as well

as children with special needs. COGENT consists of five distinct modules, each designed to activate different aspects of cognitive processes, language, and literacy. The tasks are also designed to enhance phonological awareness and working memory and spatial relationships expressed in statements provided by the facilitator. Further elaboration of the COGENT program is provided by Das (2009) and in a study by Hayward, Das, and Janzen (2007). This study is important because they studied the effects of PREP and COGENT on Canadian First Nations children who often have reading problems. Forty-five grade 3 students from a reservation school in Western Canada were divided into remedial groups and no-risk control groups. One remedial group was given the cognitive enhancement program (COGENT) throughout the school year. The second group received COGENT for the first half of the year followed by a pull-out cognitive-based reading enhancement program (PREP). Results showed significant improvements word reading and comprehension for those exposed to COGENT.

🐾 TEST YOURSELF 🐾

1. **What is the key difference between the CAS2 and traditional IQ?**
   a. The CAS2 is based on Army mental testing methods.
   b. The CAS2 is designed to be used for intervention planning.
   c. The CAS2 is based on a specific neurocognitive theory.
   d. The CAS2 does not include verbal and quantitative tests.
   e. All choices are true except (a).

2. **Which ability test yields the smallest group differences and is the best to use for nondiscriminatory assessment?**
   a. WISC-V
   b. WJ-IV
   c. KABC-II
   d. CAS2

3. **The CAS2 includes all of the following scales except which choice?**
   a. PASS
   b. Full Scale
   c. Executive Function
   d. Fluid Reasoning
   e. Working Memory

4. **Which ability test yields distinct scale profiles for students with specific learning disabilities?**
   a. WISC-V
   b. WJ-IV

  c. CAS2
  d. KABC-II
5. Which ability test correlates the highest with academic achievement test scores?
  a. WISC-V
  b. CAS2
  c. WJ-IV
  d. KABC-II

Answers: 1. e; 2. d; 3. d; 4. c; 5. b

Two

ADMINISTRATION AND SCORING OF THE CAS2, CAS2: BRIEF, AND CAS2: RATING SCALE

T he purpose of this chapter is to summarize a number of important details about administration of the CAS2, CAS2: Brief, and CAS2: Rating Scale. This will include some basic issues (e.g., seating and rapport) and points specific to each of the CAS2 tools (e.g., starting rules and spoiled subtests). Specific issues relating to the administration of the CAS2, CAS2: Brief, and CAS2: Rating Scale are provided to ensure that practitioners will be able to give the three measures effectively.

APPROPRIATE TESTING CONDITIONS

The CAS2 and CAS2: Brief need to be administered and scored as indicated in the respective tests' manual. Although it is the obligation of the user to ensure that administration procedures are consistent with applicable professional standards, it is also assumed that examiners will create an appropriate environment for the standardized measures. Development and maintenance of rapport with a child as well as a teacher, for example, are critical to obtaining good data. Similarly, the importance of following directions precisely cannot be overstated. This text, however, is not intended to provide a description of good testing practices similar to that provided elsewhere, for example, Sattler (2008). Instead some issues that are specific to administration of the three CAS2 measures are addressed.

Seating Arrangement

Proper administration is facilitated if the examiner is within reach of the child and can closely observe the child's actions. This is especially important for the Planning subtests, which involve recording the strategies used by the child (see the "Strategy Assessment" section in this chapter). Examiners would likely find sitting across from the child or across the corner of a table most appropriate for this instrument.

Administration Directions

The CAS2 and CAS2: Brief instructions typically involve verbal and nonverbal instructions. Examiners need to carefully observe the gestures (indicated in parenthetical statements following or preceding the text) that correspond to the oral directions. For example, the administration directions for the CAS2 subtest Number Detection are shown in Figure 2.1. Note that the oral instructions for the child are accompanied by directions for the examiner to point at particular times and in

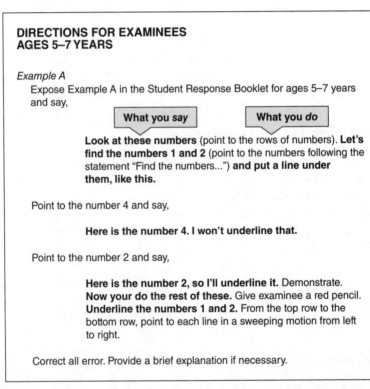

Figure 2.1   Example of CAS2 and CAS2: Brief Verbal Instructions and Gestures That Accompany Them

particular ways to the rows, numbers, and sections of the Response Book. Examiners are instructed to point "From the top row to the bottom row, point to each line in a sweeping motion from left to right" to ensure that the child understands the sequence in which the task must be completed.

DON'T FORGET 2.1

Be sure to follow the administration directions exactly. Pay special attention to the oral statements and associated gestures that are designed to guide the child's attention to the materials on the CAS2 and CAS2: Brief.

Administration Information

There are two places in the CAS2 that provide information about administration of the test—the administration and scoring manual and the record form. Both sources provide identical information about various administration issues in a text box at the top of their respective sections. This information includes what pages are used in the response or stimulus books, if a stopwatch or red pencil is needed, time limits, which items to give, and so on. For example, Figure 2.2 shows the administration box for Planned Number Matching, which appears in the administration and scoring manual, and Figure 2.3 shows the box that appears in the record form. This redundancy provides examiners ample opportunity to obtain information about how to give the subtests.

The CAS2: Brief does not have a separate administration and scoring manual. Instead, all information about administration of the CAS2: Brief subtests is provided directly on the examiner's record form as shown in Figure 2.4.

Core and Extended Batteries

There are two versions of the CAS2: a 12-subtest Extended Battery and an 8-subtest Core Battery. Each of the two batteries is composed of Planning, Attention, Simultaneous, and Successive subtests. If the Core Battery is administered, the first two subtests in each of the four PASS Scales are given. The subtests included in the Core Battery are clearly noted in several ways on the record form and in the administration and scoring manual. Figure 2.5 shows that those subtests that form the Core Battery appear in dark blue boxes on the front of the record form. Regardless of which version is administered, both yield PASS scale and Full Scale standard scores with a mean of 100 and SD of 15.

Planned Number Matching

DESCRIPTION

The examinee's task is to find and underline the two numbers that are the same in each row. Each item set has eight rows of numbers, and each row contains six numbers. This subtest is included in the Extended Battery only.

Materials	Examiner Record Form, page 4 Student Response Booklet (ages 5–7), pages 23–25 Student Response Booklet (ages 8–18), pages 26–29 Red pencil Stopwatch Scoring template
Administer	Ages 5–7: Demonstration, Examples A & B, Item Sets 1 & 2 Ages 8–18: Demonstration, Examples A & B, Item Sets 2–4
Time Limit	180 seconds (3:00 minutes) per item set
Record	Time in seconds Number correct Strategy assessment

Figure 2.2 CAS2 Administration Box for Planned Number Matching

⩵ *Rapid Reference 2.1*

The CAS2 Extended Battery consists of all 12 subtests, and the Core Battery has 8 subtests.

Subtest Order

It is necessary that the CAS2 and the CAS2: Brief subtests be administered in the prescribed order to retain the integrity of the test and reduce the influence

Planned Number Matching

Materials	Administration and Scoring Manual, pages 22–28
	Response Booklet (ages 5–7), pages 23–25
	Response Booklet (ages 8–18), pages 26–29
	Red pencil
	Stopwatch
Administer	Ages 5–7: Demonstration, Examples A & B, Item Sets 1 & 2
	Ages 8–18: Demonstration, Examples A & B, Item Sets 2–4
Time Limits	180 seconds (3:00 minutes) per item set
Record	Time in seconds
	Number correct
	Strategy assessment

Figure 2.3 Administration Information in the CAS2 Record Form

---

Simultaneous Matrices

Administration:
Age-based entry points: apply ceiling (ceiling of 4: basal of 2. if needed)

Materials:
CAS2: Brief Stimulus Book (pp. 1–90): #2 pencils

Objective:
Examinees should select the option that best completes the matrix.

Entry Points and Basals: If an examinee age 12–18 fails the first item, administer previous items in reverse order until two consecutive correct answers have been obtained (basal). Record the response in the appropriate column, and then score the response (1 = *correct.* 0 = *incorrect*) for each item.

Discontinue Rule: Discontinue subtest if examinee receives four consecutive incorrect responses.

Directions for All Examinees:
Show example in the CAS2: Brief Stimulus Book (p. 1), and say, **Look at this page. There is a piece missing here** (point to the question mark). **Which one of these** (point to the five options in a sweeping motion) **goes here?** (Point to the question mark.) If the response is correct, say, **Yes, that's the right one because it's all yellow.** If incorrect, point to Option 3 and say, **This is the right one because it's all yellow.** (If necessary, provide a brief explanation.) Continue with directions for the appropriate age group.

Figure 2.4 Administration Information in the CAS2: Brief Record Form

Examiner Record Form

Jack A. Naglieri   J. P. Das   Sam Goldstein

Section 2. Subtest and Composite Scores

Subtest	Raw Score	Scaled Score			
		PLAN	SIM	ATT	SUC
Planned Codes (PCd)					
Planned Connections (PCn)					
Planned Number Matching (PNM)					
Matrices (MAT)					
Verbal-Spatial Relations (VSR)					
Figure Memory (FM)					
Expressive Attention (EA)					
Number Detection (ND)					
Receptive Attention (RA)					
Word Series (WS)					
Sentence Repetition/ Questions (SR/SQ)					
Visual Digit Span (VDS)					

Figure 2.5 CAS2 Extended and Core Batteries as Shown on Page 1 of the Record Form

of extraneous variables on the child's performance. The Planning, Simultaneous, Attention, and Successive order was determined to maximize the validity of the scales. The Planning tests are administered first because they provide the least restrictions on how the child may complete the task. This gives the child considerable flexibility to solve the subtest in any manner. By contrast, the Attention subtests must be completed in the prescribed order (e.g., left to right, top to bottom). By administering the Planning subtests before the Attention subtests the amount of constraint increases over time. If the Attention subtests were administered before the Planning ones, some children could be inhibited by the more structured instruction. The Simultaneous subtests are given after Planning subtests to give the examinee a respite from responding on paper. Successive processing subtests are given last because they typically take less time.

Age Partition

Instructions and in some cases sets of items differ across the age ranges for which the CAS2 and CAS2: Brief are administered. This enables tailoring of specific items to particular age groups. In addition, two of the Attention subtests have different types of materials so that the content of the test would be more appropriate for children in the two age groups. Specialized content was necessary to ensure that younger children would easily understand the items and those older children would not view subtests as too simple. For example, the CAS2 Expressive Attention subtest for 5- to 7-year-olds contains pictures of animals but the version for 8- to 17-year-olds is composed of words. The subtests with different versions include Expressive Attention and Receptive Attention. The subtest Expressive Attention on the CAS2: Brief also has different content for ages 4 to 7 and 8 to 18 years.

Subtests Given by Age

All of the CAS2 subtests, except one, are given to all children regardless of age. The exception is Sentence Repetition, which is administered only at ages 5–7 years, and Sentence Questions, which is given only to children 8–18 years of age. All four subtests in the CAS2: Brief are given to all ages. The information regarding which items to give by age is designated in the administration and scoring manual and the record form. The items that are to be given for children ages 5–7 or 8–18 years are also provided in the way the record form is graphically constructed, as shown in Figure 2.6 for the Planned Connections subtest. The form includes boxes that are arranged so that they are filled in only when the test was given. Note that the column labeled "Ages 5–7" has seven boxes below it. This indicates that in addition to the demonstration and sample A Items, items 1–4 are given. Similarly, the column labeled "Ages 8–18" has seven boxes that correspond to items 5–11, indicating that these items are given in addition to the samples.

Start and Reverse Rules

The CAS2 and CAS2: Brief Simultaneous and Successive subtests have designated starting points. For example, whereas children below age 8 always begin with the

Planned Connections

Materials   Administration and Scoring Manual,
            pages 16–21
            Response Booklet (ages 5–7), pages 11–21
            Response Booklet (ages 8–18), pages 10–24
            Red pencil
            Stopwatch

Administer Ages 5–7: Demonstration, Example A, Items 1–7
            Ages 8–18: Examples A & B, Items 5–11

Time Limits See below

Record   Time in seconds
            Strategy assessment

	Item	Time Limit	Time in Seconds Ages 5–7	Time in Seconds Ages 8–18
5–7 Years	Demonstration			
All Ages	Example A			
5–7 Years	1.	60" (1:00)		
	2.	60" (1:00)		
	3.	60" (1:00)		
	4.	90" (1:30)		
		+		
8–18 Years	5.	90" (1:30)		
	6.	150" (2:30)		
	7.	150" (2:30)		
	5–7 Stop			+
	Example B			
	8.	150" (2:30)		
	9.	150" (2:30)		
	10.	180" (3:00)		
	11.	180" (3:00)		
	8–18 Stop			
	Raw Score			
			Sum of Items 1–7 Total Seconds	Sum of Items 5–11 Total Seconds

Figure 2.6 CAS2 Planned Connections Subtest Items Administered by Age

first item, those 8 and above begin with a more advanced item. For example, examinees age 8 and above begin with item 5 on the Word Series subtest. When a child age 8 to 18 years fails the first item administered, the preceding items are administered in reverse order until two consecutive correct answers have been obtained. Then continue forward administration if the discontinue rule has not been met.

Discontinue Rule

The administration of the Simultaneous and Successive subtests of the CAS2 and CAS2: Brief is discontinued after four consecutively numbered item failures. The Expressive Attention subtest (ages 8 to 18) may be discontinued when the examinee has difficulty reading the colored words or difficulty identifying colors.

Time Limits

Time limits for items on the CAS2 and CAS2: Brief vary and are therefore provided in the administration directions manual and in the record form. These limits are provided in total seconds (e.g., 150") as well as minutes and seconds (e.g., 2:30) to accommodate professionals who use digital or analog stopwatches. The point at which to begin timing is clearly indicted in the administration and scoring manual. Following these instructions carefully will ensure accurate evaluation of the time children take to complete the items. In those instances when time limits are not provided (e.g., Nonverbal Matrices), examiners should exercise good judgment when encouraging the child to attempt the next item.

Rates of Presentation

There are several subtests that require stimuli to be presented at a specific rate or for an exact period of time. On the CAS2 this includes Figure Memory, Word Series, Sentence Repetition/Sentence Questions, and Visual Digit Span. Word Series requires administration at the rate of one word per second, and words are presented at the rate of two words per second on Sentence Repetition and Sentence Questions. Figure Memory requires stimuli be presented for exactly 5 seconds. Visual Digit Span items are presented for the number of seconds that is equal to the number of digits in the item up to a maximum of 5 seconds. The items on the CAS2: Brief Successive Digits subtest are administered at the rate of one per second. These time limits must be followed exactly to ensure comparison to the normative sample.

Strategy Assessment

All the CAS2 and CAS2: Brief Planning subtests include an observational phase called *strategy assessment*. This means that the examiner records if the examinee used strategies to complete the items. Strategy assessment was developed to obtain information about how the child completed the items and is used to help describe the standard scores that were obtained (see the respective test manuals for more information). This information enables the examiner to go beyond the score and understand the methods the child used during Planning. The specific strategy used is then interpreted in relation to the standard score and the percentage of children who used that strategy in the standardization sample. This can help explain a particularly high or low Planning score and be integrated into the overall pool of data that comprises the entire evaluation.

Strategy assessment includes two parts: observed strategies and reported strategies. Observed strategies are those seen by the examiner through nonobtrusive means when the child completes the items. Examiners often evaluate how children complete test items through careful observation during testing, and this method provides information that goes beyond the Planning score. Reported strategies are obtained following completion of the item(s) of each Planning subtest. The examiner obtains this information by saying "Tell me how you did these." or "How did you find what you were looking for?" or a similar statement. The strategies can be communicated by the child through either verbal or nonverbal (gesturing) means.

≡ *Rapid Reference 2.2*

Strategy assessment is conducted at the end of administration of each of the Planning subtests on the CAS2 and CAS2: Brief.

To facilitate recording of strategies that were both observed and reported, a strategy assessment checklist is included in the appropriate sections of the record form (see Figure 2.7). Examiners indicate which strategy or strategies were used by placing a check mark (or the numbers 1, 2, 3, or 4) to facilitate recall of a specific strategy used by the child on one or more of the stimulus tasks (e.g., 2 = child scanned left to right on stimulus 2) in the appropriate location(s) during the observation and reporting stages. Unique strategies can be recorded in the space provided. Spontaneous verbalizations made by the child either before, during, or after each task should be recorded as well if they provide further insight (e.g., a child spontaneously commenting on the presentation of the second planned codes

Strategy Checklist			
Observed	**Reported**	**Description of Strategy**	**Item Set**
✓	✓	1. Coded left to right, top to bottom	*1*
		2. Said codes to self out loud	
	✓	3. Coded one letter at a time (e.g, did As, then Bs)	*3–6*
		4. Coded neatly and slowly	
✓		5. Used a pattern found in a previous item	*2*
	✓	6. Looked for the pattern in the item	*3–6*
		7. Looked at codes already completed, rather than using the key	
Other: Observed _____ Reported _____			

Figure 2.7 Example of Strategy Assessment Checklist from the CAS2: Brief Planned Codes Subtest

stimulus—"oh you tried to fool me, you changed the pattern"—or asking before the task begins, "are you timing how long I take" or "do I have a certain amount of time and then you stop me?").

Provide Help Guidelines

The instructions for administration of the CAS2 and the CAS2: Brief have been written to ensure that the child will understand the demands of every subtest. Several methods have been used to ensure that the child understands what is being requested. This includes sample and demonstration items as well as opportunities for the examiner to clarify the requirements of the task. For example, after the first sample in Expressive Attention, the child is asked if he or she is ready to begin. If the child does not seem ready or appears in any way confused or uncertain, the examiner is instructed to "provide a brief explanation if necessary." This instruction is intended to give the examiner the freedom to

DON'T FORGET 2.2

Once standardized administration directions have been given, if the examinee does not seem ready or appears in any way confused or uncertain, the examiner may "provide a brief explanation if necessary." Explanations may be in the form of gestures, verbal statements, or communication in another language. Be careful not to inadvertently teach the child the task; rather, explain what is required.

explain what the child must do in whatever terms are considered necessary so as to ensure that the child understands the task. This interaction can be in any form including gestures, verbal statements, or communication in any language. The intent of this instruction is to give the examiner full decision making to make clear the demands of the subtest and to enable the examiner to be certain that the child was well-informed about what to do. *This instruction, however, is not intended to teach the child how to do the test but rather to tell the child what is required.*

≡ Rapid Reference 2.3

....

Provide help guidelines on the CAS2 and CAS2: Brief give the examiner the option to restate the subtest directions in any language or any manner to ensure the child knows the demands of the task.

Bilingual or Hearing-Impaired Children

The CAS2 and CAS2: Brief instructions for administration were designed to give the examiner flexibility to interact with the child to ensure that good data are obtained. It is assumed that the child has an adequate working knowledge of English so that he or she will benefit from the samples and demonstrations provided. It is, as discussed previously, possible to augment the English instructions when the statements "provide a brief explanation if necessary" or "provide additional help when needed" is given. That is, during introductory portions of the subtests examiners who have the knowledge to interact with the child in his or her native language or through another means such as sign language may do so when instructed to provide assistance. The child's need for information in another language or method can become obvious when the child asks for help using another language, if it is apparent that the child is hearing impaired, or if the child does not respond to the instruction. In such instances it is the responsibility of the examiner to decide when to use another method of communication. It is also the responsibility of the examiner to determine if, because he or she does not know the child's other language, another examiner should evaluate the child.

Spoiled Subtests or Omitted Ratings

If a subtest from the 12-subtest Extended Battery is spoiled during administration, there are two options. First, the PASS and Full Scale scores can be computed for the 8-subtest Core Battery version. The second option is to prorate the sum of three subtest scaled scores from the sum of the two that were not spoiled using Table 3.2 in the CAS2 administration and scoring manual. To use this table, enter the first column with the sum of the scaled scores for the two subtests. Read across the table to obtain the estimated sum of three subtests based on the sum of the two. This value is used to obtain the appropriate Planning, Attention, Simultaneous, and Successive scale index scores. Use the prorated sum of scaled scores when summing the PASS scores to obtain the Full Scale score.

If one of the Core Battery subtests is spoiled during administration, practitioners have the option to give the last subtest on that scale. That subtest scaled score can be used as one of the two scores needed to obtain a Core Battery sum of scaled scores and the Full Scale index score.

There is no alternative subtest to give if one of the subtests on the CAS2: Brief is spoiled. The only option would be to administer the CAS2 8-subtest version.

In the event that a teacher omits ratings on the CAS2: Rating Scale, the examiner may request that the item(s) be completed. If that is not possible, then the scores on the respective PASS scales will be underestimates and should be interpreted accordingly. In these instances, the examiner may have to readminister the scale to another teacher.

ADMINISTRATION OF CAS2

In this section some specific issues that are important to consider when administering each of the CAS2, CAS2: Brief, and CAS2: Rating Scale are provided. This text is organized by measure and subtest in the order of administration. Each section contains a brief description of the subtest and specific comments regarding administration of the items followed by scoring guidelines. For more details, readers should consult the manuals for each of these measures.

Planned Codes

This subtest contains four items, each with its own set of codes and particular arrangements of rows and columns. A legend at the top of each page shows which letters correspond to which codes (e.g., A, B, C, D with OX, XX, OO, XO, respectively). Just below the legend are four rows and eight columns of letters without the codes. Children write the corresponding codes in empty boxes beneath each of the letters. The items differ in the correspondence of letters to codes and the position of the letters on the page. In the first item, the letters appear in columns for A, B, C, and D. That is, all the As appear in the first column, all the Bs in the second column, all the Cs in the third column, and so on. On the second item, the letters are configured in a diagonal pattern.

Administration Comments
- The child may fill in the boxes in any order, and in fact they are instructed "You can do it any way you want." This is to enable the child to use strategies such as doing all the As first or completing the page by skipping around.
- Although self-corrections are permitted, the children are discouraged from spending more than a second or two erasing. If necessary the examiner should tell the child to keep going. Similarly, if the child stops prior to the expiration of the time limit, the examiner instructs the child to keep going.
- Strategy assessment is conducted after the last item, number 4, is completed.

Planned Connections

This subtest contains two types of items. The first seven items require children ages 5–7 years to connect numbers in sequential order. For older children, the last four items require the examinee to connect numbers and letters in sequential order, alternating between numbers and letters (e.g., 1-A-2-B-3-C). If the examinee makes a mistake, the examiner directs the child back to the previous correct position. Children 5–7 years of age are administered items 1–7. Children 8–18 years of age are administered items 5–11. The items are constructed so that children never complete a sequence by crossing one line over the other. This provides a means of reducing the areas to be searched when looking for the next number or letter.

Administration Comments
- There are two important points about starting each Planned Connections item. First, timing begins when the examiner says "Now do this one. Begin here" and points to the number 1. Second, the examiner always tells the child where to begin by pointing to the number 1.
- It is imperative that children complete the sequence correctly and therefore errors are corrected immediately. An error is defined as the connection of two boxes that are not in correct sequence. If the child makes an error the examiner is instructed to immediately say, "Wait, you made a mistake. Begin again from here" (and point to the previous correct location). Instructions do not allow the child to erase an error because the timing does not stop during this instruction.

- In order to correct the child as the task is being completed the examiner must be able to keep track of the child's progress. This is not too difficult when the items are numbers in sequence, but it is more complicated with the items that involve alternating numbers and letters. The best way to score these items as the child progresses is for the examiner to use a look-back strategy. For example, if the

child is on the letter D, the examiner looks back to the previous point (the number 3) and then instantly knows that the number 4 follows the letter D.
- Occasionally a child may stop before reaching the last number or letter. In such instances the examiner must immediately say to keep going.

Planned Number Matching

The child's task is to find and underline two numbers that are the same in each row. Each item is composed of eight rows of numbers with six numbers per row. Two of the six numbers in each row are the same. The length of numbers differs on the various rows. Numbers increase in digit length from one digit on the first row of item 1 to seven digits on the eighth row of item 4. There are four rows for each digit length and a total of four pages of numbers. Children ages 5–7 are provided an example followed by two test items. Children ages 8–18 are provided a different example and two test items. Each row of numbers was carefully developed to maximize benefits of strategy use in the identification of correct matches. This approach resulted in items with some rows that contain numbers that start with unique numbers, some rows that include numbers with similar digit strings, and some rows in which the beginning numbers are more similar than those at the end of the row.

Administration Comments
- Examiner should always fold back the response book so that the child sees only one page at a time.
- When necessary, it is permissible to remind the child to indicate when he or she is finished by saying, "Tell me when you're finished."

- Although the child may self-correct, do not allow the child to spend more than a second or two crossing out. If the child takes too much time, say, "Keep going."
- Sometimes children stop before the time limit has expired. If necessary the examiner should say, "Keep going."
- Strategy assessment is conducted during and at the end of this subtest. Be sure to fill in the strategy assessment checklist on the record form.

Matrices

Nonverbal Matrices is a 44-item multiple-choice subtest. Each item uses geometric shapes and designs that are interrelated through spatial or logical organization. Children are required to decode the relationships among the parts of the item and choose the best of six options. The Matrices subtest items are composed of a variety of formats, including completion of geometric patterns, reasoning by analogy, and spatial visualization originally included in the Matrix Analogies test (Naglieri, 1985) and its most recent revision (Naglieri Nonverbal Ability Test, Second Edition; Naglieri, 2007).

Administration Comments

- This subtest has a starting rule (item 12) for children ages 12–18 years. If a child ages 12–18 years fails item 12, then administer the preceding items in reverse order until two consecutive correct answers have been obtained. Examinees ages 12 and above with suspected cognitive disability begin with item 1.
- It is important to note that for the sample and first items that are given the examiner tells the child the answer regardless of whether the child is correct or not. This is designed to ensure that all children receive the same information about the item.
- Discontinue the subtest after four consecutively numbered items are failed.

Verbal-Spatial Relations

This subtest is composed of items that require the comprehension of logical and grammatical descriptions of spatial relationships. Children are presented with items with six drawings and a printed question at the bottom of each page. The examiner reads the question aloud and the child selects the option that matches the verbal description. The items require the evaluation of logical grammatical relationships, which demands simultaneous processing with verbal content.

Administration Comments
- The examiner always reads every question printed at the bottom of the page, even if the child is capable of reading it alone.
- The examiner should read the questions in a very clear manner, in a normal reading voice, at the rate of about two words per second.
- Each question can only be read one time.
- This subtest has a starting rule (item 7) for children ages 8–18 years. If the child age 8–18 years fails item 7, then administer the preceding items in reverse order until two consecutive correct answers have been obtained. Examinees ages 8 and above with suspected cognitive disability begin with item 1.
- If a child fails four consecutive items, discontinue the subtest.
- The items are printed at the bottom of each page in the stimulus book, and they also appear in the administration and scoring manual following instructions for the subtest.

Figure Memory

The child's task is to identify a two- or three-dimensional geometric figure that was shown for 5 seconds when it is embedded within a more complex design. Children are asked to identify the original design that is embedded within the larger figure. The child reproduces the figure on the response page by drawing over the lines that make the figure using a red pencil. For a response to be scored correct, all lines of the design have to be indicated without any additions or omissions.

Administration Comments
- Children ages 5–7 and older children with suspected cognitive disability begin with item 1, and those ages 8–18 start with item 10. If a child age 8–18 years old fails item 8, then administer the preceding items in reverse order until two consecutive correct answers have been obtained.
- The discontinue rule is four consecutively numbered items failed.
- The exposure time for each item is 5 seconds.
- The sequence of administration is as follows (see Figure 2.8):
  1. Examiners should place the stimulus book in front of the child so the bottom edge of the book (as seen by the child) is about 7–8 inches from the edge of the table. This allows for placement of the response book between the child and the stimulus book.
  2. Expose each stimulus figure for exactly 5 seconds.
  3. Then turn the stimulus page to remove the item from the child's view.

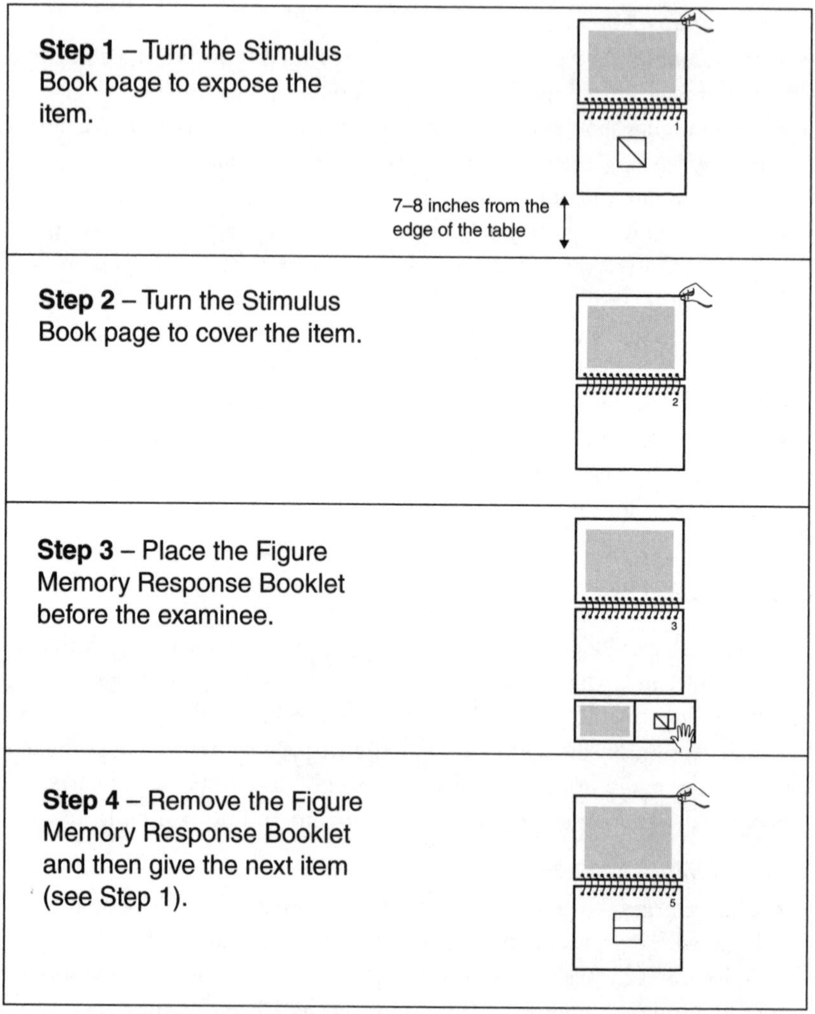

Step 1 – Turn the Stimulus Book page to expose the item.

7–8 inches from the edge of the table

Step 2 – Turn the Stimulus Book page to cover the item.

Step 3 – Place the Figure Memory Response Booklet before the examinee.

Step 4 – Remove the Figure Memory Response Booklet and then give the next item (see Step 1).

Figure 2.8 Sequence of Events When Administering the CAS2 Figure Memory Subtest

4. Next, immediately place the appropriate page of the response book in front of the child.
5. Then remove the response book after the child has responded.
6. Begin the sequence again for the next item.
- During the sample and item 1, it is permissible to clarify the directions by using another word, such as *trace*.

- Sometimes it is necessary to communicate to the child that self-corrections are permitted. Examiners are free to explain that corrections can be made by either crossing out or erasing.
- Examiner must score the child's responses during the administration so that the discontinue rule can be determined. To assist the examiners, the answers for the demonstration and sample items as well as all the remaining items appear in the administration and scoring manual. Note that the diagrams are presented as seen by the child (the view that would also be seen by the examiner sitting next to the child) and as seen by the examiner (if the examiner is sitting across from the child).

> **DON'T FORGET 2.5**
>
> ....
>
> The exposure time for the CAS2 Figure Memory items is exactly 5 seconds. Be ready to turn the page that covers the stimulus before the 5 seconds has elapsed.

Expressive Attention

Expressive Attention is composed of two different types of items on each of three pages. The first set of three is administered to children ages 5–7. The child's task is to identify the pictures of animals as either large or small, regardless of their relative size on the page. There are three pages of animals (each page is considered an item). In the first item all the animals are the same size. On the second, the animals are sized relative to actual size. The third item is the most sensitive to attention because the animals are usually sized opposite to their actual size.

The second set of items is administered to children ages 8–18. There are also three items in this version. First, the child reads words such as *blue* and *yellow*; second, the child identifies colors of a group of rectangles; and finally the child identifies the color ink in which words are printed. It is the last page that is sensitive to attention because the child has to focus on one variable (the color) and not read the word (a more automatic response).

> **DON'T FORGET 2.6**
>
> ....
>
> The demonstration for Expressive Attention for children younger than 8 years of age is designed to ensure that the child knows or can learn which animals are big and which are small. Go through the demonstration carefully and provide a brief explanation if necessary on the CAS2 and CAS2: Brief.

Administration Comments

- All three items in the appropriate item set are administered to each child. The first two are used to compute the Speed/Fluency scale. The last item is used to measure attention because that page requires the examinee to focus on one aspect (e.g., for those younger than 8 years of age, the size of the animal in real life) and resist responding on the basis of the size on the page.

- If a child makes more than five errors on sample A, or cannot read, or has difficulty seeing the colors, do not administer the subtest.

- Synonyms for the words *big* and *small* (e.g., *large* or *little*) are acceptable. Similarly, if a child calls the bird a robin or a blue jay, say, "Yes, and it's a bird."

- Unlike Planning subtests that can be completed in any manner, all Attention subtests require that the child complete each item row by row, from left to right and from top to bottom. If the child deviates, the examiner must immediately say, "Do it this way." (Point across the rows from the child's left to right.)

- Self-corrections are permitted on this subtest and scored as correct. They do, however, increase the time taken and therefore appropriately influence the child's score.

- Timing is begun when the child says the first word and stopped when the child says the last word.

Number Detection

This subtest consists of four items (pages) of rows of numbers that contain targets (numbers that match the stimuli) and distractors (numbers that do not match the stimuli). The child's task is to underline numbers on a page that match stimuli at the top of the page. There are four pages of numbers (each page is considered an item). Each page has different targets. For example, for ages 5–7, children find the numbers 1 and 2 on the first two pages and the numbers 5 and 6 on the last two pages. Each page has 12 numbers on each of 18 rows.

Administration Comments

- In contrast to Planning subtests, which allow the child a method to complete the page, this subtest must be competed row by row, from left to right and from top to bottom. If the child deviates, the examiner must say, "Do it this way." (Point across the rows from the child's left to right.) Similarly, if the child skips a row, the examiner must immediately say, "Do this row first." (Point to the skipped row.) These instructions block the application of plans.

- After completion of the page, some children may want to go back and check their work (a good plan). Because this test is designed to measure attention, do not allow the child to review or modify responses after completing the page.

- Because time is an important variable in this test, if the child indicates a desire to change a response, say, "Cross out your mistake and keep going." This encourages rapid completion of the page.
- Timing begins when each item (page) is exposed and the instruction "begin" is given.

Receptive Attention

The examinee's task is to find and underline pairs of pictures or pairs of letters that are the same on each item (page). Each item consists of rows of pictures or letters that contain targets (pairs that match) and distractors (pairs that do not match). For ages 5–7, the picture pairs match either on the basis of physical appearance or category (name). For ages 8–18, children must underline pairs of letters that are physically the same or have the same name.

Administration Comments

- The child must complete the task row by row, from left to right and from top to bottom. If the child deviates, say, "Do it this way." (Point across the rows from the child's left to right.)
- If necessary, instruct the child not to spend too much time drawing the lines neatly.
- Do not allow the child to review or modify responses after completing the page.
- Timing begins when each item (page) is exposed and the instruction "begin" is given.

Word Series

The child's task is to repeat a series of single-syllable high-imagery words in the same order in which the examiner said them.

Administration Comments

- The words are presented in a uniform pitch at the rate of one word per second.
- The examiner must drop his or her voice when the last word of the series is spoken so that the child knows when the presentation is completed.
- Mispronunciations (e.g., *tee* for *key*) and word-ending changes are not counted as errors.

- Discontinue the subtest if a child fails four consecutively numbered items.
- Children ages 8–18 year begin with item 5. If a child in this age group fails item 4, then give item 1 (using the directions for ages 5–7) and administer forward until the discontinue rule has been met.
- During the introduction of the test, the examiner tells the child all the words that are used.

Sentence Repetition (Ages 5–7 Only)

The child's task is to repeat a series of sentences spoken by the examiner. Each sentence contains color words in place of content words. For example, instead of "The boy ran," the item might read "The red blued."

Administration Comments
- The examiner reads the sentences in a normal reading voice at the rate of about two words per second.
- Normal intonation and dropping of the voice is used when the last word of every sentence is spoken or at the end of phrases.
- The longer sentences contain commas, which indicate how the words should be grouped.

> # CAUTION 2.1
> ....
> Be sure to read the items for Sentence Repetition, Sentence Questions, and Verbal-Spatial Relations in a normal reading voice at about the rate of two words per second.

- Each sentence is read one time only.
- When the child fails four consecutively numbered items, the subtest is discontinued.
- The items appear in the administration and scoring manual and the record form.

Sentence Questions (Ages 8–17 Only)

The child's task is to answer a question about a sentence read by the examiner. Each sentence is in the same format as the Sentence Repetition subtest and contains color words in place of content words.

Administration Comments
- The examiner should read the items in a normal reading voice at the rate of about two words per second. Normal intonation and dropping of the voice is used when the last word of every sentence is spoken or at the end of phrases.

- The longer sentences contain commas, which indicate how the words should be grouped.
- If the child requests the sentence and question be repeated, the examiner may do so, but only one time.
- If a child fails four consecutive items the subtest is discontinued.

Visual Digit Span

The examinee's task is to repeat a series of numbers in the same order as shown on a stimulus page.

Administration Comments
- Each item of lengths less than five is exposed for the same number of seconds as there are digits. Thus, a two-digit item is presented for 2 seconds, a three-digit item for 3 seconds, and a four-digit item is shown for 4 seconds. The maximum exposure time for longer items is 5 seconds.
- For items 13–30 the stimulus exposure time is 5 seconds.
- Exposure times for each item appear on the record form.
- If a child fails four consecutive items the subtest is discontinued.
- If an examinee age 8–18 fails the first item given, administer preceding items in reverse order until two consecutive correct answers have been obtained.

> **CAUTION 2.2**
>
> The CAS2 Visual Digit Span subtest items of two, three, and four digits are exposed for 2, 3, and 4 seconds, respectively. Items with five and more digits are exposed for *only* 5 seconds.

SCORING THE CAS2

There are two options for scoring the CAS2. The first option is to use the CAS2 Online Scoring and Report System (Naglieri, 2014). This online program allows for entry of each item score or entry of subtest scaled raw scores. The CAS2 Online Scoring and Report System converts either indi-

> **DON'T FORGET 2.7**
>
> CAS2 Online Scoring and Report System provides a fast and accurate way to obtain all scores as well as a narrative report that provides interpretation of all scores the test yields.

vidual item scores or subtest raw scores on the front of the CA2 record form to standard scores having a mean of 10 and a standard deviation of 3. If items scores are entered for each subtest, the program will automatically calculate raw scores, ratio scores, and apply the appropriate start and discontinue rules to calculate the subtest raw score. The program will also search for a correct entry item or two consecutive items awarded credit that are closest to the entry point and will automatically assign a score of 1 to all items below these items. Additionally, the program will identify the proper discontinue point and will automatically assign a score of 0 to any administered items above these items. Next, the PASS and Full Scale as well as supplemental scales (mean of 100 and standard deviation of 15) are automatically computed. All of the comparisons included on page 2 of the CAS2 record form will be made and results described in a narrative report. The narrative report can be obtained as a PDF or Word document and contains text describing the PASS, Full Scale, and all supplemental scales as well as subtest and scale comparisons.

The second option for scoring is traditional hand scoring. One of the advantages of the CAS2 is that the scoring does not include analysis to determine if a response should be scores 0, 1, or 2 as traditionally has been necessary. All item raw scores for each subtest are summed and converted to scaled scores. These are summed to obtain PASS and Full Scale scores and supplemental scales are similarly computed. The steps needed to obtain all the CAS2 scores and the corresponding conversion tables will be described in the next sections.

Step 1: Subtest Raw Scores to Scaled Scores

The CAS2 subtest raw scores are calculated using several different methods based on what aspects of the child's performance are being measured. These methods include one or more of the following: (1) the number correct, (2) time to completion, (3) and number of false detections. These methods of evaluating a child's performance are used either in isolation or in combination based on the goals of the subtest. Some subtest raw scores, therefore, are based on (1) number correct; (2) total time; (3) number correct and total time; and (4) number correct, total time, and number of false detections. Each raw score method is presented for the appropriate subtests in the following section.

Number Correct:
The raw score for the Matrices, Verbal-Spatial Relations, Figure Memory, Word Series, Sentence Repetition, Sentence Questions, and Visual Digit Span subtests is the number of items correct. This score is obtained by summing the number of correct items and assigning credit for those items not administered

below any starting point. Note that items on Matrices, Verbal-Spatial Relations, Word Series, Sentence Repetition, Sentence Questions, and Visual Digit Span are scored 1 for correct and 0 for incorrect.

Figure Memory:
Figure Memory items are also scored as 1 or 0. The child must draw a red line on each of the lines that make up the figure to receive credit. The child does not, however, have to draw the lines precisely as long as each of the lines of the figure is drawn (see Figure 2.9). Notice that in the response scored as 0 the child did not draw a line on the bottom of the square. That is, instead of drawing five lines as required (the four sides of the box and the diagonal) the child produced only four of them (three sides of the box and the diagonal).

Examiners should score the child's responses to Figure Memory during administration to determine if the discontinue rule has been met. To facilitate scoring, the administration and scoring manual includes diagrams of the response book page with the correct answer indicated as it would be seen from the child's and examiner's perspectives. If the examiner is sitting across from the child, then the part of the manual that shows the examiner's view would be used. Similarly, if the examiner is sitting next to or diagonally from the child, then the section of the manual that shows the correct answer from the child's perspective may be most helpful.

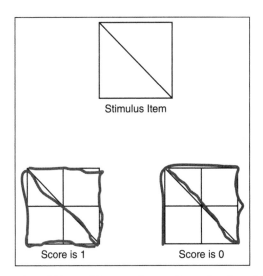

Figure 2.9 Examples of Figure Memory Items Scored as 1 and 0

Word Series, Sentence Repetition, and Sentence Questions:
The raw score for Word Series is the number of items correctly repeated. To be given a score of 1, the child must reproduce the entire string of words (e.g., *book-key-wall*) in the correct order. The child is scored 0 if the order is changed in any manner or if a word is deleted from the item. Mispronunciations of the words and word distortions, however, are not counted as errors.

Sentence Repetition and Sentence Questions:
Although Sentence Repetition and Sentence Questions are scored as pass or fail, the way the items are scored varies. In Sentence Repetition the child must repeat the entire sentence exactly as stated by the examiner. Any inaccuracy, such as word substitutions, omissions, additions, reversals, and changes in word endings, are considered as errors and results in a score of 0 for the item. Mispronunciations such as *wed* for *red,* however, are not counted as errors. Sentence Questions items are also scored either correct (1) or incorrect (0), but the rules are very different. The administration and scoring manual and the record form each contains the items and a list of the possible correct answers. The possible answers are indicated using parentheses that indicate those parts of the answers that are not required. The examiner scores the items based on whether the child produces all the words or word fragments that are not included within parentheses. This is illustrated in Table 2.1. Note that any combination of words or word endings that are contained within the parentheses can be omitted or added. What is essential for a score of 1 is the text "yellow purple" in that order. That is, if the child says "purple yellow" then the item is failed.

Time in Seconds:
The raw score for the CAS2 Planned Connections subtest is the sum of the time in seconds to complete all items. The number correct is not a part of the scoring

Table 2.1 Example Scoring Sentence Questions on the CAS2

Item	Correct Response as Shown on the CAS2 Record Form	Possible Responses That Are Correct
The yellow blues the red the green. What does the yellow do?	Blue(s) (the) red (the) green.	Blue red green.
		Blues red green.
		Blue the red green.
		Blues the red green.
		Blue red the green.
		Blues red the green.
		Blue the red the green.
		Blues the red the green.

because the examiner redirects an examinee every time an error is made. (See the administration and scoring manual for more details.) To compute the raw score, simply add the time scores for items 1–7 for ages 5–7 years or items 5–11 for ages 8–18, as shown in Figure 2.10.

Accuracy (Time and Number Correct):

> ### CAUTION 2.3
> ....
>
> Remember that when you are using a digital stopwatch and have item time scores that are greater than 1 minute, you have to add 60 seconds for each minute. When scoring time on the CAS2 and CAS2: Brief, if your digital stopwatch reads 1:20, that means 80, not 120 seconds.

The raw score for the CAS2 Planned Codes, Planned Number Matching, and Expressive Attention subtests is based on the combination of time and number correct. Time is recorded in total seconds for each item, then the number correct

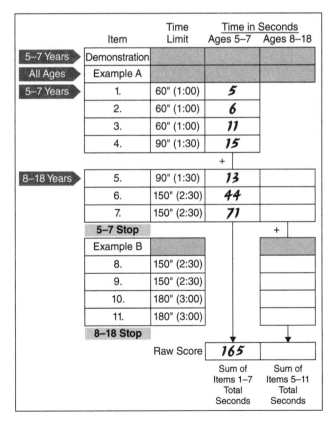

	Item	Time Limit	Time in Seconds Ages 5–7	Time in Seconds Ages 8–18
5–7 Years	Demonstration			
All Ages	Example A			
5–7 Years	1.	60" (1:00)	*5*	
	2.	60" (1:00)	*6*	
	3.	60" (1:00)	*11*	
	4.	90" (1:30)	*15*	
			+	
8–18 Years	5.	90" (1:30)	*13*	
	6.	150" (2:30)	*44*	
	7.	150" (2:30)	*71*	
5–7 Stop				+
	Example B			
	8.	150" (2:30)		
	9.	150" (2:30)		
	10.	180" (3:00)		
	11.	180" (3:00)		
8–18 Stop				
	Raw Score		*165*	
			Sum of Items 1–7 Total Seconds	Sum of Items 5–11 Total Seconds

Figure 2.10 Recording Time Scores for Planned Connections

per item is determined (this is best accomplished for Planned Number Matching using the scoring templates). The raw score for these subtests is the number correct and time for each item combined into a ratio score called "Accuracy" in the conversion table that appears on pages 17–18 of the record form.

Ratio Section of Record Form:

The Ratio Score Conversion Table included in the record form and shown in Figure 2.11 includes a heading called "Accuracy Score" at the top. The leftmost column contains time scores in 3-second intervals. To combine the number correct and time into a ratio score, enter the row that contains the item time in seconds, then find the column for the accuracy score earned by the child. The number at the intersection of the row and column is the ratio score for that item. For example, if a child earned a total time score of 22 seconds with an accuracy score of 15, then the ratio score is 28.

The ratio scores for each item are summed, as indicated on the record form, to obtain a raw score for the subtest. An illustration is given for Planned Number Matching in Figure 2.12 (use the same method to obtain the raw scores for Planned Codes and Expressive Attention). Note that the age of the child is irrelevant, as the scores are converted to ratio scores based on time and accuracy.

Ratio Score Conversion Table

Time (seconds)	Accuracy Score: Number Correct (PNM, PCd, EA) or Number Correct Minus False Detections (ND, RA)									
	13	14	15	16	17	18	19	20	21	22
0–2	200	200	200	200	200	200	200	200	200	200
3–5	132	144	156	169	182	196	200	200	200	200
6–8	76	82	89	97	104	112	120	129	137	146
9–11	53	58	63	68	73	78	84	90	96	102
12–14	41	44	48	52	56	60	65	69	74	79
15–17	33	36	39	42	46	49	53	56	60	64
18–20	28	30	33	36	38	41	44	47	51	54
21–23	24	26	28	31	33	36	38	41	44	47
24–26	21	23	25	27	29	31	34	36	38	41
27–29	19	21	22	24	26	28	30	32	34	37
30–32	17	19	20	22	24	25	27	29	31	33
33–35	16	17	18	20	21	23	25	26	28	30
36–38	14	16	17	18	20	21	23	24	26	28

Figure 2.11 Ratio Conversion Table for Combining Number Correct and Time or Number Correct, False Detections, and Time

	Item Set	Time Limit	Time in Seconds	Accuracy Score (Number Correct)	Ratio Score (see page 17)
All Ages	Example A				
	1.	60" (1:00)	*61*	*21*	*16*
	Example B				
	2.	60" (1:00)	*61*	*8*	*5*
	3.	60" (1:00)	*58*	*10*	*7*
	Example C				
	4.	60" (1:00)	*61*	*9*	*6*

Raw Score: = *34*

Sum of ratio scores

Figure 2.12 Calculation of Ratio Scores for CAS2 Planned Number Matching

Determination of the number correct for Planned Codes and Planned Number Matching is obtained using a scoring guide included in the spiral-bound scoring templates booklet. Place the completed response book under the appropriate template (the book is divided into sections for children 5–7 and 8–17 years of age). Align the page completed by the child with the scoring template. The template is a translucent paper that contains the correct answers and allows for easy determination of the number correct for the item. Record the number correct for each item in the accuracy score column of the record form. Because the child responds orally to the Expressive Attention items, this subtest does not require the use of a template.

Accuracy (Time, Number Correct, and False Detections):
The raw scores for Number Detection and Receptive Attention are also obtained using ratio scores but the accuracy score is defined differently for these subtests. Accuracy is the number of correct responses minus the number of false detections (the number of times the child underlined a stimulus that is not a target). The scoring templates booklet is used to identify how many targets (what the child is instructed to look for) and false detections the child responded to as described previously in this chapter. In addition to counting the number of correct answers (targets that appear in circles), count the number of nontargets underlined (false detections). Subtract the number of false detections from the number correct to obtain the accuracy score. Then convert the time and accuracy scores to a ratio

	Item Set	Time Limit	Time in Seconds	Number Correct	Number of False Detections	Accuracy Score (Number Correct Minus False Detections)	Ratio Score (see page 17)
5–7 Years	Example A						
	1.	60" (1:00)	61	20 ⟨–⟩	0 ⟨=⟩	20	15
	2.	60" (1:00)	61	28 ⟨–⟩	2 ⟨=⟩	26	21
	Example B						
	3.	60" (1:00)	61	25 ⟨–⟩	1 ⟨=⟩	24	19
	4.	60" (1:00)	61	24 ⟨–⟩	0 ⟨=⟩	24	19
5–7 Stop							
						Raw Score	74

Figure 2.13 Calculation of Ratio Scores Using Time, Number Correct, and False Detections

> ### DON'T FORGET 2.8
> ....
> The accuracy score is made up of either (1) time and number correct or (2) time, number correct, and false detections.

score in the usual fashion as previously described. This is illustrated for Number Detection (use the same method to obtain the raw score for Receptive Attention) in Figure 2.13 for a child age 5 years 8 months.

Step 2: Converting Raw Scores to Subtest Scaled Scores

The CAS2 subtest scaled scores (mean of 10 and standard deviation of 3) are obtained using age-based tables included in Appendix A.1 of the administration and scoring manual. The appendix is divided according to the child's chronological age in years, months, and days. Locate the appropriate conversion table (the first page of the subtest norms section includes an index showing which pages in the manual apply to each age group).

Step 3: PASS Scale Standard Scores from the Sum of Subtest Scaled Scores

Each of the four PASS scales is derived from the sum of the subtest scaled scores. For the Extended Battery, sum all three subtest scaled scores within each PASS scale. For the Core Battery, sum only the first two subtests within each PASS scale. The Full Scale is obtained from the sum of scaled scores for the Extended and Core Batteries and is calculated by summing the four "Sum of Subtest Scaled Scores" values found on the front page of the record form. See Figure 2.14.

DON'T FORGET 2.9

When converting the sum of scaled scores to obtain the CAS2 PASS and Full Scale scores, use three subtests per scale for the Extended Battery (Appendix B1–5) and two per scale for the Core Battery (Appendix B6–10).

Step 4: Obtaining PASS Scale Standard Scores

The PASS scales (mean of 100 and standard deviation of 15) are derived from the sum of subtest scaled scores using Appendix B in the CAS2 administration and scoring manual. Tables B.1 to B.5 are used to obtain scores for the Extended Battery and Tables B.6 to B.10 for the Core Battery. Each PASS scale has its own table. The table provides the standard score, percentile, and confidence intervals (90% and 95%). Note that the confidence intervals are the estimated true score type (see CAS2 interpretive and technical manual for more information).

If a subtest is spoiled when the 12-subtest Extended Battery is being administered, the practitioner has two options. One is to revert back to the 8-subtest Core Battery version for calculation of the PASS and Full Scale standard scores. Another option is to prorate the sum of three subtest scaled scores from the sum of the two that were not spoiled. Then a sum of subtest scaled scores for the spoiled PASS scale can be obtained using only two subtests. Table 3.2 in the CAS2 administration and scoring manual (page 104) is used to obtain an estimated sum of subtest scores for this purpose. To use this table, enter the first column with the sum of the scaled scores for the two subtests. Read across the table to obtain the estimated sum of three subtests based on the sum of the two. This value is used to obtain the appropriate Planning, Simultaneous, Attention, and Successive scale standard score. Use the prorated sum of scaled scores when summing the PASS scores to obtain the Full Scale.

If one of the Core Battery subtests is spoiled during administration, practitioners have the option to give the last subtest on the scale. That subtest scaled score could be used as one of the two scores needed to obtain a Core Battery sum of scaled scores and the Full Scale. This practice should be limited to those rare instances when limitations demand variation from the usually prescribed method of calculating scores for the Core Battery.

Examiner Record Form

Section 2. Subtest and Composite Scores

Subtest	Raw Score	Scaled Score			
		PLAN	SIM	ATT	SUC
Planned Codes (PCd)	34	7			
Planned Connections (PCn)	165	8			
Planned Number Matching (PNM)	10	8			
Matrices (MAT)	20		10		
Verbal-Spatial Relations (VSR)	18		11		
Figure Memory (FM)	16		10		
Expressive Attention (EA)	48			9	
Number Detection (ND)	74			10	
Receptive Attention (RA)	43			9	
Word Series (WS)	11				7
Sentence Repetition/ Questions (SR/SQ)	8				7
Visual Digit Span (VDS)	10				6

	PLAN	SIM	ATT	SUC	FS
Sum of Subtest Scaled Scores	23 (+)	31 (+)	28 (+)	20 (=)	102
PASS Composite Index Scores	84	102	96	79	87
Percentile Rank	14	55	39	8	19
% Confidence Interval — Upper	92	108	104	87	92
% Confidence Interval — Lower	79	96	89	74	83

Figure 2.14 Examples of a Completed CAS2 Record Form for Subtest, PASS, and Full Scale Scores

Step 5: Obtaining Full Scale Standard Scores

The CAS2 Full Scale (mean of 100 and standard deviation of 15) is obtained from the sum of the subtest scaled scores from the four PASS scales using Appendix B of the CAS2 administration and scoring manual. The Full Scale is computed from the sum of 8 or 12 subtests if the Core and Extended Batteries, respectively, are given. Similar to the PASS raw to standard score conversion tables, Appendix B provides the standard score, percentile, and confidence intervals (90% and 95%) for all possible raw scores.

≡ Rapid Reference 2.4

PASS and Full Scale standard scores are found in Appendix B of the CAS2 administration and scoring manual. Supplemental scale standard scores are found in Appendix D of that same manual.

Step 6: Obtaining Supplemental Scale Standard Scores

The five CAS2 supplemental scales (mean of 100 and standard deviation of 15) are obtained from the sum of the scaled scores from specific combinations of subtests using Appendix D of the CAS2 administration and scoring manual. The CAS2 supplemental scores table on page 2 of the record form (and Figure 2.15) provides information about which subtests are used to obtain the five additional scales. Appendix D also provides the standard score, percentile, and confidence intervals (90% and 95%) for all possible scores.

ADMINISTRATION OF CAS2: BRIEF

Planned Codes

This CAS2: Brief subtest, similar to the CAS2, contains four items, each with its own set of codes and particular arrangements of rows and columns. A legend at the top of each page shows which numbers (1, 2, 3, 4) correspond to different codes (a combination of Os and Xs). The items differ from those in the CAS2 in the correspondence of numbers rather than letters and the position of the numbers on the page.

Administration Comments
- Children may fill in the boxes in any order, and, in fact, they are instructed, "You can do it any way you want." This is to allow the child to use strategies such as doing all the As first or completing the page by skipping around.

Supplemental Composite Scores

Subtest	Scaled Score				
	EF w/o WM	EF w/ WM	WM	VC	NvC
Planned Codes					7
Planned Connections	8	8			
Matrices					10
Verbal-Spatial Relations		11	11	11	
Figure Memory					10
Expressive Attention	9	9			
Receptive Attention				9	
Sentence Repetition/Questions		7	7	7	
	EF w/o WM	EF w/ WM	WM	VC	NvC
Sum of Subtest Scaled Scores	17	35	18	27	27
Composite Index Scores	91	91	94	93	92
Percentile Rank	27	27	34	32	30
% Confidence Interval — Upper	101	99	101	101	99
% Confidence Interval — Lower	84	85	88	87	86

Note: EF w/o WM = Executive Function without Working Memory;
EF w/WM = Executive Function with Working Memory;
WM = Working Memory; VC = Verbal Content; NvC = Nonverbal Content.

Figure 2.15 Examples of a Completed CAS2 Record Form for Supplemental Scales

- Although self-corrections are permitted, the children are discouraged from spending more than a second or two erasing. If necessary the examiner should say, "Keep going." Similarly, if the child stops prior to the expiration of the time limit, the examiner instructs the child to "keep going."
- Strategy assessment is conducted after item 4 is completed.

Simultaneous Matrices

The CAS2: Brief Simultaneous Matrices subtest is a 44-item multiple-choice subtest. The items are different than those used in the CAS2, even though each item uses geometric shapes and designs that are interrelated through spatial or logical organization. The CAS2: Brief items have a different color scheme (yellow, blue, teal, and black) from those in the CAS2 (yellow, blue, and black). The items are also not the same. Similar to the CAS2, the items are composed of formats originally included in the Matrix Analogies subtest (Naglieri, 1985) and its most recent revision (Naglieri Nonverbal Ability Test, Second Edition; Naglieri, 2007).

Administration Comments

- This subtest has a starting rule (item 11) for children ages 12–18 years. If the child age 12–18 years fails item 11, then administer the preceding items in reverse order until two consecutive correct answers have been obtained. Examinees ages 12 and above with suspected cognitive disability begin with item 1.
- It is important to note that for the sample and first items that are given, the examiner tells the child the answer regardless of whether the child is correct or not. This is designed to ensure that all children receive the same information about the item.
- Discontinue after four consecutively numbered items are failed.

Expressive Attention

The CAS2: Brief Expressive Attention, similar to that found on the CAS2, is composed of two different types of items. The first is administered to children ages 5–7. The child's task is to identify the pictures of animals as either large or small, regardless of their relative size on the page. There are three pages of animals (each page is considered an item). In the first item all the animals are the same size. On the second, the animals are sized relative to actual size. The third item is the most sensitive to attention because the animals are usually sized opposite to their actual size. All the stimuli are different from the CAS2, but the same pictures are used.

The second set of items is administered to children ages 8–18. There are also three items in this version. First, the child reads words such as *blue* and *yellow*; second the child identifies colors of a group of rectangles; and finally the child identifies the color ink in which words are printed. It is the last page that is sensitive to Attention because the child has to focus on one variable (the color) and not read the word (a more automatic response). All the stimuli are different from the CAS2 but the same pictures are used except that the color green is not used.

Administration Comments
- If a child makes more than five errors on sample A, or cannot read the words, or has difficulty seeing colors, do not administer the subtest.
- Synonyms for the words *big* and *small* (e.g., *large* or *little*) are acceptable. Similarly, if a child calls the bird a robin or a blue jay, say, "Yes, and it's a bird."
- Unlike Planning subtests that can be completed in any manner, all Attention subtests require that the child complete each item row by row, from left to right and from top to bottom. If the child deviates, the examiner must immediately say, "Do it this way." (Point across the rows from the child's left to right.)
- Even though all three items in the appropriate item set are administered to each child, only the last item is used to measure attention because only the last page requires the examinee to focus on one aspect (e.g., for those less than 8 years of age, the size of the animal in real life) and resist responding on the basis of the size on the page.
- Self-corrections are permitted on this subtest and scored as correct. They do, however, increase the time taken and therefore appropriately influence the child's score.
- Timing is begun when the child says the first word and stopped when the child says the last word.

Successive Digits

The child's task is to repeat a series of numbers in the same order in which the examiner said them.

> **DON'T FORGET 2.10**
> ···
> When administering CAS2: Brief Successive Digits subtest, present the numbers at the rate of one per second using a uniform pitch and drop your voice when the last number of the series is spoken.

Administration Comments
- The numbers (1–9) are presented in a uniform pitch at the rate of one word per second.
- The examiner must drop his or her voice when the last numbers of the series is spoken so that the child knows when the presentation is completed.

- Discontinue the subtest if a child fails four consecutively numbered items.
- Children ages 8–18 years begin with item 3. If a child in this age group fails item 4, then administer the preceding items in reverse order until two consecutive correct answers have been obtained. Then continue forward until the discontinue rule is met.

SCORING THE CAS2: BRIEF

Accuracy (Number Correct):
The raw scores for Simultaneous Matrices and Successive Digits are computed by summing the item scores. Credit is given for those items not administered below the entry point, as indicated in the examiner record form.

Accuracy (Time and Number Correct):
The combination of time and number correct is used to compute a raw score for the Planned Codes and Expressive Attention subtests. The number correct for Planned Codes is obtained using the scoring templates. To score each item, place the student response booklet under the appropriate template. Record the number correct for each item in the accuracy score column of the examiner record form. The accuracy score for Expressive Attention is the number correct for item set 3 (ages 4–7 years) or item set 6 (ages 8–18 years), as shown in Figure 2.16.

The number correct and time for each item are combined into a ratio score using the ratio score conversion table in the CAS2: Brief examiner record form. Similar to the CAS2, this conversion table is organized in columns and rows. The number at the top of each column is the accuracy score earned by the student; read down the table to locate the row that contains the item time in seconds.

	Item Set	Time Limit	Time in Seconds	Accuracy	Ratio
4–7 Years	Demonstration				
	Example A				
	1.	180" (3:00)	*148*		
	Example B				
	2.	180" (3:00)	*157*		
	Example C				
	3.	180" (3:00)	*168*	*38*	*14*

Figure 2.16 Example of Excessive Attention Subtest Scoring

DON'T FORGET 2.11

The ratio score conversion tables for the CAS2 and CAS2: Brief appear on the last pages of the respective record forms.

The number at the intersection of the row and columns is the ratio score for that item. Record the ratio score in the appropriate place on the examiner record form. Sum the ratio scores for the appropriate items, as indicated on the examiner record form.

ADMINISTRATION OF CAS2: RATING SCALE

DON'T FORGET 2.12

It is important to remember to tell the teacher who completes the CAS2: Rating Scale to answer every question so that an accurate score may be obtained.

Administration of the CAS2: Rating Scale should begin with an explanation of the reason for the assessment and to direct the rater's attention to the instructions printed on the front of the rating form. Examiners should also emphasize the importance of reading the additional directions that appear before each set of items for the Planning, Simultaneous, Attention, and Successive scales. It is equally important to encourage the rater to respond to every one of the 40 items. Once a teacher's rating scale has been returned, the examiner should check to ensure that all the items were rated before scoring the protocol. If the teacher is reluctant to respond to some of the items, the examiner should encourage the rater to answer each one to the best of his or her ability.

SCORING THE CAS2: RATING SCALE

Scoring the CAS2: Rating Scale is accomplished by adding the numbers corresponding to each rating that were circled within each of the PASS scales (e.g., 0, for never, through 4, for always) and writing the sum in the space at the bottom of each column, as shown in Figure 2.17. These PASS scale raw scores are converted into standard scores, percentile ranks, and confidence intervals using Tables A.1 through A.25 in Appendix A in the CAS2: Rating Scale administration and scoring manual. The separate PASS scale raw scores are converted to standard scores (mean of 100 and standard deviation of 15), which are added and converted to a total score, as shown in Figure 2.18.

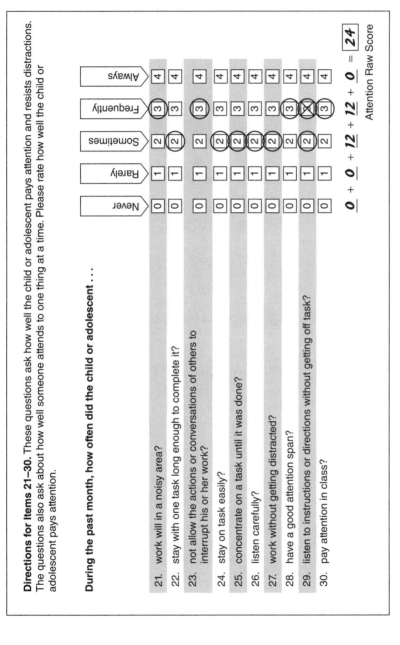

Directions for Items 21–30. These questions ask how well the child or adolescent pays attention and resists distractions. The questions also ask about how well someone attends to one thing at a time. Please rate how well the child or adolescent pays attention.

During the past month, how often did the child or adolescent . . . .

	Never	Rarely	Sometimes	Frequently	Always
21. work will in a noisy area?	0	1	2	③	4
22. stay with one task long enough to complete it?	0	1	②	3	4
23. not allow the actions or conversations of others to interrupt his or her work?	0	1	2	③	4
24. stay on task easily?	0	1	②	3	4
25. concentrate on a task until it was done?	0	1	②	3	4
26. listen carefully?	0	1	②	3	4
27. work without getting distracted?	0	1	②	3	4
28. have a good attention span?	0	1	2	③	4
29. listen to instructions or directions without getting off task?	0	1	②	⊗	4
30. pay attention in class?	0	1	2	③	4

$\underline{0} + \underline{0} + \underline{12} + \underline{12} + \underline{0} = \boxed{24}$

Attention Raw Score

Figure 2.17 Scoring Example for CAS2: Rating Scale Attention Items

PASS Scale	Raw Score	Standard Scores			
		Planning	Simultaneous	Attention	Successive
Planning	19	95			
Simultaneous	31		115		
Attention	24			100	
Successive	11				85

	Planning	Simultaneous	Attention	Successive	Sum of Standard Scores
Standard Scores	95 ⟨+⟩	115 ⟨+⟩	100 ⟨+⟩	85 ⟨=⟩	395
Total Scores					99
Percentile Rank	37	84	50	16	47
% Confidence Interval — Upper	100	120	105	92	102
Lower	90	108	95	80	96

Figure 2.18 Scoring Example for CAS2: Rating Scale

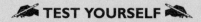

⚓ TEST YOURSELF ⚓

1. **The CAS2, CAS2: Brief, and CAS2: Rating Scale yield standard scores that are set at a mean and standard deviation of which of the following?**
   a. 100 and 16
   b. 50 and 8
   c. 100 and 15
   d. 50 and 10
2. **What is the discontinue rule for the Simultaneous and Successive scales' subtests on the CAS2 and CAS2: Brief?**
   a. Two consecutively numbered errors
   b. Three consecutively numbered errors
   c. Four consecutively numbered errors
   d. Five consecutively numbered errors

3. **What is the rate of presentation for CAS2 Word Series subtest and CAS2: Brief Successive Digits?**

    a. One word per second

    b. Two words per second

    c. Three words per second

4. **Providing help guidelines on the CAS2 and CAS2: Brief allow the examiner to accomplish what end?**

    a. Repeat the standardized instructions

    b. Restate the instructions in his or her own words

    c. Explain the requirements of the test in any language

    d. All of the above

5. **What is the rate of presentation for Sentence Repetition, Sentence Questions, and Verbal-Spatial Relations?**

    a. One words per second

    b. Two words per second

    c. Three words per second

6. **What is the exposure time for Figure Memory items?**

    a. 2 seconds

    b. 3 seconds

    c. 4 seconds

    d. 5 seconds

7. **What is the exposure time for Visual Digit Span?**

    a. 3 seconds for all

    b. 5 seconds for all

    c. As many seconds as digits up to 5

8. **During Word Series the words are spoken by the examiner at the rate of ___ per second, but in Verbal-Spatial Relations, Sentence Repetition, and Sentence Questions the items are read at the rate of about ___ per second.**

    a. two; two

    b. one; one

    c. two; one

    d. one; two

9. **When do you start timing the child on the Expressive Attention subtest?**

    a. When the page is exposed

    b. When the directions are completed

    c. When the child says the first word

10. **Should you change the order of administration of CAS2 subtests?**
    a. It is permissible.
    b. It is not advised.

11. **How many subtests do the CAS2: Extended and Core Batteries have?**
    a. 12 and 10
    b. 12 and 8
    c. 8 and 4
    d. 10 and 8

12. **About how long do the CAS2: Extended, CAS2: Core, and CAS2: Brief take to administer?**
    a. 60, 40, 20 minutes
    b. 20, 40, 60 minutes
    c. 90, 60, 40 minutes
    d. 60, 60, 20 minutes

13. **How many items are there in each PASS scale on the CAS2: Rating Scale?**
    a. 5
    b. 10
    c. 15
    d. 20

14. **Figure Memory items are exposed for how long?**
    a. 10 seconds
    b. 15 seconds
    c. 5 seconds
    d. As much time as the child needs

15. **On the CAS2 Core Battery, if one subtest is spoiled the examiner has the option to administer the last subtest on that scale.**
    a. True
    b. False

16. **On the CAS2, the examiner is always allowed to provide a brief explanation of how to do the task.**
    a. True
    b. False

17. **Subtests of the CAS2 can be administered in any order.**
    a. True
    b. False

18. **On the Visual Digit Span subtest each item of lengths less than five is exposed for the same number of seconds as there are digits.**
    a. True
    b. False

19. **In order for the examinee to receive credit on a Figure Memory item, the student must draw a red line on each of the lines that make up the figure and the lines must be drawn precisely.**

   a. True
   b. False

Answers: 1. c; 2. c; 3. a; 4. d; 5. b; 6. d; 7. c; 8. d; 9. c; 10. b; 11. b; 12. a; 13. b; 14. c; 15. a; 16. b; 17. b; 18. a; 19. b

Three

INTERPRETATION

The interpretation of the CAS2 scores is based on the idea that PASS measures neurocognitive function—or in plain language, *thinking*. In this chapter we explain how the scores from the CAS2 for the four types of thinking that represent the PASS theory are related to achievement test scores, behavior ratings, and measures of ability. A key component of this analysis is to understand the cognitive processing demand(s) of any task from the PASS perspective. For this reason, it is important to ask two critical questions about a test item or any academic task:

- What does the student have to know (i.e., achievement) to answer the question?
- How does the student have to think (i.e., PASS) to answer the question?

Consider the three test questions that appear in Figure 3.1. The verbal analogy requires *knowledge* of verbal concepts (e.g., girl, woman, boy, etc.) and relationships among those concepts. In order to answer the question, the child needs to understand that a girl becomes a woman and similarly a boy becomes a man. The relationships between the young and older person need to be comprehended to arrive at the correct answer. The second question requires *knowledge* of a number series. The child has to examine the series and detect that the numbers double from 2 to 16. In both of these examples, the examinee must know certain facts in order to understand the relationships among the words or numbers. In the third example, in which only shapes are provided, the relationships among the shapes must be understood (small diamond becomes big; so small circle becomes big) to answer the question, but knowledge of the names of the shapes is not needed; what is needed is *thinking about the relationships* between the shapes in the top and bottom rows.

What these three questions have in common is the requirement that thinking (Simultaneous processing from PASS) about relationships among the

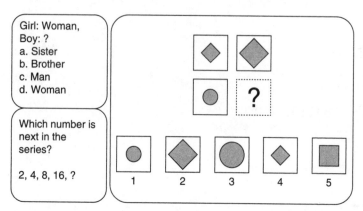

Figure 3.1 Three Kinds of Test Items Typically Used in Measures of Ability

information that was provided must be fully understood to arrive at the answer. What distinguishes the different tasks is the fact that answering the verbal and math questions requires knowledge whereas the item presented using shapes requires very little knowledge. This distinction is critically important when any test scores are interpreted.

The CAS2 test items on each of the PASS scales were designed to measure thinking (PASS) with a minimum amount of knowledge. A person's CAS2 scores will often be compared, for example, to some test scores that may require a considerable amount of knowledge (e.g., reading, math, and writing). It is essential that the relative contribution of knowledge and thinking on ability test scores be understood. The contribution thinking (e.g., PASS) has to everything we do to meet the demands of our world is what this chapter is about.

The goal of this CAS2 interpretation chapter is to help the user translate the PASS scores into theory-based explanation of a child's or adolescent's neurocognitive processing abilities that underlie functioning in all areas of life. We will explain how to examine the scores for the CAS2 (English and Spanish), CAS2: Brief, and CAS2: Rating Scale from a normative basis (comparing the student to the standardization sample) and from an ipsative perspective (comparing scores to the individual who was tested). This analysis will include a method for determining if there is a pattern of strengths or weaknesses that has relevance to educational programming, eligibility determination, differential diagnosis, as well as intervention planning.

CAS2 INTERPRETATION

The CAS2 measures are unique among ability tests in that they were conceived and built on the PASS neurocognitive theory, which provides the foundation for development of the test questions and interpretation of the test scores. This means that the focus of test score interpretation is on the child's ability to think using PASS neurocognitive constructs. The four PASS scales yield scores that provide the most important information about the examinee—more important than the Full Scale or the subtest scores. The CAS2 Full Scale (similar to the CAS2: Brief and CAS2: Rating Scale Total Scores) provides a reliable overall description of a child's neurocognitive processing abilities but does not inform the user of the PASS strengths or weaknesses. *Interpretation of PASS profiles is the key to understanding a student's successes and difficulties in school and social-interpersonal situations. PASS interpretation is also the key for eligibility determination and intervention planning.* Similarly, individual subtest score variability has little value, and efforts to reinterpret subtests from informally derived perspectives should be avoided.

The purpose of having multiple subtests in the CAS2 was to provide highly reliable PASS scales (and supplemental scales) using subtests that measure each of the neurocognitive processes in a slightly different manner. For example, only one of the Simultaneous subtests involves verbal content, only one requires memory, and the third has neither a verbal or memory requirement but does require reasoning. The varying content of these complementary measures provides a broad evaluation of Simultaneous processing. When subtest scores do vary, they should be interpreted only when additional data are compelling and when other pertinent information provides a strong reason to do so. Having one subtest score that is different from the others in that scale does not necessarily mean that the score for that scale is not interpretable (this will be more fully discussed further on in this chapter). Even in such cases the focus of interpretation of the CAS2 is on the PASS scale level.

What the CAS2 Scales Measure

The scales of the CAS2 measure Planning, Attention, Simultaneous, and Successive neurocognitive processing abilities. These are briefly described as follows.

Planning:

Planning is a neurocognitive ability used to determine, apply, and self-correct thoughts and actions so that effective solutions to problems can be achieved. Planning provides the means to solve problems for which no method or solution is immediately apparent and may involve retrieval of information as well as use of the other PASS abilities to process information. All of the CAS2 Planning subtests involve the use of strategies for efficient performance and the application of these strategies to novel tasks of relatively reduced complexity.

Attention:

Attention is a neurocognitive ability used to selectively focus on a particular stimulus while inhibiting responses to competing stimuli presented over time. Successful performance on the CAS2 Attention subtests requires attention to be focused, selective, sustained, and sometimes quite effortful. All CAS2 Attention subtests present tasks that require focus on one stimulus and resistance to responding to distractions over time.

Simultaneous:

Simultaneous processing is a neurocognitive ability used to understand how separate elements fit together into a conceptual whole often involving visual-spatial stimuli or understanding logical-grammatical verbal statements. Regardless of the content, Simultaneous processing subtests included in CAS2 require perception of parts into a single gestalt, understanding of relationships, and synthesis of parts into integrated groups, which occur either through examination of the stimuli during the activity or through recall of the stimuli.

Successive:

Successive processing is a neurocognitive ability used to integrate information into a specific serial order in which each element is related only to those that precede it, and the stimuli are not interrelated. The serial aspect of Successive processing involves working with stimuli in sequence, the ordering of thoughts and ideas, and forming sounds and movements in order. Successive processing subtests in the CAS2 require perception and reproduction of the serial order of information, and others require comprehension of complex linear relationships, which also involve working memory.

What the CAS2: Brief and CAS2: Rating Scale Measure

The CAS2: Brief and the CAS2: Rating Scale yield four PASS scores that have the same meaning as the four scales included in the CAS2. The only difference is that on the Brief version of the CAS2 one subtest is used for each of the four PASS scales. The selection of which test to include was carefully made based on theoretical and practical considerations. For example, Simultaneous Matrices was used on the CAS2: Brief because, similar to the other subtests, it has been considered a marker for that processing ability and it is less complex than Verbal-Spatial Relations and Figure Memory. Similar logic for the other selections are described in the manual.

The scores obtained using the CAS2: Rating Scale reflect *behaviors* a teacher can observe in the classroom that are associated with the four PASS constructs.

Table 3.1 How PASS Is Measured by the CAS2, CAS2: Brief, and CAS2: Rating Scale

	CAS2 Rating: Scale Items ask how well the child …	CAS2	CAS2: Brief
Planning	Thinks before acting, creates plans, and uses strategies to achieve a goal	Planned Codes Planned Connections Planned Number Matching	Planned Codes
Attention	Can focus attention to one thing at time and resists distractions	Expressive Attention Number Detection Receptive Attention	Expressive Attention
Simultaneous	Understands how parts combine to make a whole and see the big picture	Matrices Verbal-Spatial Relations Figure Memory	Simultaneous Matrices
Successive	Works with numbers, words, or ideas that are arranged in a specific series	Word series Sentence Repetition or Sentence Questions Visual Digit Span	Successive Digits

The aim was to represent Planning through observations about the strategies a student may use, Attention by how well the student can focus and resist distractions in the classroom, Simultaneous by how well the student can get the big picture, and Successive by how well the student works with information in a sequence. These behaviors provide a view of how the student uses PASS in the classroom. It is important to note, however, that environmental factors such as instruction that discourages or encourages strategy use can influence the behaviors a student shows in the classroom (see Table 3.1).

ESSENTIAL STEPS FOR CAS2, CAS2: BRIEF, AND CAS2: RATING SCALE

The interpretive approach we will specify here applies to all three CAS2 measures, especially when separate PASS scale scores are being examined. The process begins with examination of the scores for the four PASS scales. This puts emphasis on the theoretical level of analysis, which is the most informative. Next the Full Scale (CAS2) or total score (CAS2: Brief and CAS2: Rating Scale) results are examined. In each case, when there is significant variability in the PASS scales it will be very important to state that the Full Scale or total score will sometimes be higher and other times lower than the four scales in this test—rendering it an imprecise description of the examinee. We will provide specific methods for review of the test scores and interpretation.

≣ *Rapid Reference 3.1*

Summary of CAS2, CAS2: Brief, and CAS2: Rating Scale Interpretation Steps

Step 1: Interpret the scores for the four PASS scales.
Step 2: Interpret the Full Scale (CAS2) or total score (CAS2: Brief and CAS2: Rating Scale).
Step 3: Compare CAS2 and CAS2: Brief with CAS2: Rating Scale.

Good test interpretation begins with a careful analysis of the scores a test yields using statistically sound methods. Comparing CAS2 scores must take into consideration the reliability of the scales and in particular the reliability of the difference between the scores. We will use statistical guidelines when comparing all scores within the CAS2, CAS2: Brief, and the CAS2: Rating Scale, as well as when comparing across these scales and comparing these measures to other tests.

Step 1: Interpreting the PASS Profile

The first step in interpretation of the CAS2, CAS2: Brief, and the CAS2: Rating Scale is to examine the scores on the four PASS scales. In every instance these scores will be described with a confidence interval, percentile rank, and categorical label. The confidence interval and percentile rank for all scores can be found in the standard score conversion tables in the CAS2, CAS2: Brief, and CAS2: Rating Scale manuals. Each of these manuals includes a categorical system for describing the scores, which is shown in Table 3.2.

Table 3.2 Categories for CAS2 Scale and Subtest Scores

Full Scale, PASS, and Supplemental Scores	Subtest Scores	Category
130 and above	17–20	Very superior
120–129	15–16	Superior
110–119	13–14	Above average
90–109	8–12	Average
80–89	6–7	Below average
70–79	4–5	Poor
Less than 70	1–3	Very poor

Determining if the four PASS scores differ is accomplished by comparing the variance between any individual PASS scale score and the average of the student's four PASS scores. This method, which is known as an *ipsative comparison,* has been used often in intelligence testing (see Kaufman, 1994; Naglieri, 1999, 2011a) because it has the advantage of providing statistical guidelines for examining individual profiles relative to the student's level of functioning.

Analysis of the differences among the four PASS scores provides a way to describe the student's profile of neurocognitive processes. The values provided in Table 3.3 are needed to use this approach. These values are the differences required for significance (at $p = .10$ and .05 levels) when comparing each PASS score to the individual child's average PASS score. Note that the values are different for the CAS2 Core and Extended Batteries and across the three CAS2 measures.

Naglieri (1999) suggested that significance of the difference between a child's average score and one of the scores used to create that average was not sufficient to define a weakness or strength in one or more of the PASS processing scores. He suggested that only when a PASS score is significantly lower than the person's average and is *also* below the national average (below a standard score of 90) should it be considered a weakness appropriate for eligibility determination or diagnosis. For example, Table 3.4 Example 1 provides an illustration in which the

Table 3.3 Differences Between PASS Scale Standard Scores and the Student's Average PASS Score Required for Significance for the CAS2 Extended and Core Batteries, CAS2: Brief, and CAS2: Rating Scales

Scale	Age	p	Planning	Simultaneous	Attention	Successive
CAS2 Extended	5–7	.05	9.5	9.3	8.0	9.4
		.10	8.5	8.3	7.2	8.4
	8–18	.05	9.3	8.3	9.5	9.1
		.10	8.4	7.4	8.6	8.2
CAS2 Core	5–7	.05	11.2	10.1	9.0	10.7
		.10	10.1	9.0	8.1	9.6
	8–18	.05	10.2	9.1	10.9	10.4
		.10	9.2	8.1	9.8	9.3
CAS2: Brief	4–7	.05	9.9	11.5	9.4	12.0
		.10	8.9	10.3	8.5	10.8
	5–18	.05	9.1	10.8	11.3	11.8
		.10	8.2	9.7	10.1	10.6
CAS2: Rating Scale	5–7	.05	9.9	11.5	9.4	12.0
		.10	8.9	10.3	8.5	10.8
	8–18	.05	9.1	10.8	11.3	11.8
		.10	8.2	9.7	10.1	10.6

Table 3.4 Examples of PASS Profiles and Their Interpretation for CAS2 Extended Battery

	Score	Difference	Significant or Not	Strength Weakness
			Example 1: Planning Weakness	
Planning	84	−12.0	Sig	Wk
Simultaneous	111	15.0	Sig	Str
Attention	96	0.0	NS	-
Successive	93	−3.0	NS	-
Child's Average	96.0			
			Example 2: Successive Weaknesses	
Planning	90	−1.3	NS	-
Simultaneous	102	10.8	Sig	-
Attention	95	3.8	NS	-
Successive	78	−13.3	Sig	Wk
Child's Average	91.3			
			Example 3: Successive Strength	
Planning	94	−13.0	Sig	
Simultaneous	104	−3.0	NS	-
Attention	112	5.0	NS	
Successive	118	11.0	Sig	Str
Child's Average	107.0			
			Example 4: Breaking the Rule	
Planning	84	−6.3	NS	Wk*
Simultaneous	102	11.8	Sig	-
Attention	96	5.8	NS	-
Successive	79	−11.3	Sig	Wk
Child's Average	90.3			

*Even though the 84 does not meet the two rules for a weakness we designate it as such.

Successive score of 84 is significantly lower than the average score of 96 *and* that score is considerably below the average range. This qualifies as a weakness because it is low for this individual and in relation to the norm (i.e., the standardization sample). In this case we have found a weakness (score that is significantly lower than the student's mean score and falls below the normative average) that has both instructional and diagnostic implications.

Working the Numbers

In Table 3.4, Example 1, the average score of the four PASS scores is 96.0. The differences needed for significance are obtained by subtracting the mean score from each PASS scale score. Negative values mean the score is below the average and positive scores indicate the value is above the average. These illustrations are based on the 12-subtest Extended Battery so the differences needed for significance are found in Table 3.3 in this book for ages 5–18 years (values by age are found in the CAS2 interpretive manual, Appendix A, Table A.1). Differences between the individual score and average PASS score that are equal to or greater than the value in the table are considered significantly different from the student's average PASS score. In this example, the Planning score of 84 is 12 points below the child's PASS average (a value of 8.4 is needed at $p = .10$), indicating that the Planning score is significantly different from the average PASS score *and* the score is below the average range (90–109) and therefore designated as a weakness. By contrast the Simultaneous score of 111 is above the child's average PASS score by 15 points (a value of 7.4 is needed) and is statistically significant, and because this score is in the above average range (110–119) it would be designated as a strength. The Attention score of 96 is very similar to the child's average (a difference of 8.6 is needed for significance) and not considered a strength or weakness. The same is true of the Successive scale score of 93, which is 3 points below the child's mean (a value of 8.4 is needed). This profile is often found for individuals who have been diagnosed with ADHD (Naglieri & Otero, 2012) and who lack control of their behavior and thinking.

In Example 2, the average score of the four PASS scores is 91.3. The Planning scale score of 90 is not significantly different from the child's average PASS score. The Simultaneous score of 102 is above the child's average PASS score by 10.8 points, and the difference is statistically significant, but because this score is within the average range (90–109) it would not be described as a strength. However, it would be appropriate to describe the Simultaneous score as the student's strongest area of ability and use this strength when identifying or developing instructional methods that emphasize a big-picture perspective on information (e.g., story maps and webbing, from Naglieri & Pickering, 2010). The Attention score of 95 is 3.8 points above the child's average and is neither a strength nor weakness. The Successive score of 78 is 13.3 points below the child's average, which is statistically significant *and,* importantly, because the score is below the average range this score is considered a weakness because it is the student's lowest score and it falls well below the average range. This score indicates that the student has considerable difficulty working with information (words, numbers, motor movements, thoughts) arranged in a specific order. This profile is often found when young students have reading decoding problems because they struggle working with working with letters, sounds, and words arranged in a specific order (Naglieri & Otero, 2012).

In Example 3, the average score of the four PASS scores is 107. The Planning scale score is 13 points below the child's PASS average and significantly different from the average PASS score, but the score is within the average range and therefore not considered a weakness. This does not mean the score is unimportant; on the contrary, because the Planning score is the lowest relative to the remaining PASS neurocognitive abilities, it has implications for the child's educational planning and self-esteem. That is, teachers should be mindful that a student with relatively low Planning may not do equally well in all settings. Such a student may not perform his or her best when tasks demand developing and using strategies, organizing ambiguous tasks, and figuring out how to get things done, especially in comparison to tasks that demand sequencing (Successive) or sustained focus while resisting distractions (Attention). In fact the Successive score of 118 is 11 points above the child's average and is considered a strength. The Simultaneous score of 104 is close to the child's average PASS so it would not be described as a strength or weakness. The same is true for the Attention score of 112, which is 5 points from the child's average.

DON'T FORGET 3.1

It is important to note that determining PASS scores as a strength or weakness has two essential requirements:

- A significant difference between a PASS score and the student's average PASS score
- A PASS score either above (strength) or below (weakness) the average range (90–109)

≡ Rapid Reference 3.2

Comparing the difference between any individual PASS scale score and the mean of the student's four PASS scores is known as an *ipsative analysis*. This method provides a way to determine if one or more of these scores is significantly higher or lower than the student's own overall level of performance. We also compare any PASS scale that is significantly different from the student's average to the average range (90–109) to determine strengths and weaknesses. Strengths are PASS scores that are significantly greater than the student's mean score *and* fall above the average range. Weaknesses are PASS scores that are significantly lower than the student's mean score *and* fall below the average range.

Example 4 is the most interesting PASS profile, which demands that the rules be more flexibly applied. In this case, the average score of the four PASS scores is 90.3. The Simultaneous score of 102 is significantly above the child's average PASS score by 11.8 points, but because this score is within the average range it would not be described as a strength. Nevertheless, as in Example 2, it would be reasonable to describe the Simultaneous score as the student's strongest area of ability and recommend instructional methods that emphasize a big-picture perspective on information (e.g., story maps and webbing, from Naglieri & Pickering, 2010). The Attention score of 96 is 5.8 points above the child's average and neither a strength or weakness. The Successive score of 79 is 11.3 points below the child's average, which is statistically significant *and*, importantly, because the score is below the average range, this score is considered a weakness. This weakness has educational and diagnostic implications. Importantly, the Planning score of 84 is 6.3 points below the child's PASS average and, although not significantly different from the child's average PASS score, it is well below the average range. In this case it would reasonable to interpret Planning as a weakness, especially because the Successive score has had a big impact on the average PASS score. The detection of a Successive and Planning weaknesses such as these has tremendous implications for a student, especially in early elementary grades, when there is considerable emphasis on sequencing, and, if the student has difficulty, he or she will have limited ability to use strategies to be successful.

Summary of the Rules
1. If a CAS2 scale's score is significantly different from the child's average, it is important for understanding personal strength or weakness.
2. If a CAS2 scale's score is significantly different from the child's average and it is below the 90 (the average range is 90–109), it is important for understanding personal strength or weakness, *and* it should be labeled a *weakness*.
3. If a CAS2 scale's score is significantly different from the child's average and it is above the 109 (the average range is 90–109), it is important for understanding personal strength or weakness, *and* it should be labeled a *strength*.

DON'T FORGET 3.2

Ipsative values for determining the significance of the differences among the PASS scales are different if the Core (8 subtests) or Extended (12 subtests) versions of the CAS2 are used. The values for the CAS2: Brief and CAS2: Rating Scale are also unique to those measures.

DON'T FORGET 3.3

An analysis of relative PASS strengths and weaknesses can assist examiners in making a diagnosis, eligibility determination, and developing interventions.

Step 2: Examine the Full Scale or Total Score.

The next step in interpretation is to examine the Full Scale (CAS2) or total score (CAS2: Brief and the CAS2: Rating Scale). Similar to the individual PASS scores, these scores will be described with a confidence interval, percentile rank, and categorical label. It is always important to clarify that the Full Scale on the CAS2 as well as the total score on the CAS2: Brief and CAS2: Rating Scale is made up of four PASS scales. When significant variability of the four PASS scales is not found, the overall score can be considered an adequate description of the child or adolescent. By contrast, when significant PASS score variability is found, it should be clearly stated that the overall score will sometimes be higher and other times lower than the four scales. This means that the Full Scale or total score will not be representative of all of the four PASS scales. The goal of this statement is to recognize the importance of the PASS score variability and deemphasize the Full Scale or total score.

DON'T FORGET 3.4

The CAS2: Brief and CAS2: Rating Scale interpretation is limited to Step 1 (examination of PASS scale variability) and Step 2 (interpretation of the total score).

≡ *Rapid Reference 3.3*

The CAS2 Full Scale score is made up of separate scales called Planning, Attention, Simultaneous, and Successive neurocognitive abilities. When there is any significant variation (not necessarily a strength or weakness) among the PASS scales, it is important to report that the Full Scale will sometimes be higher and other times lower than any one of the PASS scales. Any PASS scale strengths and weaknesses found will have important implications for instructional programming and, if the CAS2 is used, eligibility determination.

Step 3: Compare CAS2 or CAS2: Brief with CAS2: Rating Scale

The comparison of PASS scores based on the CAS2 and PASS scores based on behaviors observed in the classroom is accomplished by comparing scores of the CAS2 or CAS2: Brief with those obtained from the CAS2: Rating Scale. It is important to recognize that the CAS2: Rating Scale, similar to any observational measure, is as much related to the environment a child has been immersed in as his or her PASS neurocognitive abilities. For this reason, PASS scores from CAS2 and those from the Rating Scale may differ because of the impact of environment, especially schooling, on a child. For example, a student may have a good Planning score yet not demonstrate behaviors related to planning in the classroom if taught to follow a specific method of solving a math question rather than using strategies to devise several ways of completing a problem. In this example a student's instruction reduces the role of planning and increases the need to remember exactly the solution taught by the teacher. The underlying message to the student is to think less about possible ways to do things and remember more of what was taught (Meltzer, 2010). In such instances the CAS2 or CAS2: Brief score may be different from the CAS2: Rating Scale score. This is valuable information to have, especially when devising interventions. But how different do the scores have to be to have a significant difference?

The values needed for significance when comparing the CAS2 and CAS2: Brief with the CAS2: Rating Scale at the $p = .05$ and .10 levels are provided in Table 3.5

Table 3.5 Values Needed for Significance When Comparing the CAS2 or CAS2: Brief with CAS2: Rating Scale

	CAS2: Rating Scale									
	$p = .05$					$p = .10$				
	Total	Plan	Sim	Att	Succ	Total	Plan	Sim	Att	Succ
CAS2 Standard Battery (12 Subtests)										
Full Scale	7	8	9	7	9	5	7	8	6	7
Planning	9	10	11	10	11	8	9	9	8	9
Simultaneous	8	10	11	9	10	7	8	9	8	9
Attention	10	11	12	11	12	8	9	10	9	10
Successive	9	10	11	10	11	8	9	9	8	9
CAS2 Core Battery (8 Subtests)										
Full Scale	8	9	10	9	10	7	8	8	7	8
Planning	10	11	12	11	12	8	9	10	9	10
Simultaneous	9	10	11	9	11	7	9	9	8	9
Attention	12	13	13	12	13	10	11	11	10	11
Successive	11	12	12	11	12	9	10	10	9	10
CAS2: Brief										
Full Scale	8	10	11	9	10	7	8	9	8	9
Planning	9	10	11	9	11	7	9	9	8	9
Simultaneous	11	12	13	11	13	9	10	11	10	10
Attention	11	12	12	11	12	9	10	10	9	10
Successive	12	13	13	12	13	10	11	11	10	11

(using the procedure described by Anastasi & Urbina, 1997, p. 111). To use this table, simply compare values for the CAS2: Rating Scale with the CAS2 or CAS2: Brief with those obtained for an individual student. If the difference is equal to or greater than the tabled values, then the finding is significant. This table will typically be used to compare the same PASS score obtained from the two different measures of PASS. It could also be used, for example, to determine if a difference between Simultaneous and Successive scores found on the CAS2 as well as the CAS2: Rating Scale was significant.

ADVANCED STEPS FOR CAS2 INTERPRETATION

≡ *Rapid Reference 3.4*

Advanced Steps for the CAS2 Interpretation

Step 4: Compare PASS scores to achievement using the Discrepancy/Consistency Method.

Step 5: Examine supplemental scales (Executive Function, Working Memory, Verbal Content, Nonverbal Content, Visual/Auditory Comparison).

Step 6: Examine the subtest scores within each of the four PASS scales.

Step 7: Compare CAS2 scores with other tests:
  a. EF Composite with CEFI Full Scale
  b. CAS2 Working Memory With CEFI Working Memory
  c. CAS2 and WISC-V
    1. CAS2 Verbal and WISC-V Verbal
    2. CAS2 Nonverbal and WISC-V Nonverbal
    3. CAS2 Working Memory and WISC-V Working Memory

Step 4: Compare PASS to Achievement Using the Discrepancy/Consistency Method

Comparing PASS scores to achievement test scores is a fundamental step in understanding if a cognitive processing strength corresponds to an academic strength and if a cognitive processing weakness corresponds to an academic weakness. The method of comparing scores on CAS2 and a variety of achievement tests can be accomplished using the same method as comparing CAS2 with CAS2: Rating Scale following from Anastasi and Urbina (1997). The values needed for significance were computed using the standard errors of measurement reported in the technical manuals of the KTEA-3 (Kaufman & Kaufman, 2015); WIAT-III (Wechsler, 2015); WJ-IV (McGrew, LaForte & Schrank, 2014), Feifer Assessment of Reading (FAR; Feifer, 2015); Feifer Assessment of Math (FAM; Feifer, 2016); and the Bateria-III (Muñoz-Sandoval, Woodcock, McGrew, & Mather, 2005). The comparisons between ability (PASS neurocognitive) and achievement (reading, math, etc.) are effectively accomplished by the CAS2 because the PASS test items do not rely heavily on knowledge. That is, there is no vocabulary, general information, or arithmetic questions on the CAS2 (see Naglieri, 2014, for more discussion), which makes the comparisons free from content overlap. Importantly, despite the fact that CAS2 items require very little knowledge, PASS scores are highly correlated with achievement (Naglieri & Rojahn, 2004).

Working the Numbers

The values needed for significance when comparing the PASS scores from the CAS2 with achievement test scores from, for example, the WIAT-III are provided in Appendix B. To use this table, simply compare values for the CAS2 and achievement test standard scores obtained for an individual student to the values in the table. If the difference (ignore the sign) is equal to or greater than the tabled values then the finding is significant. For example, if a student earned scores of 84 in Planning, 102 in Simultaneous, 96 in Attention, and 79 in Successive (a weakness) on the CAS2 Extended Battery, these scores could be compared to the subtest and composite scores from the WIAT-III. If the student earned scores of 80 and 77 on the Pseudoword Decoding and Basic Reading subtests, respectively, these scores would be significantly lower (at $p = .10$) than the Simultaneous and Attention scores. However, the Pseudoword Decoding and Basic Reading scores would *not* be significantly different from the Planning and Successive scores. The differences among the PASS scales (Planning and Successive significantly below the child's average PASS score), and the differences between the high-ability scores (Simultaneous and Attention) in contrast to low achievement, and the similarity between the low-ability scores on Planning and Successive with low achievement, form the basis of the Discrepancy/Consistency Method for SLD determination, which will be described next.

Pattern of Strengths and Weaknesses Using the Discrepancy/Consistency Method for SLD Determination

Three methods for detecting a pattern of strengths and weaknesses (PSW) that can be used as part of the process of identifying a student with a specific learning disability (SLD) have been suggested by Naglieri in 1999, Hale and Fiorello in 2004, and by Flanagan, Ortiz, and Alfonso in 2007. These authors share the same goal: to present a procedure to detect a PSW in scores that can be used

DON'T FORGET 3.5

....

The essence of the Discrepancy/ Consistency Method is two discrepancies and one consistency.

Discrepancy 1:
Significant variability among the PASS scores indicating a weakness in one or more of the basic psychological processes

Discrepancy 2:
Significant difference between high PASS scores and low achievement test scores

Consistency:
No significant difference between low PASS scores and low achievement

to identify an SLD (sometimes referred to as a third option; Zirkel & Thomas, 2010). Despite differences in the composition of the scores used and the definitions of what constitutes a basic psychological process, these methods all rely on finding a combination of differences as well as similarities in scores across academic and cognitive tests. Our approach to operationalizing a PSW is called the Discrepancy/Consistency Method (DCM) for the identification of SLD. Determining SLD is essentially based on the combination of PASS and achievement test scores. The method involves a systematic examination of variability of PASS and academic achievement test scores, which has two main ingredients. First, there must be evidence of a PASS cognitive weakness as described in Step 1 of this chapter, and, second, achievement test scores should show substantial variability that aligns with the high and low PASS scores. What results is a combination of PASS scale discrepancies that are significant relative to the child's overall performance (a significant difference within the student) with one or two PASS scores that are substantially below what would be considered typical (the normal range) *and* achievement scores that are consistent with the high PASS and low PASS scores. Such a finding provides evidence that a child has a disorder in the basic psychological processes necessary for SLD identification (Naglieri, 2005, 2011a). The steps for the DCM are provided in Figure 3.2, and a graphic representation of approach is found in Figure 3.3.

Finding a specific PASS weakness (in this case Successive and Planning) provides evidence that the student is not equally competent in each of four basic neurocognitive processes (Discrepancy 1). This weakness in working with information that demands sequencing can be easily related to the demands of, for example, the Pseudoword Decoding task, which also requires working with serial information. The lack of a significant difference (the consistency) between the low Successive score and reading scores for this illustration provides possible evidence of a cause of the academic failure (assuming adequate instruction, motivation to learn, etc.). The significant difference between the two high PASS scores (Simultaneous and Attention) and the two low reading scores (Discrepancy 2)

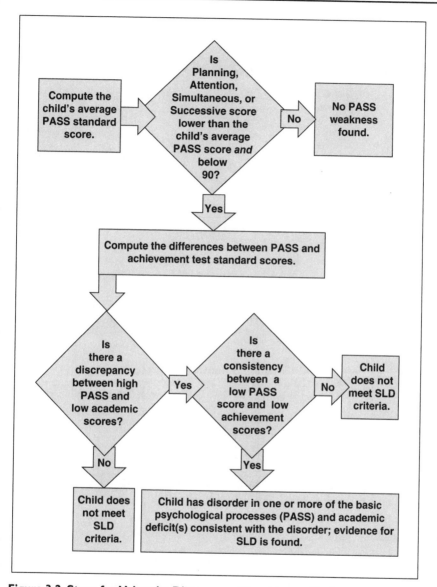

Figure 3.2 Steps for Using the Discrepancy/Consistency Method

further suggests that the student's achievement is below his or her ability to attend, shift focus and resist distraction (Attention), and work with information that forms a whole (Simultaneous). This evidence, in conjunction with other relevant data, supports eligibility as a student with an SLD when other inclusionary or exclusionary conditions are also met.

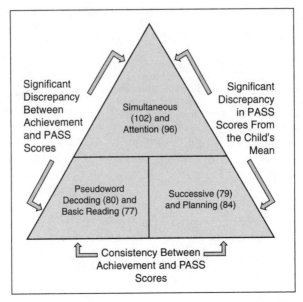

Figure 3.3 PASS and Achievement Scores for the Discrepancy/Consistency Method

Step 5: Examine the CAS2 Supplemental Scales

The supplemental scales included in the CAS2 provide additional information about a student's performance in several areas of interest. These scores provide a way to integrate results from CAS2 with other measures (e.g., executive function [EF] or working memory) or other concepts (e.g., verbal/nonverbal or visual/auditory). Because the CAS2 is intended to be used as a part of a larger comprehensive assessment, these scores are useful for comparing this instrument to other measures of ability and behavior. Even though our view is that PASS is the most valid and reliable way to interpret the CAS2, connecting this test's scores with commonly used concepts is important. When doing so, practitioners should follow a few guidelines.

PASS scales represent the best way to understand the CAS2 subtests; therefore, these scales are the focus of interpretation. When a strength or weakness on any of the PASS scales is found, then interpretation at the theoretical level (e.g., PASS) is conducted. When the results from CAS2 are integrated into a larger comprehensive assessment the supplemental scales enable a way to connect findings to PASS. For example, perhaps one of the measures in the comprehensive evaluation includes a rating scale of EF such as the Comprehensive Executive Function

Inventory (CEFI; Naglieri & Goldstein, 2013). It would be reasonable to expect that any rating scale of EF is best compared to those subtests included in the CAS2 that are most closely related to the research on the cognitive manifestations of EF. This is precisely what the EF scales on the CAS2 were developed to do. Keep in mind, however, that a cognitive test of EF from CAS2 may yield different results than a behavioral measure of EF, because scores from a rating scale of observable behaviors are more influenced by experiences than a neurocognitive score. See Naglieri and Otero (2014) for further discussion.

The CAS2 provides two EF scales: one that includes and one that excludes measures of working memory. We did this because there is considerable variability in the field as to which of these two approaches is best. Providing both gives you, the user, the option to choose. So, for example, the simplest way to decide which to use would be to select the Executive Function Without Working Memory score when you are comparing the Working Memory scale on the CAS2 with some other measure of Working Memory. The definition, research basis, and CAS2 subtests used for each of the supplemental scales are presented in the next section.

Executive Function Scales

There is no universally agreed-on definition of EF, especially in regard to the role working memory may play (Goldstein, Naglieri, Princiotta, & Otero, 2014). For this reason, the CAS2 provides two supplemental scales to measure EF: Executive Function Without Working Memory and Executive Function With Working Memory. The Executive Function Without Working Memory composite is composed of the Planned Connections and Expressive Attention subtests, which are most closely aligned with the research on this concept. For example, Weyandt et al. (2014) found that the well-known trail-making (our Planned Connections) and Stroop tests (our Expressive Attention) are the most widely used measures of EF. These tests measure two important components of EF: shifting and inhibition (Georgiou, Das, & Hayward, 2008), respectively. The Executive Function With Working Memory composite is composed of the Planned Connections and Expressive Attention as well as Verbal-Spatial Relations and Sentence Repetition (ages 5–7 years) or Sentence Questions (ages 8–18 years) subtests. This combination of subtests adds the working memory concept described by Baddeley and Hitch (1974), which is central to some theories of EF.

The CAS2 Executive Function With Working Memory scale can be compared to the Full Scale score on the CEFI (Naglieri & Goldstein, 2013). Conceptually, this comparison would enable you to determine if cognition as measured by the CAS2 is consistent with behavior as measured by the CEFI. This comparison will indicate if a student's ability (CAS2) to think strategically, apply a solution, determine if it is working, modify the plan as needed, and successfully complete the task as consistent with behaviors observed by a parent or teacher or reported by the student. Keep in mind that you should not assume that these scores should be similar, because behaviors will be greatly influenced by the environment within which the student functions. Differences in scores can indicate the need for a change in the way adults interact with the student. For example, if the nature of the educational experiences the student has had values explicit instruction of how to complete assignments, then the student's opportunity to think about different ways to solve problems is inhibited. Behaviors related to EF will be reduced in favor of solutions provided by the teachers. This can lead students with good scores on the Executive Function scale of the CAS2 to demonstrate few behaviors related to EF and consequently have a low score on the CEFI.

Working the Numbers

The differences between the CAS2 and the CEFI Parent, Teacher, and Self-Rating scores are provided in Table 3.6. This comparison is easily achieved because, unlike other behavioral measures of EF, the scores on the CAS2 and CEFI are scaled in the same manner. Both are set at a mean of 100 and standard deviation of 15 in which the higher the score the better. To use this table, begin by selecting the level of significance desired and the rater and whether you want to include or exclude Working Memory from EF. Then simply interpret scores that are equal to or greater than the tabled values as significant.

Working Memory Scale

Georgiou, Das, and Hayward (2008) described working memory as the capacity of the individual to store information for a short period of time and manipulate

Table 3.6 Values Needed for Significance When Comparing the CAS2 Executive Function Scale With CEFI Teacher, Parent, and Self-Ratings

| | CEFI Full Scale Score | | | | | |
| | $p = .05$ | | | $p = .10$ | | |
	Parent	Teacher	Self	Parent	Teacher	Self
Supplemental Scales of CAS2						
Executive Function Without Working Memory	12 11 11	11	12	10 10	9 9	10
Executive Function With Working Memory	10 9 9	9	10	8 8	8 8	8

it using two concepts introduced by Baddeley and Hitch (1974): the phonological loop and visual-spatial sketchpad. Engle and Conway (1998) described the visual-spatial sketchpad as a mental image of visual and spatial features. The phonological loop component of working memory refers to retention of information from speech-based systems that is particularly important when order of information is required (Engle & Conway, 1998). Because the Verbal-Spatial Relations and Sentence Repetition/Sentence Questions subtests have cognitive demands similar to those of the Visual-Spatial Sketchpad and Phonological Loop, respectively, they were selected to comprise the Working Memory scale on the CAS2.

The most obvious comparison of the CAS2 Working Memory scale score would be to the WISC-V and WPPSI-III Working Memory scales. This comparison seems straightforward based on the identical names of the scales on these two tests, but they are complicated by the differences in the subtests used to measure this concept. For example, the CAS2 subtests selected to comprise the Working Memory scale closely represent the concepts of the Visual-Spatial Sketchpad and Phonological Loop (Baddeley & Hitch, 1974; Engle & Conway, 1998). The WISC-V Working Memory Index is composed of Digit Span and Picture Span. We can assume that Digit Span Forward (similar to the CAS2 Sentence Repetition and Sentence Questions) has a strong Successive processing demand, but as shown by Schofield and Ashman (1987), Digit Span Backwards involves Successive and Planning processes. It is not clear what processes are involved in the WISC-V Digit Span Sequencing subtest. It is also not clear what the cognitive demands of Picture Span may be, although we suspect it may involve some Successive processing. The WPPSI-III Working Memory Index is composed of Picture Memory and Zoo Locations. The child views a page of pictures and then identifies those pictures on a second page in Picture Memory. Zoo Locations requires the child to identify where certain animals were placed in a spatial array. The cognitive requirements of these tasks need to be experimentally determined; however, taking at face value that they can be used as measures of Working Memory, we provide comparisons to the CAS2.

Working the Numbers

The values needed to compare the CAS2 and WISC-V and WPPSI-III Working Memory scales are provided in Table 3.7. When the difference between the two Working Memory standard scores are equal to or greater than the values presented at .05 or .10 level, then the result is significant. This table also provides the values needed for comparing the Verbal and Nonverbal scores, which can be obtained by the WISC-V or WPPSI-IV with the CAS2 (see Tables 3.7 and 3.8).

Table 3.7 Values Needed for Significance When Comparing Similar Scales on the WISC-V and CAS2

| | WISC-V | | | | | |
| | p = .05 | | | p = .10 | | |
CAS2	Verbal (VCI)	Nonverbal (NVI)	Working Memory (WMI)	Verbal (VCI)	Nonverbal (NVI)	Working Memory (WMI)
Verbal	12	11	12	10	9	10
Nonverbal	12	10	12	10	9	10
Working Memory	12	10	12	10	9	10

Table 3.8 Values Needed for Significance When Comparing Similar Scales on the CAS2 and WPPSI-IV

| | WPPSI-IV | | | | | |
| | p = .05 | | | p = .10 | | |
Supplemental Scales of CAS2	Verbal (VCI)	Nonverbal (NVI)	Working Memory (WMI)	Verbal (VCI)	Nonverbal (NVI)	Working Memory (WMI)
Verbal	11	11	12	9	9	10
Nonverbal	11	11	12	9	9	10
Working Memory	11	11	12	9	9	10

Verbal and Nonverbal Scales

The use of verbal and nonverbal measures of ability was initiated in 1917 when the US Army developed the Alpha and Beta tests (Naglieri, 2015). The verbal (Alpha) tests were intended for those who had been educated and the nonverbal (Beta) tests were intended for those who were illiterate. Yoakum and Yerkes (1920) stated that the purpose of the Beta (nonverbal) tests were "to avoid injustice by reason of unfamiliarity in English" (p. 19) and that the Alpha (verbal) tests would *not* measure intelligence reliably for those with a limited knowledge of English (p. 51). The Alpha and Beta tests are what David Wechsler based the Wechsler-Bellevue, published in1939, on, and which became the most widely used test of intelligence.

The Wechsler Intelligence Scale for Children, Fifth Edition (WISC-V; Wechsler, 2014) includes verbal and nonverbal tests. The Verbal Comprehension scale is composed of subtests (Vocabulary and Similarities) intended to measure "verbal concept formation and abstract reasoning," "word knowledge and verbal concept formation" (p. 7), as well as "a child's ability to acquire, retain, and retrieve general factual knowledge" (p. 8) and "verbal reasoning and conceptualization, verbal comprehension and expression, the ability to evaluate and use past experience, and the ability to demonstrate practical knowledge and judgment" (p. 8). The Wechsler Preschool and Primary Scale of Intelligence (WPPSI-IV; Wechsler, 2012) Verbal Comprehension scale is composed of the Information and Similarities subtest. In the CAS2, we wanted to measure thinking with verbal content but with questions that required as little factual knowledge as possible and that required less expressive language skill.

The Verbal scale on the CAS2 was designed to measure verbal reasoning but with less of a demand on English and on general knowledge. The CAS2 Verbal scale is composed of Verbal-Spatial Relations, Receptive Attention, and Sentence Repetition (ages 5–7 years) or Sentence Questions (ages 8–18 years), which are derived from the Simultaneous, Attention, and Successive processing scales, respectively. The CAS2 Verbal scale is different from verbal IQ measures found on traditional IQ tests because it is not as dependent on academically related verbal knowledge (e.g., there are no vocabulary or word analogies tests). Instead, the CAS2 Verbal scale demands the use of language across three of the four PASS scales and meets the goals expressed by Suzuki and Valencia (1997) as well as Naglieri and Bornstein (2003) for a measure of ability that has greatly reduced English skills and general factual knowledge demands but still measures thinking with language. Comparing the WISC-V or the WPPSI-IV and CAS2 Verbal scales using the values presented in Table 3.7 or 3.8 enables the practitioner to determine if the child can work with the English language whereas the WISC-V Verbal Index score will reflect how much the child knows *as well as* working with English.

The so-called nonverbal tests were originally described by Wechsler as a Performance scale, which has been split into Visual Spatial and Fluid Reasoning in the WISC-V, although a Nonverbal Index score is also included. Nonverbal tests have gained popularity as the US population has gotten more diverse (see Bracken & McCallum, 2009; Naglieri & Brunnert, 2009). These tests typically demand that the examinee recognize patterns in the way shapes are placed in the matrix and understand the logic of changes in shape, color, and rotation. The CAS2 subtests Matrices, Figure Memory, and Planned Codes are used to create a nonverbal scale that (1) requires reasoning, (2) has a visual spatial memory component, (3) gives the opportunity to see if a child would use strategies when solving a task, and (4) has minimal language requirements. This scale involves Simultaneous and Planning processes. The WISC-V Nonverbal Index score is composed of six subtests: Block Design, Matrix Reasoning, Coding, Figure Weights, Visual Puzzles, and Picture Span. For the WPPSI-IV these would be Block Design, Object Assembly, Picture Memory, and Zoo Locations. We suggest that this Nonverbal Index involves Simultaneous processing (Block Design, Visual Puzzles, and Matrix Reasoning), perhaps some Successive processing (Picture Span), and quantitative knowledge (Figure Weights). For the WPPSI-IV we suggest the Nonverbal Index involves Simultaneous processing (Block Design, Object Assembly, and Zoo Locations and perhaps some Successive processing on Picture Memory). Practitioners should recognize that differences between the CAS2 and WISC-V Nonverbal scores may reflect the different cognitive demands of these scales.

Visual Versus Auditory Subtest Comparisons

The comparison of performance between visual and auditory stimuli has been of interest for a long time. In order to compare scores on tasks that are very similar in their PASS demands we use the CAS2 Word Series and Visual Digit Span subtests. These tests provide an efficient way to compare visual (Visual Digit Span) and auditory (Word Series) information when both tests demand the same cognitive ability (Successive processing). If the two subtests' scores differ by 3 points (one standard deviation), then the difference is statistically significant (see CAS2 interpretive manual, Table B.3) and the modality of stimuli for that child may be an important factor to consider.

> ## DON'T FORGET 3.6
> ....
> When the difference between Visual Digit Span and Word Series subtest scores is 3 points, then there is a significant difference ($p = .05$) between visual and auditory presentation. Further inquiry should be considered.

Speed/Fluency Scale

The concept of fluency as measured by how fast a person responds can be understood from the PASS theory following Goldberg's (2009) description of how the right and left hemispheres of the brain acquire new information and skills. In his book *The New Executive Brain* Goldberg states that when a task is new (not yet learned) brain activity is maximized but as the task is learned and it is fluently (i.e., quickly) executed, the role of the brain shifts from thinking about how to solve the task to remembering, executing the solution with automaticity (Fluency). The transition from novel to fluent (which Goldberg calls *routinization*) is the path taken during the acquisition of everything we learn well enough to do with little effort (see Figure 3.4). Fluency, therefore, is the result of the interaction of many factors, such as instruction, motivation, intention, and opportunity, but especially PASS, because PASS provides a foundation for learning. Additionally,

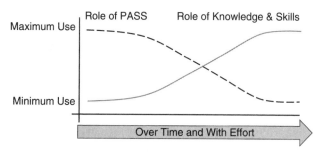

Figure 3.4 From PASS to Fluency

doing things smoothly, efficiently, and rapidly denotes Speed/Fluency. The transition from needing to put forth greater effort to less effort not only represents a change in hemispheric dominance from right to left but also represents greater vertical organization of the task. That is, as any task is learned there is not only a shift in cortical dominance but also greater involvement of the cerebellum activity, representing greater cortical to subcortical dominance. It is the cerebellum that drives the speed, force, and accuracy of the expression of what is learned.

We can measure Speed/Fluency with the first two pages of the Expressive Attention subtest on the CAS2. These tasks require that the student respond to very well-known stimuli (either the size of well-known animals or reading the same words or naming the same set of basic colors) as quickly as possible. Performance on these tasks provides a way to measure the extent to which a person has learned simple information so well that answering the question (e.g., is it a big or little animal or is the rectangle blue or yellow) requires fluent retrieval of knowledge but little thinking (PASS).

Step 6: Examine the Subtest Scores Within Each of the Four PASS Scales

The method for determining if there is variation among the CAS2 subtests is different for the 12-subtest Extended and 8-subtest Core Batteries. When the Extended Battery is used, the subtest scores within each of the four PASS scales are compared to the mean of the subtest scores for that scale. The differences are tested for significance using the ipsative comparison method and compared to the average range (8–12) using the same logic as the PASS scales. That is, the difference needs to be significant and the subtest score must be below 8 (weakness) or above 12 (strength). The values needed for significance are provided in Table 3.9. These variations should first be interpreted within the context of the PASS theory, consideration of strategy use, and other relevant variables.

Table 3.9 Differences Needed When Comparing Subtest Scores to the Child's Mean Within Each PASS Scale for the 12-Subtest Extended Battery (Ages 5–18 Years)

Subtest Extended Battery	$p = .05$	$p = .10$
Planned Codes	2.2	2.0
Planned Connections	2.5	2.2
Planned Number Matching	2.4	2.2
Matrices	2.0	1.8
Verbal-Spatial Relations	1.9	1.7
Figure Memory	2.2	1.9
Expressive Attention	2.1	1.9
Number Detection	2.5	2.2
Receptive Attention	2.4	2.1
Word Series	2.4	2.1
Sentence Repetition (Ages 5–7)	2.3	2.1
Sentence Questions (Ages 8–18)	2.3	2.1
Visual Digit Span	2.4	2.1

DON'T FORGET 3.7

....

A single subtest within a PASS scale that is significantly low means that the child could not *consistently* demonstrate the ability required to complete the task. Importantly, this finding does not diminish the validity of the scale when the score can be interpreted within the PASS theoretical perspective.

DON'T FORGET 3.8

....

Strategy assessment is an important part of the CAS2 and the CAS2: Brief because it augments interpretation of the Planning subtest scores, so be sure to complete the strategy checklist during (for observed plans) and after (for reported plans) on each Planning subtest.

These procedures provide a way to determine if a weakness within any of the PASS scales has potential importance. For example, a student may have a low score on Planned Number Matching, and analysis of strategy use indicated that no plan was used. If the child used strategies on the other two Planning subtests, the low score and observation of no plan would indicate that strategy use was inconsistent across the three Planning subtests. Similarly, a low score on Planned Codes may reflect a lack of self-monitoring if the child completes the page vertically because it was appropriate on a previous page without recognizing that the conditions have changed. These low scores are consistent with the concept of Planning and indicate a weakness in cognition that should, and does, influence the overall Planning scale score.

Table 3.10 Differences Needed When Comparing Two Subtests Scores Within Each PASS Scale for the 8-Subtest Core Battery.

Subtest Core Battery	$p = .05$	$p = .10$
Planned Codes and Planned Connections	3	3
Matrices and Verbal-Spatial Relations	3	2
Expressive Attention and Number Detection	4	3
Word Series and Sentence Repetition (5–7 years)	3	3
Word Series and Sentence Questions (8–18 years)	3	3

Comparisons of subtests within each PASS scale for the 8-subtest Core Battery are evaluated by comparing the two subtests in each scale. To determine when two subtests within each of the four PASS scales differ significantly, calculate the difference between the two (ignore the sign) and compare the result to the values in Table 3.10. If the difference obtained is equal to or greater than that found in the table, then the two scores can be considered significantly different. If a significant difference is found, review the performance within the PASS perspective whenever possible. For example, if a student obtained a higher score on the Word Series than Sentence Repetition subtests and you observed that the higher score was associated with a chunking strategy, then the use of a plan influenced the results for the Successive scale. The difference between the two subtest scores illustrates how much better the student can do on a task that requires Successive processing when a strategy is used. Whereas the best estimate of Successive processing is the lower score, the higher score indicates what can be expected when the student applies Planning processing to the task. This has considerable implications for intervention, so encourage the use of plans when completing work, especially work that demands Successive processing (see Naglieri & Pickering, 2010).

USING CAS2 ONLINE

The purpose of this illustration is to show the features of the CAS2 online scoring and interpretive report (Naglieri, 2014). This program is designed to provide an efficient way to convert all raw scores to derived scores, complete all scoring and comparisons of scales within the CAS2, and give a narrative describing each scale, the scores obtained, and what they mean. After either the item-level scores or subtest raw scores are entered in the online program, which looks like the CAS2 record form, the results are provided in either PDF or a Word document. Two reports can be obtained: a score summary as well as a scoring and interpretive report, which appear in Figures 3.5 and 3.6. We suggest that the interpretive report provides the essential findings that could be included within

CAS2 Cognitive Assessment System

Second Edition

Examiner Record Form

Jack A. Naglieri   J. P. Das   Sam Goldstein

Student's Name: Tony N
Sex: M   Grade: 6
School: Bull Run
Examiner: Temp User

	Year	Month	Day
Date Tested	2015	08	03
Date of Birth	2009	05	17
Age	6	2	16

Subtest and Composite Scores

Subtest	Raw Score	Scaled Score			
		PLAN	SIM	ATT	SUC
Planned Codes (PCd)	17	7			
Planned Connections (PCn)	250	8			
Planned Number Matching (PNM)	6	8			
Matrices (M)	20		13		
Verbal-Spatial Relations (VSR)	17		11		
Figure Memory (FM)	14		11		
Expressive Attention (EA)	40			11	
Number Detection (ND)	36			9	
Receptive Attention (RA)	29			8	
Word Series (WS)	11				8
Sentence Repetition/ Questions (SR/SQ)	11				10
Visual Digit Span (VDS)	9				9

	PLAN	SIM	ATT	SUC	FS
Sum of Subtest Scaled Scores	23	35	28	27	113
PASS Composite Index Scores	84	111	96	93	95
Percentile Rank	14	76	39	32	37
90% Confidence Interval — Upper	92	116	104	100	99
90% Confidence Interval — Lower	79	104	89	87	91

Subtest and Composite Profiles

Figure 3.5 Completed CAS2 Record Form Provided by the CAS2 Online Scoring and Interpretive Report Writer

PASS Scale Comparisons

	Index Score	d value	Sig/ NS	Strength Weakness	% in sample
Planning	84	-12	Sig	W	19.2
Simultaneous	111	15	Sig	S	12.3
Attention	96	0	NS		100.0
Successive	93	-3	NS		79.1
PASS Mean	96				

Subtest Analysis

	Scaled Score	d value	Sig/ NS	Strength Weakness	% in sample
Planned Codes	7	-0.7	NS		>25
Planned Connections	8	0.3	NS		>25
Planned Number Match	8	0.3	NS		>25
Planning Mean	7.7				

	Scaled Score	d value	Sig/ NS	Strength Weakness	% in sample
Matrices	13	1.3	NS		<1
Verbal-Spatial Relations	11	-0.7	NS		>25
Figure Memory	11	-0.7	NS		>25
Simultaneous Mean	11.7				

	Scaled Score	d value	Sig/ NS	Strength Weakness	% in sample
Expressive Attention	11	1.7	NS		<1
Number Detection	9	-0.3	NS		>25
Receptive Attention	8	-1.3	NS		<1
Attention Mean	9.3				

	Scaled Score	d value	Sig/ NS	Strength Weakness	% in sample
Word Series	8	-1	NS		>25
Sentence Repetition/ Sentence Questions	10	1	NS		>25
Visual Digit Span	9	0	NS		>25
Successive Mean	9				

Supplemental Composite Scores

Subtest	Scaled Score				
	EF w/o WM	EF w/ WM	WM	VC	NVC
Planned Codes					7
Planned Connections	8	8			
Matrices					13
Verbal-Spatial Relations		11	11	11	
Figure Memory					11
Expressive Attention	11	11			
Receptive Attention				8	
Sentence Repetition/ Questions		10	10	10	
	EF w/o WM	EF w/ WM	WM	VC	NVC
Sum of Subtest Scaled Scores	19	40	21	29	31
Composite Index Scores	97	100	103	97	101
Percentile Rank	42	50	58	42	52
90% Confidence Upper	106	107	109	104	108
Interval Lower	89	93	96	90	94

NOTE: EF w/o WM = Executive Function Without Working Memory; EF w/ WM = Executive Function With Working Memory; WM = Working Memory; VC = Verbal Content; NvC = Nonverbal Content.

Visual-Auditory Comparison

	Scaled Score
Word Series	8
Visual Digit Span	9
Difference	1
Significance	Not Significant

Figure 3.5 (Continued)

a comprehensive report. Of course, the user should always modify or add interpretive statements as needed. The case example is not a real one but intended to illustrate the functionality of the online system.

The PASS scores for the interpretive Example 1 presented in Table 3.4 in this chapter were used to generate the CAS2 online report, which includes a summary of scores and a narrative interpretation. The summary report is, essentially, the first two pages of the CAS2 record form, which contains all the raw and derived scores as well as the analysis of the PASS profile and subtest scaled score differences. The scores for the supplemental scales are provided on the second page as are the results of the Visual and Auditory comparison. As discussed previously in this chapter, Example 1 illustrates a PASS profile with a weakness in Planning and a strength on the Simultaneous scales. There was no significant subtest variability. This suggests that the PASS perspective yields critically important information, and there is little need for interpretation of the supplemental scales beyond comparison to scores from other measures. This means that in this case, the portions of the scoring and interpretive report that are most important are those that discuss the PASS and Full Scale results. The reports are provided in Figures 3.5 and 3.6.

CAS 2 Cognitive
Assessment
System
Second Edition

Scoring and Interpretive Report
Jack A. Naglieri

Name: Tony N
Age: 6
Gender: Male
Date of Birth: 05-17-2009
Grade: 6
School: Bull Run

This computerized report is intended for use by qualified individuals. Additional information can be found in the CAS2 Interpretive Manual.

Figure 3.6 Interpretive Report Provided by the CAS2 Online Scoring and Interpretive Report Writer

FULL SCALE

Tony earned a Cognitive Assessment System, Second Edition (CAS2) Full Scale score of 95, which is within the Average classification and is a percentile rank of 37. This means that his performance is equal to or greater than that of 37% of children his age in the standardization group. There is a 90% probability that Tony's true Full Scale score falls within the range of 91 to 99. The CAS2 Full Scale score is made up of separate scales called Planning, Attention, Simultaneous, and Successive cognitive processing. Because there was significant variation among the PASS scales, the Full Scale will sometimes be higher and other times lower than the four scales in this test. The Planning Scale was found to be a significant cognitive weakness. This means that Tony's Planning score was a weakness both in relation to his average PASS score and when compared to his peers. This cognitive weakness has important implications for diagnosis, eligibility determination, therapeutic and educational programming. The Simultaneous Scale was found to be a significant cognitive strength. This means that Tony's Simultaneous score was a strength both in relation to his average PASS score and when compared to his peers. This cognitive strength has important implications for instructional and educational programming.

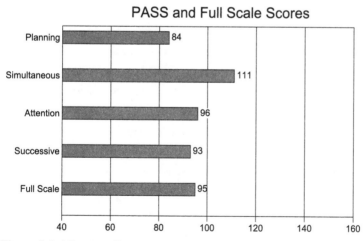

Figure 3.6 (Continued)

PLANNING SCALE

Tony's Planning score was significantly lower than his average PASS score and below the average range. This means that Tony performed particularly poorly on tests that required strategies for solving the problems on the Planning tests. He had trouble with development and use of good strategies, control of behavior, self-monitoring, and self-correction when completing these tests. Tony earned a CAS2 Planning Scale score of 84 which is within the Below Average classification and is a percentile rank of 14. The percentile rank indicates that Tony did as well as or better than 14% of others his age in the standardization group. There is a 90% probability that Tony's true Planning score is within the range of 79 to 92. This cognitive weakness has important implications for diagnosis, eligibility determination, and educational and therapeutic programming because children who are weak on the Planning Scale often have problems with tasks requiring strategies, completing schoolwork and other tasks on time, impulse control, self-monitoring, and social situations. There was no significant variation among his three subtest scores in the Planning Scale.

SIMULTANEOUS SCALE

Tony's Simultaneous score was significantly above his average PASS score and well above the Average range. This means that Tony performed particularly well on tests that required working with information that is organized into groups and forms a cohesive whole. This scale required an understanding of how shapes as well as words and verbal concepts are interrelated. He earned a CAS2 Simultaneous Scale score of 111 which is within the Above Average classification and is a percentile rank of 76. The percentile rank indicates that Tony did as well as or better than 76% of others his age in the standardization group. There is a 90% probability that Tony's true Simultaneous score is within the range of 104 to 116. This cognitive strength has important implications for educational programming because youth who are strong in Simultaneous skills have exceptional ability to understand relationships among words and images, especially spatial tasks like orientation in space and getting the big picture. Instructional methods that involve this learning strength in Simultaneous processing should be utilized. There was no significant variation among his three subtest scores in the Simultaneous Scale.

Figure 3.6 (Continued)

ATTENTION SCALE

Tony's Attention score reflects his ability to focus and resist distractions. Tony earned an Attention Scale score of 96, which is within the Average classification and is a percentile rank of 39. This means that Tony did as well as or better than 39% of the children in the standardization group. There is a 90% probability that Tony's true Attention score is within the range of 89 to 104. There was no significant variation among his three subtest scores in the Attention Scale.

SUCCESSIVE SCALE

Tony's Successive score reflects his ability to repeat information, such as words or sentences, in order, and an understanding of verbal statements when the meaning was dependent on the sequence of the words. Tony earned a Successive Scale score of 93, which is within the Average classification and is a percentile rank of 32. This means that Tony did as well as or better than 32% of the children in the standardization group. There is a 90% probability that Tony's true Successive score is within the range of 87 to 100. There was no significant variation among his three subtest scores in the Successive Scale.

SUPPLEMENTAL CAS2 COMPOSITES

The CAS2 supports the calculation of five supplemental composite scores: Executive Function Without Working Memory, Executive Function With Working Memory, Working Memory, Verbal Content, and Nonverbal Content. Tony's performance on these scales will be reviewed below.

EXECUTIVE FUNCTION

Tony's Executive Function score was within or close to the average range. This means that he performed about average on tests that required control of thinking, behavior, and attention (Planned Connections and Expressive Attention). He obtained a score of 97 on Executive Function, which measures inhibition (Planned Connections subtest) and shifting attention (Expressive Attention subtest). This score falls within the Average classification and is a percentile rank of 42. The percentile rank indicates that Tony did as well as or better than 42% of others his age in the standardization group. There is a 90% probability that Tony's true Executive Function score is within the range of 89 to 106.

Figure 3.6 (Continued)

WORKING MEMORY

Tony's Working Memory score was within or close to the average range. This means that he performed about average on tests that required evaluating and working with information that had to be remembered for a short period of time (Verbal-Spatial Relations and Sentence Repetition). Tony earned a Working Memory score of 103, which is within the Average classification and is a percentile rank of 58. The percentile rank indicates that Tony did as well as or better than 58% of others his age in the standardization group. There is a 90% probability that Tony's true Working Memory score is within the range of 96 to 109.

EXECUTIVE FUNCTION WITH WORKING MEMORY

Tony's Executive Function With Working Memory score was within or close to the average range. This means that he performed about average on tests that required control of thinking, behavior, and attention when working with information that had to be evaluated and remembered for a short period of time. He obtained a score of 100, which is within the Average classification and is a percentile rank of 50. The percentile rank indicates that Tony did as well as or better than 50% of others his age in the standardization group. There is a 90% probability that Tony's true score on this scale is within the range of 93 to 107.

VERBAL CONTENT

Tony's score on the Verbal Content scale was within or close to the average range. This means that he performed about as expected on tests that involved working with both simple and more complex verbal concepts (Receptive Attention and Verbal-Spatial Relations) and understanding verbal statements when the meaning was derived from the sequence of the words (Sentence Repetition). Tony earned a Verbal Content score of 97, which is within the Average classification and is a percentile rank of 42. The percentile rank indicates that Tony did as well as or better than 42% of others his age in the standardization group. There is a 90% probability that Tony's true Verbal Content score is within the range of 90 to 104.

Figure 3.6 (Continued)

NONVERBAL CONTENT

Tony's score on the Nonverbal Content scale was within or close to the average range. This means that he performed about as expected on tests that involved reasoning with visual spatial designs (Matrices), devising and using strategies (Planned Codes), and remembering geometric shapes (Figure Memory) when the content of the tests did not include words. Tony earned a Nonverbal Content score of 101 on the Nonverbal Content scale, which is within the Average classification and is a percentile rank of 52. The percentile rank indicates that Tony did as well as or better than 52% of others his age in the standardization group. There is a 90% probability that Tony's true Nonverbal Content score is within the range of 94 to 108.

Supplemental Composite Scores

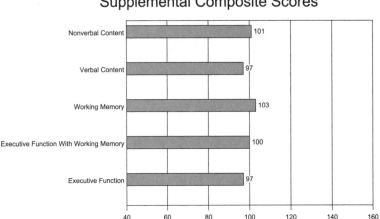

VISUAL-AUDITORY COMPARISON

Tony's scores on the subtests in the Successive processing scale that involved visual (Visual Digit Span) or auditory (Word Series) presentation of information were compared to determine if the difference in the modality of the task may have had relevance. There was not a significant difference between the two subtests that measured Successive processing when the information was given using an auditory (Word Series) or visual (Visual Digit Span) presentation. Tony's score of 9 on the visual subtest falls within the Average classification and is not significantly higher than his score of 8 on the auditory subtest, which falls within the Average classification.

Figure 3.6 (Continued)

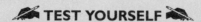

TEST YOURSELF

1. **The Discrepancy/Consistency Method is used to do which of the following?**
   a. Operationalize a method to identify gifted students
   b. Help identify students with a specific learning disability using the pattern of strengths and weaknesses approach
   c. Determine if a student has a cognitive weakness
   d. Determine if a student has a relative weakness

2. **The CAS2, CAS2: Brief, and CAS2: Rating Scale all have which of the following scales?**
   a. Planning, Attention, Simultaneous, Successive
   b. Executive Function
   c. Working Memory
   d. Verbal/Nonverbal
   e. Only (a)

3. **How are the CAS2, CAS2: Brief, and CAS2: Rating Scale all interpreted?**
   a. Traditional Verbal/Nonverbal/Quantitative format
   b. CHC model
   c. PASS theory
   d. None of the above

4. **When is the CAS2 Full Scale score most valuable?**
   a. When there is significant variability among the PASS scales
   b. When there is no significant PASS strength or weakness
   c. When only one PASS scale is a strength or weakness
   d. None of the above

5. **Who can use the CAS2 Rating Scale?**
   a. Teachers
   b. Counselors
   c. School psychologists
   d. All of the above

6. **The CAS2: Brief has how many subtests?**
   a. Two
   b. Four
   c. Six
   d. Eight

7. **The CAS2 has Core and Extended Battery versions that contain how many subtests?**
   a. 2 and 4, respectively
   b. 4 and 8, respectively
   c. 8 and 12, respectively
   d. 12 and 16, respectively

Answers: 1. b; 2. a; 3. c; 4. b; 5. d; 6. b; 7. c

Four

ASSESSMENT OF ENGLISH LANGUAGE LEARNERS

CONTEXT FOR UNDERSTANDING THE NEED FOR FAIR ASSESSMENT WITH ENGLISH LANGUAGE LEARNERS

There is a continuing and growing role of non-English languages as part of the national fabric. Fueled by long-term historic and more recent immigration patterns, the language diversity of the United States has increased over the past six decades. Immigration to the USA from 1970 to 2015 has steadily increased from 9.6 million to approximately 42.5 million (Zong & Batolova, 2016). Information from the 2011 census about speakers of non-English languages and their English-speaking ability tabulated 291.5 million people ages 5 and over, 60.6 million people (21% of this population), spoke a language other than English at home (native-born, legal immigrants, and illegal immigrants). The largest increases from 2010 to 2013 were for speakers of Spanish, Chinese, and Arabic. Spanish speakers who were non-Hispanic, White, Black, or Asian were more likely to speak English "very well" compared with those who were Hispanics (US Census Bureau, 2012).

According to the US Census Bureau's population estimates as of July 1, 2014, there are roughly 55 million Hispanics living in the United States, representing approximately 17% of the US total population, making people of Hispanic origin the nation's largest ethnic or race minority. Population projections released in 2014 predict that by 2060 it is estimated the Hispanic population will reach 128.8 million, constituting approximately 31% of the US population. Among Hispanic subgroups, in 2012, Mexicans ranked as the largest at 64%. Following Mexicans were Puerto Ricans (9.4%), Salvadorans (3.8%), Cubans (3.7%), Dominicans (3.1%), Guatemalans (2.3%), and the remaining 13.7% were people of other Hispanic or Latino origins.

In 2012, 23.3% of elementary and high school students and 6.8% of college students were Hispanic. Many Hispanics live in households where Spanish is also spoken. There were reported to be 38.3 million US residents 5 years and

> **DON'T FORGET 4.1**
> ....
>
> • Hispanics are the largest ethnic minority in the nation.
>
> • Almost one-fourth of the students in schools are Hispanic.
>
> • In 2012, 38.3 million US residents 5 years and older were reported to speak Spanish at home.

older who speak Spanish at home in 2012, constituting 13.0% of US residents and 78% of Hispanics (US Census Bureau, 2012, Table B16066). This is a 121% increase since 1990 when there were 17.3 million Spanish speakers (US Census Bureau, 2012). Enrollment of English language learner (ELL) students in schools across the nation has been on the rise with percentages ranging from 23% in California to a low of 0.6% in West Virginia. The majority of states have experienced double-digit percentage increases in the number of ELL students since the new millennium; however, states such as South Carolina, Indiana, and Arkansas reported a percentage increase of 800, 400, and 300, respectively, between 1997 and 2008 (Batalova & McHugh, 2010). More astonishing, however, is the growth within school districts, with some districts experiencing growth rates of more than 4,000% in the prior 5-year period (National Clearinghouse for English Language Acquisition, 2011).

UNDERSTANDING LANGUAGE DEVELOPMENT AND ELLS

It is now clear that ELL students represent the fastest-growing segment of the school population across all regions of the United States. Psychologists are more likely than ever to work with at least one ELL student directly or indirectly at some point. Therefore, it is very important to have a basic understanding of second-language learning. Not having such an understanding has historically lead to disproportionate representation of students from diverse backgrounds in special education, specifically those diagnosed with a learning disability (Shifrer, Muller, & Callahan, 2011). A particular challenge emerges for psychologists given that ELLs who display well-developed conversational skills can appear deceptively proficient in the second language, even though they're actually in the early stages of language development.

Students are more likely to progress in learning the societal language (i.e., English) when they are surrounded by peers who have higher levels of language proficiency than they do. If they are in neighborhoods and schools where there are too few native English speakers and where instruction may be poor, they will lag in acquiring English language proficiency. There are two types of language proficiencies: basic interpersonal communication skills (BICS) and cognitive academic language proficiency (CALP). BICS are language skills needed in social situations (Cummins, 1981). It is the day-to-day language needed to interact socially with other people. ELLs employ BICS when they are on the playground, in the lunchroom, on the school bus, at parties, playing sports, and talking with friends on the telephone. Because these social interactions are contextual, they are meaningful but are not cognitively demanding. For recent arrivals to the US educational system, these language skills develop over 6 months and up to 2 years. School personnel and support service personnel may assume a student is proficient in the language because he or she demonstrates adequate social language skills. CALP refers to formal academic learning, which includes listening, speaking, reading, and writing about subject area content material. This level of language learning is essential for students to succeed in school. This usually takes from 5 to 7 years. If a child has no prior schooling or has no support in native language development, it may take 7 to 10 years for ELLs to catch up to their peers. Academic language acquisition isn't just the understanding of content area vocabulary. It includes skills such as comparing, classifying, synthesizing, evaluating, and inferring. Academic language tasks are context specific and become more cognitively demanding when ideas, concepts, and language are presented at the same time.

It is important for psychologists and educators to understand this distinction between BICS and CALP as well as the importance of noting a student's language proficiency before or during the evaluation process. Confusion regarding a student's level of language proficiency has often led to an overreliance of tests that that are inappropriate for use with ELLs referred for special education (Klingner, Artiles, & Mendez Barletta, 2006), specifically, relying on tests that measure language, knowledge, and quantitative concepts. Reliance on these types of tests not only raises a red flag of potential legal and ethical concerns but also certainly is not best practice.

Acculturation factors in cognitive assessment must also be considered when evaluating students from linguistic and culturally different backgrounds. Acculturation refers to acquiring or adopting the dominant culture's values and norms by underrepresented groups living within that society. Acculturation is developmental and occurs across the continuum. Traditional tests of cognitive ability measure abilities that are inherently biased, given that they are based on values and norms of the culture in which they were created. Cognitive assessments measure the ability to access the culturally influenced information that is embedded in the test itself (Lau & Blatchley, 2009).

ELL students come from diverse educational, linguistic, experiential, and cultural backgrounds. Therefore, there are several factors unique to many ELL

DON'T FORGET 4.2

....

- When assessing ELLs, remember BICS and CALP are not the same. BICS describes social, conversational language used for oral communication. CALP is the context-reduced language of the academic classroom.

- It takes 5 to 7 (in some occasions up to 10) years for ELLs to become proficient in the language.

- Traditional tests of cognitive ability assess culturally influenced information.

- There are unique factors that need to be taken into account when conducting an evaluation and considering the results of many ELL students.

students that need to be taken into account when conducting, evaluating, and interpreting the results. Collecting multiple points of information regarding previous schooling the student received, including the type of educational placement (public or private); classroom variables (e.g., number of students, their ages, educational preparation of the teachers); frequency of attendance; disruption in schooling and the reasons; the amount of exposure the student has had to the native and second language; and a description of the curriculum are all important units of information to best understand the student and guide examiners in test selection and interpretation. When possible, it is important to examine the student's parents' level of education, literacy levels, languages spoken in the home (and what percentage of the time), social economic status, as well as other relevant culture characteristics (Blatchley & Lau, 2010).

THE CHALLENGES OF ELL ASSESSMENT

Tests that have traditionally been used to measure cognitive strengths and weaknesses or to diagnose fall short in their attempt to appropriately and adequately consider the role of second language learning and environmental and institutional factors that may contribute to the student's academic problems (Klinger et al., 2006). ELL students are heterogeneous relative to their emerging skills in English and their unique blend of cultural backgrounds (Geva & Wiener, 2015). Furthermore, emergent bilingual learners will likely have differing rates of language acquisition, tend to use words in both languages less then monolinguals do, and have more than one lexicon to draw from, which may hinder their speed of language processing and language retrieval. Thus, test questions that require knowledge and skills in a particular language, which is dependent on formal exposure to academic content and cultural-experiential nuances, will not accurately evaluate cognitive ability.

Traditional tests, such as the family of Wechsler scales of intelligence (Wechsler, 2003, 2012, 2014; Wechsler, Coalson, & Raiford, 2008), the Stanford-Binet V (Roid, 2003), and the Woodcock-Johnson IV (Schrank, McGrew, & Mather, 2014), for example, assume the examinee has sufficient CALP in order to understand and respond to subtest items of a verbal and quantitative nature. These tests include too many questions that do not necessarily measure how a student *thinks* but instead measure what they *know*. Furthermore, in the case of ELL students, these types of measures may be more a reflection of the student's CALP and *not* a measure of neurocognitive functioning. In order to illustrate this further let us examine specifically one of most the most widely used tests of intelligence in the field of clinical and school psychology (Braden & Athanasiou, 2005): the Wechsler intelligence scales. Weiss (Weiss, Munoz, & Prifitera, 2015) reported lower average full-scale IQs across all versions of the Wechsler scales for Hispanic samples (91.6 for the WAIS-IV, 93.1 for the WISC-IV, and 95.3 for the WPPSI-IV). The authors' reasoning for these findings is low educational attainment within the Hispanic sample being compared to the larger US normative sample. In order to "inform culturally sensitive interpretation" of test results, new Hispanic percentile norms and stratified base rate data have been provided by Weiss et al. (2015) for the Wechsler scales. We suggest that this kind of recalibration does not address the fundamental problem— which is that the content of the test questions is inappropriate for this population. Obtaining a verbal IQ score in comparison to other Hispanics with similar language and experiential backgrounds does not address the fundamental problem. Looking at test results in this way does not enhance our understanding of how the student thinks and learns and does not guide us in designing specific interventions.

We can conclude that testing cognitive ability with Hispanics has its challenges because of varying educational and cultural experiences, language development, and parental education, all of which have

DON'T FORGET 4.3

- ELL students are heterogeneous relative to their emerging skills in English and their unique blended cultural backgrounds.

- Tests that require a greater level of language encoding, processing, and retrieval, and that require knowledge based on formal exposure to academic content and cultural-experiential nuances, may have discriminatory impact.

- Many traditional tests are muddled with items that do not necessarily measure how a student *thinks* but instead measure what he or she *knows*.

a substantial impact on the students we assess. Therefore, ask yourself the following question: Should we use tests that require good language proficiency skills and knowledge when our goal is to evaluate Hispanic children and adolescents nondiscriminantly? To examine this question, in the following sections we will review what are the typical options examiners have when evaluating ELL students and then present our rationale for using PASS as operationalized through the CAS2.

CURRENT OPTIONS FOR TESTING ELL STUDENTS

Use of Translators or Interpreters

It is probably not controversial to suggest that under ideal circumstances most professionals would agree that Spanish-speaking examinees of limited English language proficiency should be evaluated by Spanish-speaking psychologists rather than through an interpreter. In situations when there are no examiners proficient in the native language of the examinee, the use of translators or interpreters for test administration, although necessary, is problematic for the same reasons previously mentioned; namely, test score validity is compromised. However, the practical challenge remains in that there simply are not enough bilingual psychologists available to meet the demand for services. Making an appropriate referral may not always be a viable option and can present significant financial and logistical hardships for many students and families. In one study Casas, Guzmán-Vélez, and Cardona-Rodriguez (2012) examined empirically whether using an interpreter to conduct neuropsychological testing of monolingual Spanish speakers affects test scores. Their results indicate that interpreter use may significantly affect scores for some commonly used tests, with this influence being greater for verbally mediated tests such as vocabulary and similarities. Although there are no ability tests that have been standardized with the use of translators or interpreters, the CAS2 offers a unique approach to administration that permits freely communicating with the examinee in any language. As described in Chapter 2 of this book, the CAS2 and CAS2: Brief instructions for administration include an opportunity to provide additional help when needed. At specific points in the directions for administration of the subtests examiners can use any language to explain the demands of the tasks. For more information consult Chapter 2 in this book and the respective CAS2 manuals.

Nonverbal Tests

Measures of general intelligence that use test questions avoiding language and using diagrams instead (so-called nonverbal tests) were developed at the start of

World War I when the Army's Alpha and Beta tests were created (Naglieri, 2015). The US Army saw a need for a quick-to-administer intelligence test to help determine what sort of advanced training a recruit would receive. Psychologists Lewis Terman, Robert Yerkes, and others collaborated to develop two versions of the test, known as the Army Alpha and Army Beta tests. The Alpha test was intended for literate recruits who had knowledge of English and math skills, and the Beta tests were deemed particularly important for those who performed poorly on the Alpha test and were suspected of illiteracy or having difficulty understanding and speaking English. Over the decades several nonverbal tests have been developed for use with individuals with limited language proficiency and poor language skills.

Critics argue that the overreliance on these tests for identification of Hispanic students for special education and gifted programs is misguided. Ortiz and Melo (2015) argue that few studies have examined the issue of validity with respect to their use as an acceptable substitute for a Full Scale IQ score derived from verbally laden tests. Wechsler and Naglieri (2006) have demonstrated concurrent validity of the Wechsler Test of Nonverbal Ability with other popular tests of cognitive ability and demonstrated virtually no difference in Full Scale scores when comparing ELLs to matched controls.

Lakin (2012) measured verbal, quantitative, and nonverbal reasoning tests that were administered to a culturally and linguistically diverse sample of students. The 2-year predictive relationship between ability and achievement scores revealed that nonverbal scores had weaker correlations with future achievement than did quantitative and verbal reasoning test scores for ELL and non-ELL students. Lakin fails to note, as has been presented elsewhere in this book, that the reason such tests may correlate higher with achievement is that the verbal and quantitative content is very similar to the content on tests of achievement.

Another potential weakness of reliance on nonverbal tests is construct underrepresentation—that is, the test measures only general ability. By contrast, tests such as the CAS2 measure a broader range of cognitive abilities or processes that are central to diagnosis and eligibility determinations of, for example, specific learning disabilities. In spite of any potential shortcomings, tests that have reduced language requirements can be particularly important when assessing Hispanic ELLs because they are more likely to have varied educational backgrounds and differing levels of English language proficiency.

Spanish Language Testing

It is intuitive to believe that the best-case scenario for evaluating ELLs is to do so in their native language with instruments that are available in Spanish. The numbers of bilingual psychologists who conduct psychometric assessments are miniscule compared to the number of ELL students in the schools, however. Demographics of the psychology work force in the United States as reported by The Center for Workforce Studies Report (July 2015) indicate less than 5.0% of active psychologists are Hispanic. The report does not break down this percentage into subspecialties, and thus it is unknown what percentages are practicing in fields in which practitioners conduct cognitive assessments. The National Association of School Psychologists membership for the 2014–2015 fiscal year is approximately 24,422 (J. Neponuecemo, director of membership, National Association of School Psychologists, personal communication, 2016); of these, approximately 2.5% identify themselves at Hispanic and bilingual. It becomes apparent that there are not enough bilingual professionals to service the growing numbers of ELL students in the United States (Peña, 2012).

Most available measures of cognitive functioning are developed and normed for monolingual populations, whether in English or Spanish. How ELL students with varying levels of language proficiency in English and Spanish perform on traditional tests of cognitive ability administered in their native language is not well known. Previous research on the relationship between proficiency and cognitive test performance was limited in scope and points mostly to the fact that bilingual individuals, as a group, tend to score about a standard deviation lower with respect to Full Scale intelligence quotient than their monolingual counterparts on all sorts of intelligence and cognitive ability tests (Bialystok, Luk, Peets, & Yang, 2010; Brigham, 1923; Cummins, 1984; Jensen, 1976; Kranzler, Flores, & Coady, 2010; Mercer, 1979; Valdés & Figueroa, 1994; Yoakum, 1921).

Sotelo-Dynega, Ortiz, Flanagan, and Chaplin (2013) investigated relationships between English language proficiency on performance on the Woodcock- Johnson Tests of Cognitive Abilities, Third Edition (WJ-III). The results provide evidence to support a linear, inverse relationship between English language proficiency and performance on tests that require higher levels of English language development and mainstream cultural knowledge. Consistent with previous research, the WJ-III General Ability Index for ELLs, on average, was significantly below the mean of the standardization sample (11 points). At the subtest level, four were lower than the normative mean of 100. The largest significant difference was measured for Verbal Comprehension (with a mean of 80.4). When compared with monolingual English speakers, ELLs as a group did perform significantly below the standardization sample mean of 100 on three of the other WJ-III subtests, including Concept Formation (standard score = 87), Visual Auditory Learning (standard score = 96), and Numbers Reversed (standard score = 95) tests. Within-group performance analysis showed that as the level of English language proficiency increases, so does the General Ability Index. These results illustrate the problems associated with a measure of ability that is unduly influenced by test questions that demand knowledge of English, an issue that is addressed by the CAS and CA2.

It is quite clear to practitioners, especially one of this book's authors, a bilingual psychologist with 25 years of experience, that low English language proficiency affects test results whenever common cognitive ability tests are used in schools and clinics. Since the original CAS became available in 1997, literally hundreds of ELL students had been evaluated, and a study was needed to examine how students performed across English and Spanish (research) versions of the CAS. For example, Naglieri, Otero, Delauder, and Matto (2007) conducted the first study of its kind to demonstrate that ELL students attained *both* similar Full Scale scores and similar patterns of performance at the subtest level, regardless of the test language, when administering the CAS, a measure of neurocognitive processing. The similarity in scores suggested that ability could be more equitably assessed across race and ethnic groups with this neurocognitive measure of ability. A second study comparing English and Spanish versions of the CAS was conducted by Otero, Gonzalez, and Naglieri (2013). Again, the Full Scale scores as well as PASS processing scale scores were compared. The data conclude no significant differences were found in Full Scale scores, and profiles were similar in the English and Spanish versions of the PASS scales.

The CAS, CAS2, and CAS2: Brief do not have high demands with respect to English language proficiency and do not include measures of word or math knowledge. Although general intelligence tests have value, there is an advantage to conceptualizing intelligence on the basis of basic psychological processes such as what PASS does. Fagan (2000) as well as Suzuki and Valencia (1997) suggested that a cognitive processing approach would avoid the knowledge base required to answer verbal and quantitative questions found on most traditional IQ tests and would be more appropriate for culturally and linguistically diverse populations.

English Language Testing

When Hispanic bilingual examiners are not available, sometimes the only recourse is to assess an ELL student with English-based assessment instruments. Before such testing is undertaken it is advisable to ensure the student has attained the appropriate level of CALP in English. Many school districts throughout the nation measure English language proficiency of ELL students on a yearly basis. For example, WIDA ACCESS for ELLs (Assessing Comprehension and Communication in English State-to-State for English Language Learners) is a large-scale English language proficiency assessment given to kindergarten through 12th graders who have been identified as ELLs. It is given annually in WIDA Consortium member states to monitor students' progress in acquiring academic English. Individually administered tests such as the Woodcock-Munoz Language Survey (Alvarado, Ruef, & Schrank, 2005) and the Bilingual Verbal Ability Test (Cummins, Alvarado, & Ruef, 1998) also provide helpful information in this area. As mentioned previously, the development of robust CALP skills under the best circumstances will take at least 7 years and may take up to 10 years. Therefore, it is likely that even students classified on a test such as the Access for ELLs as "expanding" or "bridging" (intermediate to advanced English language proficiency) will still need room to fully develop CALP. This may be one reason why in practice we observe that ELLs score lower than their native-English-speaking counterparts on verbally and linguistically loaded tasks.

Another approach that has been developed to help practitioners when testing students who are culturally and linguistically diverse (CLD) is the Culture–Language Interpretive Matrix (C-LIM; Flanagan & Ortiz, 2001). This model was originally conceptualized to answer the question of *difference* versus *disorder* when interpreting cognitive assessment results (Flanagan, Ortiz, & Alfonso, 2007). The difference versus disorder distinction attempts to differentiate whether cognitive assessment results are because of either (1) student differences in cultural and linguistic backgrounds or (2) a valid indication of an underlying cognitive disorder. The C-LIM attempts to discriminate between difference and disorder by sorting individual tests from commonly used cognitive batteries on two dimensions: linguistic demand and cultural loading. In the C-LIM framework, it is *theorized* that students' scores become lower as a function of the extent to which they are markedly different on one or both of the C-LIM dimensions (i.e., cultural loading and linguistic demand). This model, however, was based primarily on expert opinion. In an attempt to address this shortcoming, Cormier, McGrew, and Ysseldyke (2014) set out to evaluate empirically the validity of the C-LIM classifications for the Woodcock-Johnson Tests of Cognitive Abilities, Third Edition. Not surprisingly, when examining the empirical classification of the WJ-III COG tests, some patterns emerged. For example, findings indicated that the most linguistically demanding tests were all tests of Comprehension-Knowledge (*Gc*) and Fluid Reasoning (*Gf*). These tests were categorized to be high linguistic demand in the C-LIM as well. Conversely, tests with particularly low linguistic demand tended to measure domains of Visual-Spatial Processing (*Gv*) and Processing Speed (*Gs*). Additional analysis of the data collected suggested modification of the original classifications for the WJ-III was needed. Many more tests were classified as having moderate linguistic demands than what was previously thought, and fewer tests were of lower linguistic demand than originally thought. The authors suggest using caution when using and interpreting the WJ-III tests classified as having high and moderate linguistic demand, especially when testing culturally and linguistically diverse students. Although there may be some practical utility for the unseasoned practitioner to classify subtests according to degree of linguistic or cultural demands in trying to understand patterns of performances, this approach does little to help make decisions about diagnosis or eligibility.

Another study by Styck and Watkins (2013) examined the diagnostic utility of the C-LIM for the Wechsler Intelligence Scales for Children, Fourth Edition (WISC-IV) for distinguishing between a referred sample of 69 English language learners, 79 English speakers diagnosed with autism, and 216 English speakers referred for a special education evaluation. Results indicated that the WISC-IV and C-LIM did not significantly differentiate between these groups of students. Evidence from this study does not support the use of the C-LIM for making decisions about individuals in applied practice.

In examining the utility of the C-LIM, Kranzler et al. (2010) administered the Woodcock-Johnson III tests of cognitive abilities to a sample of 46 students in public schools who had not been referred for special education services. Several statistical analyses of the data were conducted. The results appeared to follow the predicted pattern suggested by C-LIM—a downward trend from higher mean scores on tests with low linguistic demand and cultural loading—but the findings were statistically nonsignificant. The data did not substantiate the predictions of the C-LIM model. The authors conclude that although children and youth from diverse backgrounds tend to score higher on cognitive tests with minimal linguistic demands, the use of the C-LIM model is yet to empirically demonstrate validity and therefore its widespread use is not recommended.

DON'T FORGET 4.4

- ELL students may be evaluated using several methods: testing limits, using interpreters, using nonverbal instruments, native language testing, and English language testing.

- In practice, choose one or a combination of approaches that best help to understand the child on a case-by-case basis.

Using CAS2 and PASS With Hispanics ELLs

As discussed elsewhere, the CAS2 is based on PASS theory, which integrates neuropsychological and cognitive psychological research and posits four distinct yet interrelated neurocognitive abilities: Planning, Attention, Simultaneous, and Successive. The PASS theory and its measurement system, the CAS2, provide a multidimensional, comprehensive assessment of essential neurocognitive abilities that go beyond general intelligence, and, more important, this approach is sensitive to specific cognitive problems related to specific academic failure, is relevant to intervention, equitably evaluates individuals from disadvantaged groups, and functions similarly across cultures and languages (see Das, 2004; Naglieri & Otero, 2011). Within the normative sample of the CAS2, Hispanic males and females were proportionally well represented consistent with the 2011 US census. According to the US census, Hispanics ages 5 to 21 years constituted 21% of the population, and the CAS2 matched this within its norm sample.

The validity of using PASS and CAS with Hispanics has been achieved through several means. Several studies have examined the CAS scores for racial and ethnic group bias. Naglieri, Rojahn, and Matto (2007) found that CAS Full Scale scores for Hispanic and White children differed 4.8 points when demographic differences were statistically controlled. They also reported that the correlations between CAS scores with achievement did not differ significantly for the Hispanic and White samples. Naglieri et al. (2007) compared PASS scores obtained on the CAS when administered in English and Spanish to bilingual children referred for reading problems. The children earned similar Full Scale scores on the English (mean of 84.6) and Spanish (mean of 87.6) versions of the CAS, and the scores from the two versions were highly correlated ($r = .96$). Additionally, Otero, Gonzales, and Naglieri (2013) studied the performance of referred Hispanic ELLs on the English and Spanish versions of the CAS and reported that the Full Scale scores on the English (mean of 86.4) and Spanish (mean of 87.1) versions were very similar and highly correlated ($r = .99$, corrected for range restriction). These findings for the CAS suggest that ability may be more fairly assessed across race and ethnic groups with the PASS neurocognitive approach.

Item selections on the CAS2 are free from gender, race, and ethnic bias. Item bias is said to exist when examinees from different racial or gender groups who have the same ability level perform differently on the same item. (See the CAS2 technical manual for a detailed description of the logistic regression procedure used to detect bias.) None of CAS2 items were determined to be statistically biased, and so we conclude that subtests on the CAS2 are also free from gender, race, and ethnic bias.

DON'T FORGET 4.5

There is considerable evidence that the CAS2 can be appropriately used with Hispanic ELLs.

Using the CAS2: Spanish

The initial translation of the CAS was undertaken by a group at the University of Puerto Rico lead by Wanda Rodriquez in 2000. Researchers used the method of back translation in which the test is translated from English to Spanish, and then it is translated back from Spanish to English. The administration and scoring manual, the test's written materials, and the test scoring sheet were translated using this method. The 12 CAS subtests were divided into two equal groups, and each group was assigned to a pair of translators. Each translator of the team worked independently on six subtests, and once the subtests were translated, the two translators on the same team compared their translations. Any disagreements were discussed and, when necessary, teams consulted a translator on the other team. When agreement was reached in the translation of their six subtests, one translator from each team joined to determine the consistency of the vocabulary used in the whole test. Once these processes were completed, the product was presented to two psychologists with broad experience in instrument translation and they in turn checked for the coherence between the English and Spanish versions. A similar approach was used for the CAS2—Spanish, but with a larger groups of experts from different geographical locations.

CASE ILLUSTRATION

One of the best ways to understand how to use the CAS2 with Hispanic ELLs is by a brief case illustration. The following is a brief version of a real case of a student with significant neurocognitive processing weakness and academic failure that was evaluated by this book's second author. The case illustrates the benefit of using a neurocognitive processing test for diagnosis and intervention.

Introduction to Alejandro

Alejandro is an 8-year-old Hispanic boy who is in second grade. His English language proficiency rating as measured by WIDA ACCESS was 1.6 (within the beginning to entering range). He was referred to the school psychologist because he was not acquiring basic literacy skills such as identifying letters, cluster sounds, and words, and had difficulty with counting and basic calculation. The classroom teacher indicated Alejandro had difficulty following directions, difficulty maintaining attention and focus, and recently had become more difficult because he would refuse to do schoolwork and was sometimes defiant.

Alejandro lives with his parents, maternal grandparents, and a younger brother. The family immigrated to the United States when Alejandro was 3 years old. Alejandro did not attend preschool or day care. Spanish is spoken in the home.

Parents and grandparents speak to each other in Spanish and the children are spoken to only in Spanish. Alejandro has conversational English and uses some English with his younger brother and with most friends at school. At school, the teacher delivers instruction in English, with Spanish support approximately 35% to 40% of the time.

According to school records Alejandro attended full-day kindergarten, and there were no concerns with attendance or disruptive behaviors. He was described as appearing distracted, inattentive, and as needing repetition of instructions, visual aids, and modeling in order to understand required tasks. Alejandro was performing significantly below grade benchmarks in reading, math, and writing since the first grade and continued notations regarding inattention-like behaviors were noted. By the middle of his second-grade academic year, Alejandro was having difficulty with decoding, phonics, and sight word vocabulary; working with math problems that involve money; understanding word problems requiring subtraction or basic multiplication, fact families, and problem-solving activities; and focusing and paying attention.

Alejandro received group reading instruction weekly and 4 months of individual and small-group reading-recovery instruction from a reading specialist, math tutoring, and preferential seating but made little progress. He became increasingly self-conscious about his level of academic success to the point of refusing to engage in academic work. After several team problem-solving meetings and special reading instruction, he continued working close to two grade levels below his peers and struggled in all basic content areas. Alejandro has responded minimally to intervention.

A complete evaluation by the school psychologist was conducted in order to better assess Alejandro's educational needs. Although friendly and cooperative, Alejandro showed some signs of anxiety. He wanted to know how he was doing and looked to the examiner for approval. Alejandro needed frequent breaks so that he could maintain his focus. Several procedures such as record reviews, classroom observations, interviews, rating scales, and direct performance measures were conducted. Select procedures are reported here in order to illustrate the use of the CAS2 and its usefulness in eligibility determination and intervention planning.

Cognitive Assessment

Alejandro was administered the Wechsler Intelligence Scale for Children, Fourth Edition (Spanish) [WISC-IV Spanish] and the Cognitive Assessment System, Second Edition (CAS2). Several of the CAS2 test results are quite revealing (Figure 4.1). First, there is a rather large discrepancy among the Full Scale scores. Second, the profile of strengths and weaknesses differs in important ways. On the

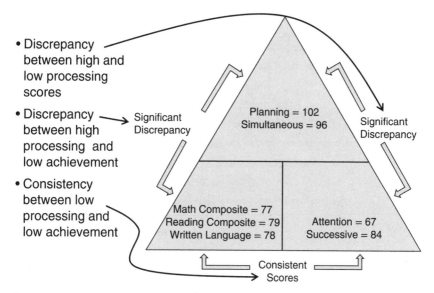

- Discrepancy between high and low processing scores
- Discrepancy between high processing and low achievement
- Consistency between low processing and low achievement

Significant Discrepancy

Planning = 102
Simultaneous = 96

Significant Discrepancy

Math Composite = 77
Reading Composite = 79
Written Language = 78

Attention = 67
Successive = 84

Consistent Scores

Figure 4.1 Alejandro's CAS2 and Achievement Test Results Based on the Discrepancy/Consistency Method

WISC-IV (Spanish), he earned a score of 75 on Verbal Comprehension, 79 on Perceptual Reasoning, 86 on Working Memory and 75 on Processing Speed (Full Scale IQ = 73). None of these WISC-IV Index scores differed significantly from Alejandro's average score, which means no strengths or weaknesses were found. On the CAS2, we observe the Full Scale score to be 10 points higher with strengths in Planning (developing and using efficient strategies) and Simultaneous (understanding relationships) processing and a significant weakness in Attention (focusing on what is relevant to the task) and Successive processing (keeping information in sequential order). As we will see, these findings have important implications for diagnosis and intervention planning.

Academic achievement testing demonstrated significantly underdeveloped skills across domains of written language, math, and reading (Figure 4.2). Reading words in isolation was somewhat better developed and was expected, given the supports Alejandro had received thus far.

Based on the data it is reasonable to suggest the possibility of a specific learning disability. How would we determine if we have met all the federal criteria to substantiate this claim? Naglieri's (1999, 2011a) Discrepancy/Consistency Method, described in this book, is one such method. The method is used to examine the variability of cognitive and academic achievement test scores. The results illustrate that Alejandro has a cognitive weakness in the basic psychological processes as measured by the CAS2 Attention and Successive scales. These weaknesses are

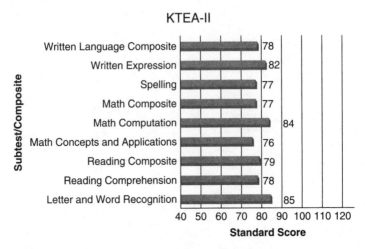

Figure 4.2 Alejandro's Academic Achievement Test Results

consistent with poor academic scores in math, reading, and written language. In contrast to these two low neurocognitive processing scores are his average scores on the Planning and Simultaneous scales. Determining whether the cognitive processing scores differ significantly and whether there is consistency between the low processing and low achievement scores is the key to not only determining whether Alejandro can be classified as having an SLD but also enables us to suggest interventions to help him be successful.

In the case of Alejandro the following can be concluded:

1. Alejandro has a disorder in one or more basic cognitive processes.
   ◦ Attention = 67 and Successive = 84
2. He has average scores in basic psychological processes.
   ◦ Simultaneous Processing = 96 and Planning = 102
3. He has documented academic failure.

DON'T FORGET 4.6

Alejandro has intra-individual differences in basic neuropsychological processes as measured on the CAS that underlie his academic difficulties. Figure 4.1 shows the application of the method in graphic form.

Alejandro's academic difficulties can be addressed in several ways when taking into account his pattern of scores on the CAS2. In *Helping Children Learn* (Naglieri & Pickering, 2010), there are several interventions linked to each of the neurocognitive processes measured by the CAS2. Teachers working with

Alejandro were given handouts titled "Graphic Organizers for Connecting and Remembering Information" (pp. 37–38), "Segmenting Words for Reading/Decoding and Spelling" (p. 76), "Chunking for Reading/Decoding" (p. 69), and "Plans for Word Syllables" (pp. 79–80). The psychologist was available to be a consultant to assist the classroom teacher in

any way necessary to provide support. These and other handouts are available in English and Spanish. Because it is common for the parents of ELL students to also have limited knowledge of English, the Spanish handouts are particularly helpful in understanding the interventions and to enhance at-home participation in helping the student.

In conclusion, Hispanic ELLs continue to be the largest growing student population in the United States. Therefore, it is imperative that we use instruments that are minimally influenced by cultural background and the impact of language. In this chapter we have shown that there is considerable empirical evidence supporting the use of the PASS theory as measured by the CAS and CAS2 with Hispanics. We believe that by using the CAS2 or CAS2: Brief, fair assessment of ELL students can be accomplished.

🖋 TEST YOURSELF 🖋

1. **Heterogeneity does not exist among Hispanics.**
   a. True
   b. False
2. **Hispanics account for approximately what percentage of the population of children under 18 years old?**
   a. 10
   b. 20
   c. 30
   d. 40
3. **Hispanic students with good basic interpersonal communication skills should do well on almost any test of cognitive ability.**
   a. True
   b. False

4. **Which of the following tests measure how students think?**
   a. WISC-V
   b. WJ-IV
   c. CAS2
   d. SB-V
5. **The effective use of the CAS2 with Hispanic ELLs has been empirically demonstrated.**
   a. True
   b. False
6. **ELLs often score low on traditional measures of cognitive ability because of which of these reasons?**
   a. Lack of vocabulary knowledge
   b. Different cultural experiences
   c. Varied educational histories
   d. Many traditional tests often including quantitative items
   e. All the above

Answers: 1. b; 2. c; 3. b; 4. c; 5. a; 6. e

Five

Jack A. Naglieri and Steven Feifer

One of the greatest strengths of the PASS theory as measured by the CAS2 is that use of this assessment provides the practitioner with an understanding of how a student learns best (a PASS strength), what obstacles to learning may exist (a PASS weakness), and what can be done to maximize learning (the purpose of this chapter). Importantly, the four neurocognitive abilities that define the PASS theory are not difficult to explain to teachers, parents, and the students. In simplest terms, PASS can be described as follows:

Planning is used when you think about how to do something before or when you act.

Attention is used when you focus your thinking on something and resist distractions.

Simultaneous processing is used when you think about how ideas or things go together.

Successive processing is used when you manage information or actions in a specific order.

These four PASS cognitive processes can underlie academic success and difficulties. If someone is strong in one of these areas, that strength can form the basis of success. If there is a weakness, this could pose an obstacle to learning. It is our job to provide information about strengths and weaknesses to maximize the probability of success in school and in life. An important question is, then, "How do we intervene?" But first we have to clarify what we mean by intervention and how that differs from instruction.

We will use the term *intervention* to indicate a specific way of teaching that is selected or developed with consideration of the PASS cognitive processing profile of the student and the relationship it has to academic performance. *Instruction* is the application of some method of teaching any subject, such as a phonics or whole language curriculum, so that a student has the opportunity to learn. The application of an instructional method without consideration of the cognitive and academic processing profiles of a student is *not* an intervention. We suggest that ordinary instruction becomes an intervention when it based on the results of an assessment that includes PASS and other relevant information such as mental health, previous educational history, home environment, and so forth. The more informed you are about the characteristics of the student, the more efficient the selection of an instructional method and the more likely the intervention will be successful.

INTERVENTION'S ESSENTIAL COMPONENTS

The interventions we present in this chapter are relevant for three essential groups: students, teachers, and parents. For maximum impact, the information from a comprehensive assessment that includes the CAS2 should be carefully described to the teachers, parents, and the students themselves. When all three of these stakeholders understand the PASS strengths and weaknesses, the relationships between cognition and academic skill acquisition, and which interventions are needed to maximize learning, the likelihood of success will increase. This process must begin with the student.

Informing the Student

When the CAS2 is used to evaluate a student referred for a suspected disability we can reasonably expect that this student's difficulties at school have adversely affected his or her self-concept. Just as success in school is often associated with being smart, the lack of success in school can lead a student to doubt his or her ability to succeed. Thinking, or simply suspecting, that he or she is not very capable of learning can lead a student to give up more easily, further reducing the likelihood of success. It is very important, therefore, that a student be informed of his or her PASS

> **DON'T FORGET 5.1**
> ....
> Remember that informing the student about his or her PASS scores is an essential step to changing the student's self-perception. Once the child knows what strengths were found, those can be used to overcome a weaknesses.

strengths and weaknesses in a manner that is age appropriate. The goal is to give the student the clear message that weaknesses *can* be managed with thoughtful effort and that PASS strengths can be used to manage PASS weaknesses. This understanding can change the student's view of him- or herself by providing reassurance that with knowledge of strengths and needs, success is possible. Therefore, practitioners should engage in a process whereby the mystery behind academic failure is replaced with a cogent explanation of PASS strengths and weaknesses.

Using the Book, Helping Children Learn

A student with a weakness in a PASS area should be informed about these four PASS thinking abilities and how information about strengths and weaknesses can be used to improve learning. There are four PASS handouts (see Naglieri & Pickering, 2010) that describe each PASS way of thinking and are intended to be discussed and given to the student. These short handouts provide students with a description of how to be smart by using a specific PASS way of thinking. Figure 5.1 shows the handout for Planning. The theme of this handout is to help the student learn that you can be smarter if you "Think smart and use a plan!" before doing things (Naglieri & Pickering, 2010, p. 63). The Planning handout is central to the intervention. It is very important that students know that one way to deal with academic problems is to "Think Smart" and be strategic. The message in the handout is that you can achieve more than you have in the past if you are strategic. This requires that the student learn to recognize when the demands of a task are particularly difficult and if that difficulty is related to PASS weakness or not enough knowledge of the topic.

To illustrate, a typical student with a specific learning disability in reading decoding has a weakness in Successive processing (Naglieri & Otero, 2011), which makes working with the sequence of sounds and letters in words very difficult. The student with a weakness in Successive processing needs to be told that *any* task that demands sequencing will be problematic and requires a strategy, for example, blending sounds to make a word, sequencing of letters or sounds to make and spell words, remembering information in order, doing things in a specific order such as tying shoelaces, combination locks, motor tasks, and so on. One approach to meeting the demands of any task that requires sequencing such as reading or spelling is to put sounds or letters in groups. There are many well-known strategies that can be used to help. For example, the handout "Chunking for Reading Decoding," which appears in Naglieri and Pickering's (2010, p. 86) book, teaches the student how to use a chunking strategy for reading decoding instead of trying to sound out and blend sounds to

How to Be Smart: Planning

When we say people are smart, we usually mean that they know a lot of information. But being smart also means that someone has a lot of ability to learn new things. Being smart at learning new things includes knowing and using your *thinking abilities*. There are ways you can use your abilities *better* when you are learning.

What Does Being Smart Mean?

One ability that is very important is called *Planning*. The ability to *plan* helps you figure out *how to do things*. When you don't know how to solve a problem, using Planning ability will help you figure out how to do it. This ability also helps you control what you think and do. It helps you to stop before doing something you shouldn't do. Planning ability is what helps you wait until the time is right to act. It also helps you make good decisions about what to say and what to do.

How Can You Be Smarter?

You can be smarter if you PLAN before doing things. Sometimes people say, "Look before you leap," "Plan your work and work your plan," or "Stop and think." These sayings are about using the ability to plan. When you stop and think about *how* to study, you are using your ability to plan.

You will be able to do more if you remember to use a plan. An easy way to remember to use a plan is to look at the picture "Think smart and use a plan!" (Figure 1). You should always use a plan for reading, vocabulary, spelling, writing, math problem solving, and science.

Do you have a favorite plan for learning spelling words? Do you use flashcards or go on the Internet to learn? Do you ask the teacher or another student for help? You can learn more by using a plan for studying that works best for you.

Think smart and use a plan!

I figured out how to do it!

Use a plan.

It is smart to have a plan for doing all schoolwork. When you read, you should have a plan. One plan is to look at the questions you have to answer about the story first. Then read the story to find the answers. Another plan is to make a picture of what you read so that you can see all the parts of the story. When you write you should also have a plan. Students who are good at writing plan and organize their thoughts first. Then they think about what they are doing as they write. Using a plan is a good way to be smarter about your work!

Figure 1. Picture reminder for using a plan.

Figure 5.1 Student Handout for Thinking Smart—Planning

You can also be better in math if you use a plan. Think about the problem, choose a way to solve it, see if that plan works, change plans if necessary, and check the final answer carefully. Use a plan to draw a diagram of the problem so that you understand the question. Using a plan is a good way to be smart!

How Can You Interact Smartly with Other People?

You should always use a plan with the people in your life. Think about how you want to behave. If what you are doing is not working, plan for another way to reach your goal. Think about what you want to say and choose your words carefully *before* you say it. Think about how the other person might feel or act after you say something. Doing these things will help other people understand you better, and you will understand them better, too. Using a plan with other people is another way to be smart!

Remembering to Plan

Remember that sometimes when you are scared, tired, or just doing too many things at one time, you might forget to plan. This is a bad way to do things. When you see that you are not using a plan, say to yourself, "Stop and use a plan." Use a plan, and you will be a lot smarter!

Resources

Goldstein, S., & Naglieri, J.A. (2007, October 22–27). Planning and attention problems in ADHD: What parents and teachers can do. *Attention*.

Naglieri, J.A., Goldstein, S., & Conway, C. (2009). Using the Planning, Attention, Simultaneous, Successive (PASS) theory within a neuropsychological context. In C. Reynolds & E. Fletcher-Janzen (Eds.), *Handbook of clinical child neuropsychology* (3rd ed.) (pp. 783–800). New York: Springer.

Pressley, M.P., & Woloshyn, V. (1995). *Cognitive strategy instruction that really improves children's academic performance* (2nd ed.). Brookline, MA: Brookline Books.

Scheid, K. (1993). *Helping students become strategic learners*. Brookline, MA: Brookline Books.

Figure 5.1 (Continued)

make a word. When a strategy is used in this way, the correct answer is arrived at by *thinking* about how to solve the problem (using a plan) rather than by trying to decode the word in segments (which demands much Successive processing). This change in the instruction changes the cognitive demands of the task because seeing letters in groups reduces the length of the sequence and involves Planning and Simultaneous processes. Shifting the cognitive processing demand of a task is an excellent intervention because not only does it help the child perform a task in a way that does not rely on his or her cognitive weakness but also it gives the child a chance to be successful.

Teaching the student about his or her strengths and needs and how to use cognitive tools to address the learning needs empowers him or her. Once empowered the mind-set shifts from "I can't do this work" to "If I think smart, I know I can do better." This transition in perspective needs to be shared and nurtured by the adults who work with the student. It is very important, therefore, that we consider the mind-set of the student. One way to understand the student's thinking about how he or she acts and thinks is to talk with the student about mind-set. In simple terms, mind-set is a description of the way a person thinks and acts when doing things, especially tasks that are demanding. The concept of growth and fixed mind-sets described by Dweck (2006) is a valuable part of the intervention process. Students with a fixed mind-set believe they cannot improve with effort, so they tend to give up easily. By contrast, those with a growth mind-set believe they *can* achieve with effort and persistence. Ensuring that the student has a growth mind-set is important, but so too is the mind-set of the parents and teachers. When informing parents and teachers about a child's cognitive strengths and weaknesses, it is critical that the content of the conversation includes a growth mind-set perspective.

DON'T FORGET 5.2

Use the handouts from *Helping Children Learn* (Naglieri & Pickering, 2010) to inform the student, parents, and teachers of ways to use PASS strengths to overcome any areas of need (see Figures 5.1, 5.2, and 5.3).

Two informal rating scales shown in Figures 5.2 and 5.3 are described as Measure of Mindset (Children-Adolescents) (MOM-CA) and Measure of Mindset (Teacher-Parent) (MOM-TP) (Naglieri & Kryza, 2015) and can be used to stimulate the discussion among the teacher, parent, school psychologist, and student. The teacher, parent, and student responses to this informal checklist can be used to help determine if the student has a growth (the first five questions) or fixed (the last five questions) mind-set. Simply add the scores for the first and second group of

Measure of Mindset (Child & Adolescent)				
Jack A. Naglieri & Kathleen M. Kryza - Copyright © 2015				

Name _____
Date _____

Instructions: These 10 questions ask about how you think and feel. The answers you give can help us know your thoughts about how you learn. Please read every question carefully and circle the number under the word that tells what you do.

	Never	Sometimes	Most times	Always
1 I don't give up easily.	0	1	2	3
2 When things get hard I say, "I Can do it"	0	1	2	3
3 When I fail I try harder until I get it done.	0	1	2	3
4 I believe that I can learn from my mistakes.	0	1	2	3
5 I think I can do almost anything if I try hard enough.	0	1	2	3
6 When I don't understand something I give up.	0	1	2	3
7 I do not like to be challenged.	0	1	2	3
8 When work is hard I think, "I can not do it."	0	1	2	3
9 When things get hard I do something else.	0	1	2	3
10 When I fail I do something else that is more fun.	0	1	2	3

Figure 5.2 Measure of Mindset: Child & Adolescent Version

Copyright © 2015 by J. A. Naglieri and K. M. Kryza. This may be duplicated for educational use only.

five questions and compare the totals. This will provide information about the student's self-perception and level of persistence when challenged. The goal of this discussion is to ensure that the student gets to the point where he or she can say, "I can't do it; *yet*. So, I am going to keep trying until I can."

Informing Teachers and Parents

PASS scores obtained from the CAS2, CAS2: Brief, or the CAS2: Rating Scale provide an explanation of how a young person learns and makes a prediction for future success. A strength or weakness in any of the four neurocognitive abilities must be taken into consideration when the learning environment is examined and when instruction or intervention is delivered. The goal is to select teaching

Measure of Mindset (Teacher & Parent)				
Jack A. Naglieri & Kathleen M. Kryza - Copyright © 2015				

Name _____
Date _____

Instructions: These 10 questions ask about a child or adolescent's attitudes toward learning. Please read every question carefully and circle the number under the word that tells what you have observed about your child.

		Never	Sometimes	Most times	Always
1	He/she doesn't give up easily.	0	1	2	3
2	When things get hard he/she says, "I can do it!"	0	1	2	3
3	Failure leads him/her to try harder until the task is finished.	0	1	2	3
4	He/she views failure as an important part of learning.	0	1	2	3
5	He/she believes that you can do anything if you try hard enough.	0	1	2	3
6	He/she is afraid of failure.	0	1	2	3
7	When things get hard he/she avoids the work.	0	1	2	3
8	He/she believes that hard work usually does not pay off.	0	1	2	3
9	He/she is fast to give up on a task.	0	1	2	3
10	He/she sees failure as proof of a person's limitations.	0	1	2	3

Figure 5.3 Measure of Mindset: Teacher & Parent Version

Copyright © 2015 by J. A. Naglieri and K. M. Kryza. This may be duplicated for educational use only.

methods with consideration of the PASS demands of the task and the correspondence of those demands with the PASS profile of the learner. This requires that the PASS processes involved in the teaching method, program, or lesson plan must be understood. For example, a child who is low in successive processing will likely have problems learning from a phonics-based reading program that demands blending sounds to read words. Therefore, when equipped with information about a student's PASS scores, the teacher can select methods that more efficiently match the characteristics of the learner. A critical part of this process is to examine the academic and PASS demands of any learning environment to determine whether a particular skill can be directly remediated, as well to determine appropriate strategies that can facilitate learning.

Figure 5.4 shows a handout for teachers that describes Simultaneous processing (Naglieri & Pickering, 2010), enhancing their understanding of the relationships

Simultaneous Processing Explained

Simultaneous processing is a mental process used to relate separate pieces of information as a group or see how parts are related to a whole. Usually Simultaneous processing is seen in tasks that involve spatial skills, such as using blocks to build a design, doing geometry, seeing patterns in numbers, seeing a group of letters as a word, understanding words as a whole, understanding a sentence as part of a paragraph, and reading comprehension. The spatial aspect of Simultaneous processing includes the perception of an object as a whole and seeing patterns. Simultaneous processing is involved in reading comprehension in that it requires the integration and understanding of word relationships, prepositions, and inflections so that a person can derive meaning based on the whole idea. Children good at Simultaneous processing easily recognize themes and how facts fit together to form a complete whole.

Example of Simultaneous Processing in the Classroom

Simultaneous processing is involved in the comprehension of spoken and written language. For example, the sentence "The black cat ran" requires a student to relate the element "cat" with the element "blackness" and relate it to the action "run." Grouping the words *flowers*, *birds*, *rocks*, and *clouds* into a group of "things you can find outside" uses Simultaneous processing because it requires the student to see how each of those things relates to the others and to the statement.

Figure Test

Draw each figure from the front, top, and side views.

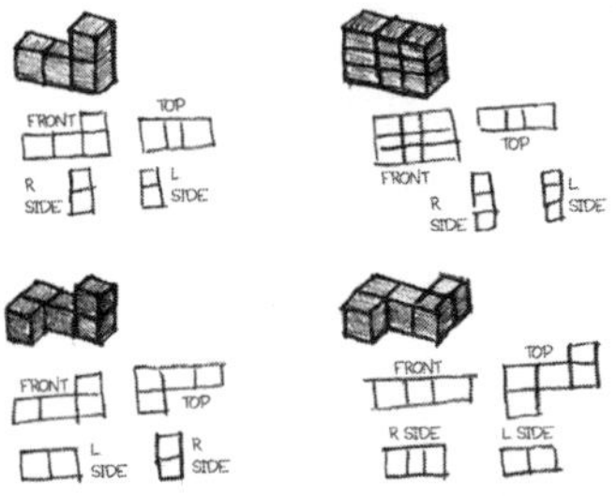

Figure 1. An example of an activity that requires Simultaneous processing.

Simultaneous processing is required for things to be seen as a whole. To recognize a shape in a collection of lines that form a cube requires Simultaneous processing, as does drawing a map (see Figure 1). Drawing or making a map requires grasping the relationship of one place to another in a meaningful way, rather than seeing a map as a bunch of shapes and lines.

A simple but common task for children in school is to draw pictures, often pictures about a story they have written or read. Simply drawing the picture and seeing how each part, color, and design fits to make the artwork meaningful requires Simultaneous processing. A drawing that includes all of the necessary parts in a well-organized group involves Simultaneous processing. Relating the picture to what was read or written requires the student to understand the story and how its parts are interrelated.

Figure 5.4 Handout for Teachers That Describes Simultaneous Processing

Simultaneous processing describes several activities.

- Relating parts into a comprehensive whole to see how things fit together
- Understanding relationships among words, pictures, or ideas
- Working with spatial relationships
- Seeing several things or integrating words into a larger idea

Here are some classroom problems related to Simultaneous processing:

- Failure to recognize sight words quickly
- Failure to interpret word, sentence, or passage meaning
- Difficulty with seeing the shapes of words or working with spatial tasks
- Failure to see patterns in text or math problems
- Failure to comprehend math word problems

Strategies for Developing Simultaneous Processing

- Do matching and categorization games (e.g., pictures, words), including opposites, with the child
- Show the child reproductions of figures in rotation and from different perspectives
- Have the child practice on jigsaw puzzles, hidden picture worksheets, and building three-dimensional objects
- Ask the child to supply missing details in stories
- Encourage rhyming
- Have the child use and create maps, both geographical and contextual
- Teach the child how to summarize stories or articles

How Is Simultaneous Processing Measured?

Simultaneous processing can be measured using the Cognitive Assessment System (CAS). The CAS gives an overall score and separate PASS scores for the four cognitive scales, including Simultaneous processing. The average score is 100. Scores below 90 are considered below average.

Resources

Kirby, J.R., & Williams, N.H. (1991). *Learning problems: A cognitive approach.* Toronto: Kagan & Woo Limited.
Naglieri, J.A. (1999). *Essentials of CAS assessment.* New York: John Wiley & Sons.
Naglieri, J.A., & Das, J.P. (1997). *Cognitive Assessment System.* Itasca, IL: Riverside.

Figure 5.4 (Continued)

between a student's PASS profile and the PASS demands of the academic tasks the student is good at or struggling with. This analysis should be conducted with two important issues in mind: (1) most tasks involve more than one PASS ability and (2) the role of PASS processes can change as the task is learned.

It is important to recognize that many academic tasks will require more than one PASS process (Naglieri & Rojahn, 2004). The key is to see how the student's PASS weakness relates to each part of the task to be learned. For example, when reading a paragraph, a student who is low in Planning may do poorly because of a failure to consider all the possible meanings of the text. A student who is poor in Simultaneous processing may do poorly because he or she cannot see how to combine all the information into a cohesive whole to arrive at the overall meaning. Another person low in Successive processing may have trouble remembering the order of events described in the paragraph and will arrive at the wrong conclusions. Finally, a student low in Attention will likely miss the subtle details and therefore fail to understand the text. Knowing the PASS strengths and weaknesses and the demands of the academic task will help the teacher anticipate the obstacles and encourage the student to approach the task with appropriate consideration of the best ways to proceed.

A second important consideration is the changing role of PASS neurocognitive abilities over the course of learning. There are two aspects to this progression. First, Goldberg (2009) stated that the PASS processes will be more involved at the initial stages of learning when knowledge is limited. When knowledge is well learned and

> ## DON'T FORGET 5.3
> ....
> PASS cognitive processes are very important when learning something new. Once the knowledge becomes well learned, it is a skill and can be demonstrated with less reliance on PASS.

can be used without much cognitive effort, then the knowledge becomes a skill. This means that educators need to recognize the student's strengths and weaknesses in each of the PASS neurocognitive abilities when any new activity is first being presented. This was previously illustrated by Figure 3.4.

Another important consideration is that knowledge of PASS scores, when paired with specific academic processing demands, provides teachers with much more precision in selecting appropriate interventions for the most challenging learners. For instance, a younger student with weaknesses in Simultaneous processing and reading may benefit from teaching word families in a manner that helps the child hear and see the similarities of words (e.g., *hat, sat, bat, mat,* etc.).

It is important to note that over the course of learning, as a new task transitions from a novel endeavor into something that is known, and ultimately to a well-learned skill, then the PASS processing demands will likely change as well. Consequently, targeted intervention strategies will also change over time.

Finally, the fourth important consideration is that despite a PASS weakness, students *can* learn. The key is to initially work around the weakness so that the student experiences some success and then to teach the student to recognize that when learning is hard to "think smart and use a plan!" (Naglieri & Pickering, 2010).

Providing Educational Services

Parents should be aware of a few basic tenets of the special education process when their child is referred for an assessment. The standard practice of student assessment is based on making special education qualification decisions according to a set of prescribed criteria as outlined by the Individuals with Disabilities Act (IDEA). Consequently, school psychologists often select a battery of tests designed to meet eligibility decision requirements as opposed to specifically crafting an assessment battery to generate targeted intervention suggestions. Oftentimes, intervention selection remains an afterthought or at best is loosely tied in with targeted test results. Herein lies the difference between an *administrative* test battery used primarily to qualify children for special education services versus an *integrative* test battery used to determine targeted processing strengths and weaknesses that can be parlayed into tangible and specific interventions.

Traditionally, most evaluators have used global academic achievement scores to determine an overall reading, math, or written language composite score. These scores represent a compilation of individual achievement skills in a particular academic area. Composite scores are often needed, and in

> **DON'T FORGET 5.4**
> ....
> The "basic psychological processes" described in the definition of a specific learning disability can be operationalized using the CAS2.

some cases are required, to establish a significant discrepancy between a child's overall cognitive ability in order to meet basic special education eligibility requirements. The basis for this method of identifying learning disorders—the *discrepancy method*—does not focus on specific neurocognitive processes inherent in reading, writing, or mathematics but rather examines global attributes of achievement in comparison to global attributes of cognition (Feifer & Della Toffalo, 2007). Regardless of whether this method is sufficient to make qualification decisions for special education services or not, we suggest that this approach offers teachers little in the way of generating targeted academic goals and recommendations individualized in a manner that best meets a student's learning needs.

With the reauthorization of IDEA in 2004, examiners no longer need to rely on significant discrepancies between aptitude and achievement in order to determine eligibility for special education services. Instead, alternative approaches focusing on the underlying cognitive processes a child uses to learn information can be cataloged and measured to determine the presence of a specific learning disorder. Because the CAS2 is a comprehensive measure of basic psychological processes for learning, and the Feifer Assessment of Reading (FAR; Feifer, 2015) is a comprehensive measure of basic cognitive and linguistic processes used for reading, both can be paired together to more precisely determine a child's learning needs as well as target specific recommendations customized to the child. This process empowers teachers to make sound educational decisions about children.

ASSESSMENT OF READING

The FAR is composed of 15 individual subtests measuring various aspects of phonological development, orthographical processing, decoding skills, morphological awareness, reading fluency, and comprehension skills. The FAR measures four specific subtypes of reading disorders, all of which are derived from deficits in one or more PASS basic psychological processes.

Phonological Index:

Students who have difficulty with the phonological components of reading that underscore accurate word recognition skills are exhibiting *dysphonetic dyslexia*. From a neuropsychological standpoint, the supramarginal gyrus, located at the juncture of the temporal and parietal lobes, is a key brain region responsible for the temporal ordering of phonological information (McCandliss & Noble, 2003; Sandak et al., 2004; Shaywitz, 2004). The primary PASS process needed for sequencing letters together to recognize words is Successive processing. The following reading intervention programs are tailored toward learning more-effective sequencing of sounds.

≡ *Rapid Reference 5.1*

Explicit Phonics Programs to Improve Successive Processing of Sounds

Wilson Reading System
  ○ Corrective Reading and REACH System
Read 180
LEXIA Strategies for Older Students
Alphabetic Phonics (Orton-Gillingham)
  ○ SRA Corrective Reading
  ○ Earobics II
  ○ LiPS Seeing Stars
  ○ LEXIA Primary Reading
  ○ Horizons
  ○ Fast Forward I
  ○ Fast Forward II
Earobics I
Saxon Phonics Program
Ladders to Literacy
Road to the Code
  ○ SIPPS
  ○ Phono-Graphics
  ○ Success for All
  ○ Scott Foresman Early Intervention Reading
  ○ Foundations

Fluency Index:

Subtests that make up the FAR's Fluency Index address the *surface dyslexia* subtype of reading disorder. These students often struggle with reading speed and automatically recognizing words in print primarily because of poor orthographic skills. In other words, these students have difficulty processing the entire visual word form as a whole and struggle reading words that are not phonetically decodable (e.g., *debt, onion, yacht,* etc.). Simply put, these children are sound-by-sound, letter-by-letter readers, which greatly slows them down and hinders fluency. The neural circuitry involved with surface dyslexia includes the left angular gyrus, an important brain region that plays a role in the orthographic assembly of the visual word form (Sakurai, Asami, & Mannen, 2010).

The primary PASS process needed for the visual-spatial recognition of the printed word form is Simultaneous processing. The following reading intervention programs are tailored toward increasing reading speed and fluency by teaching students to develop automatic word recognition skills, relying on more Simultaneous processing of the printed word form.

≡ *Rapid Reference 5.2*

Reading Fluency Programs to Improve Simultaneous Processing of Words

- Academy of Reading
- Wilson Reading System
- Laubauch Reading Series
- Read 180
- Read Naturally
- Great Leaps Reading
- Quick Read
- RAVE-O
- Fast Track Reading
- Destination Reading
- Reading Recovery
- Early Success
- Fluency Formula

Mixed Index:

The third reading disorder subtype, often referred to as *mixed dyslexia,* is the most severe type of reading disability for students. Generally, these readers have difficulty across the language spectrum, which is characterized by a combination of poor phonological processing skills, slower rapid and automatic word recognition skills, poor orthographic processing, and inconsistent text attention (Feifer & Della Toffalo, 2007). In fact, these readers are characterized by numerous PASS processing deficits including poor Successive processing to sequence letters, poor Simultaneous processing to recognize the entire printed word form, and poor Attention to recognize word cues in the passage to derive meaning from print. Oftentimes, these students require an IEP that includes one or more of the aforementioned reading programs (see Table 5.1). The key is to develop a balanced literacy program that focuses on using the student's strengths to bypass a particular weakness.

Table 5.1   Balanced Literacy Strategies and PASS for Mixed Dyslexia

Reading Process	PASS Process
Phonemic processing	Successive processing
Orthographic processing	Simultaneous processing
Morphological processing	Successive processing
Reading fluency	Simultaneous processing
Vocabulary development	Attention
Comprehension strategies	Planning and Attention
Spelling patterns	Successive processing

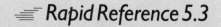

Rapid Reference 5.3

Mixed Dyslexia Interventions for Students With Poor Simultaneous and Successive Processing

Balanced Literacy:
The key to developing reading success with any student is to incorporate a balanced literacy approach. This is especially critical with students possessing mixed dyslexia, because there are often combinations of deficits including poor phonological processing skills and poor fluency skills resulting from poor Successive and Simultaneous processing. Using programs such as Read 180 or Failure Free Reading may yield more positive results than simply overrelying on phonics-based programs that overemphasize Successive processing.

Use Strengths to Bridge Weaknesses:
 Most students with severe forms of dyslexia do not respond to conventional remediation programs because of atypical development in various regions of the brain responsible for modulating the phonological aspect of reading (Noble & McCandliss, 2005; Shaywitz, 2003). Therefore, use cognitive strengths such as in Planning or Attention, which is more of a top-down methodology, to teach reading by emphasizing morphological development and vocabulary instruction.

Motivation and Confidence:
Every effort should be made to keep the reading process as enjoyable and entertaining as possible. Have students practice reading 20 minutes per day on high-interest books that they select.

Comprehension Index:

The final reading disorder subtype involves deficits in *reading comprehension* skills. In essence, these readers struggle to derive meaning from print despite good reading mechanics. Children with reading comprehension difficulties often display marked deficits on certain executive functioning skills, especially planning and working memory skills, both of which are modulated by frontal lobe functioning (Crews & D'Amato, 2009; Cutting, Materek, Cole, Levine, & Mahone, 2009; Reiter, Tucha, & Lange, 2005). The primary PASS processes needed to derive meaning from print are Planning, which helps students devise a strategy for the self-organization of verbal material, and Attention, which recognizes other cues in the passage to derive meaning from print. The following comprehension strategies are offered to assist children who struggle with both Planning and Attention.

≡ *Rapid Reference 5.4*

Reading Comprehension Strategies to Improve Planning and Attention

Stop and Start Technique:
The student reads a passage out loud, and every 30 seconds the teacher says "stop" and asks questions about the story. Eventually the time interval is lengthened.

Directional Questions:
Ask questions at the beginning of the text instead of the end so students can become more directional readers.

Story Maps:
This is a prereading activity in which graphic organizers are used to outline and organize information prior to reading the text.

Narrative Retelling:
Have the child retell the story after reading it aloud.

Read Aloud:
Reading out loud enables students to hear their own voices and can facilitate working memory.

(continued)

Multiple Exposure:
Encourage students to skim the material on reading for the first time with an emphasis on chapter and text headings. Read for detail on the second exposure of the text.

Active Participation:
Encourage active reading by getting children in the habit of note-taking or putting asterisks next to important material in the text.

Create Questions:
Have students write their own test questions about the material.

Reduce Anxiety:
Anxiety inhibits working memory and leads to ineffective recall. Children who are anxious about reading out loud in front of their classmates should be provided an opportunity to read in a "safety zone" in class. This may also help to eliminate distractions as well.

Practice Terminology:
Practice defining new terms and concepts prior to reading material with dense language. Vocabulary enrichment is often the key to improving comprehension.

CAS2 AND MATHEMATICS

The CAS2 can also be applied to mathematics to diagnose and remediate math learning disabilities. In fact, the four cognitive abilities measured by the CAS2 can be integrated with the Feifer Assessment of Mathematics (FAM; Feifer, 2016) to specifically target the mathematical needs of children. The FAM is a comprehensive test of mathematics designed to examine the underlying processes that support the acquisition of proficient math skills. The FAM is comprised of 19 individual subtests measuring various aspects of fact-retrieval skills, numeric and spatial memory, perceptual estimation skills, linguistic math concepts, and core number sense development. When paired with the CAS2, the FAM can assist practitioners to not only determine the presence of a general math learning disability (MLD) but also determine the specific subtype of dyscalculia in order to better inform intervention decisions. The following mathematical subtypes provide the theoretical framework for integrating the FAM and CAS2.

Verbal Index

The verbal subtype of dyscalculia consists of students who have difficulty retrieving or recalling stored mathematical facts of overlearned information. In essence, there is a breakdown in the verbal representations of numbers and the inability to use language-based procedures to assist in automatic fact-retrieval skills. In fact, these students often have difficulties in reading and spelling and language retrieval as well (Ashkenazi, Black, Abrams, Hoeft, & Menon, 2013). Verbal dyscalculia does not necessarily hinder a student's ability to appreciate numeric qualities and understand mathematical concepts or detract from making comparisons between numbers, but it does hinder a student's ability to encode and retrieve overlearned math facts, such as single-digit addition, single-digit subtraction, single-digit multiplication, and single-digit division.

These students often present a profile on the CAS2 of poor Planning and poor Simultaneous processing. Essentially, math-fact retrieval is often approached without a specific plan for retrieving the information. Furthermore, these students struggle to store the information as a unique whole (e.g., $7 \times 5 = 35$), which tends to reflect poor Simultaneous processing. Specific interventions include the following.

≡ *Rapid Reference 5.5*

....

Interventions for Verbal Dyscalculia

- Distinguish between reciting *number words* and *counting* (map symbol to spatial value, not verbal tag).
- Develop a forward number word sequence (FNWS) and backward number word sequence (BNWS) to 10, 20, and 30 without counting back. This helps develop better number line fluency skills and ultimately better fact-retrieval skills.
- Develop a base-10 counting strategy whereby the child can perform addition and subtraction tasks involving 10s and 1s. Learning to chunk numbers will use Successive processing strategies to bridge Simultaneous processing weaknesses.
- Reinforce the language of math by reteaching quantitative words such as *more, less, equal, sum, altogether, difference,* and so on.

Procedural Index

The procedural subtype of dyscalculia represents one or more deficits in the ability to count, order, or sequence numbers or sequence mathematical procedures (e.g., remembering the algorithm) when problem-solving. Just as younger children must ultimately link phonemes with graphemes in order to learn the phonological code for reading, children begin to develop mathematical knowledge and skills in much the same manner by learning to link nonsymbolic information with numerical symbols. After all, the meaning of numbers is ultimately represented by their subsequent relationships to other numbers within the broader number system (Cowan & Powell, 2014). Consequently, when there is a breakdown in the procedural system, the syntactical arrangement and execution of arithmetical procedures often becomes compromised. The procedural subtype not only underscores serial counting but also is involved in recalling the sequences of steps necessary to perform multi-digit tasks such as long division, multiplying or dividing multi-digit numbers, as well as working with fractions and decimals. These students often have a PASS profile on the CAS2 of poor Successive processing as well as limited Attention, which often makes them lose their place while counting on a number line. Specific interventions include the following.

≡ *Rapid Reference 5.6*

....

Interventions for Procedural Dyscalculia

- Create a class setting that is free from anxiety. Anxiety limits working memory and the ability to use Successive processing strategies.
- Use mnemonic strategies. For instance, long division requires a student to divide, multiply, subtract, and bring down. Remember this sequence with dad, mom, sister, brother).
- Talk aloud all regrouping strategies.
- Use graph paper to line up equations.

Semantic Index

The third subtype of dyscalculia is referred to as the *semantic subtype,* which consists of visual-spatial and conceptual components. A core deficit within this subtype is an inability to decipher magnitude representations among numbers (Dehaene, 2011). The semantic subtype can affect symbolic as well as nonsymbolic representation of numbers, and therefore it hinders a variety of mathematical-related skills. For instance, the *nonsymbolic* representations of math refer to the visual-spatial processes needed to perform tasks such as estimation skills, pattern-recognition skills among objects, or even aligning numbers in columns when problem-solving. These types of visually mediated tasks often require Simultaneous processing as measured by the CAS2.

The semantic subtype also involves math difficulties because of a poor conceptual understanding of a mathematical principle. These students often have poor number sense and struggle connecting the actual numeric symbol with its corresponding value (Wong, Ho, & Tang, 2015). The semantic understanding of numbers is needed in order to develop strong quantitative reasoning skills; otherwise, students tend to simply memorize equations void of any real meaning or application possibilities. Consequently, these students tend to have poor Planning ability as measured by the CAS2 and lack a plan of attack when engaged in quantitative reasoning tasks. For example, the ability to transcode challenging mathematical equations into more palatable forms of operations requires good planning skills. Take the equation $9 \times 16 = 144$. Most children would opt to use paper and pencil to determine the answer is 144 and would be hard-pressed to solve this equation very quickly. However, strong planning enables a student to convert the problem to a base 10 format of $10 \times 16 = 160$, then subtract 16, and arriving at 144 much quicker and often without the need for paper and pencil. The ability to deploy a particular mathematical strategy (Planning) is often lacking with students who have poor symbolic representation of numbers and therefore lack a basic number sense. Specific interventions may include the following.

≋ *Rapid Reference 5.7*

Interventions for Semantic Dyscalculia

- Teach students to think in *pictures* as well as *words*.
- Have students explain their strategies when problem-solving to expand problem-solving options.
- Teach estimation skills to enable effective previewing of responses.
- Have students write a math sentence from a verbal sentence.
- Construct incorrect answers to equations and have students draw a picture to demonstrate why the problem is wrong.

≡ *Rapid Reference 5.8*

Feifer Assessment of Reading

Feifer Assessment of Reading	Planning	Attention	Simultaneous	Successive
Phonological Index				X
Phonemic Awareness				X
Nonsense Word Decoding				X
Isolated Word Reading Fluency			X	X
Oral Reading Fluency			X	X
Positioning Sounds				X
Fluency Index			X	
Rapid Automatic Naming			X	
Verbal Fluency	X			
Visual Perception		X		
Irregular Word Reading Fluency			X	
Orthographical Processing		X	X	
Comprehension Index	X	X		
Semantic Concepts	X		X	
Word Recall	X	X		
Print Knowledge		X		
Morphological Processing				X
Silent Reading Fluency: Comprehension	X	X	X	

Feifer Assessment of Mathematics

Feifer Assessment of Mathematics	Planning	Attention	Simultaneous	Successive
Procedural Index				X
Forward Number Count		X		X
Backward Number Count		X		X
Numeric Capacity		X		X
Sequences	X			X
Object Counting		X		X
Verbal Index			X	
Rapid Number Naming			X	
Addition Fluency		X	X	
Subtraction Fluency		X	X	
Multiplication Fluency		X	X	
Division Fluency		X	X	
Linguistic Math Concepts	X		X	

Feifer Assessment of Mathematics	Planning	Attention	Simultaneous	Successive
Semantic Index	X		X	
Spatial Memory		X	X	
Equation Building	X		X	X
Perceptual Estimation	X		X	
Number Comparison		X	X	
Addition Knowledge	X	X		
Subtraction Knowledge	X	X		
Multiplication Knowledge	X	X		
Division Knowledge	X	X		

Discrepancy/Consistency Method of Interpretation

Examiners are encouraged to follow the Discrepancy/Consistency Method of interpretation to determine eligibility for special education services using the FAR, FAM, and CAS2. As previously stated, the identification of a basic psychological process begins with the administration of the CAS2, because one or more of the four pro-

> **DON'T FORGET 5.5**
>
> The Discrepancy/Consistency method of SLD determination tells you if the child has significant variability in PASS as well as achievement test scores and which PASS weakness is associated with the academic difficulty.

cessing scores needs to be substantially below average and discrepant from the student's average PASS score. Second, there needs to be consistency between the poor processing score(s) and lower scores in the academic skill(s) in question. With respect to reading, SLD statute defines these areas as consisting of basic reading skills, reading fluency skills, or reading comprehension skills. Third, there must be also be a consistency between lower scores on, for example, a FAR reading index score and lower cognitive processing as indicated on the CAS2. For instance, if a student has relatively poor Simultaneous processing and scores relatively low scores on the Fluency index of the FAR, this would be *indicative* of an SLD consistent with *surface dyslexia*. The following example illustrates the aforementioned discussion as well as yields more specific and targeted recommendations customized for the child.

Reason for Referral:

Nelson is a 9-year-old fourth-grade student who was referred for a comprehensive psychological evaluation because of concerns regarding his overall reading skills and difficulty completing most daily tasks in a timely manner.

Background Information:

Nelson has been attending Stony Brook Elementary School since kindergarten and began receiving targeted academic interventions in the first grade. According to school reports, Nelson was having difficulty acquiring basic sound-symbol associations, and his reading fluency was measured at just 27 correct words per minute at the completion of first grade. Nelson began receiving Tier II reading support services in second grade and worked with the school's reading specialist for approximately 30 minutes each day. He responded well to his reading intervention services and completed second-grade reading approximately 57 words per minute accurately. Nevertheless, there were additional academic concerns on entering third grade. For instance, Nelson was described as having difficulty with spelling and written language skills, struggled with math fact retrieval skills, and was inconsistent with reading comprehending skills. There were no reported attention or behavioral concerns and his teacher indicated that Nelson often put forth a good effort each day. However, he continued to struggle keeping pace with his peers and often failed to complete his work in a timely manner. The school's child development team conveyed a meeting prior to the onset of fourth grade and recommended a comprehensive psychological evaluation.

Neurocognitive Abilities:

Nelson was administered the CAS2 to assess various aspects of cognitive functioning and problem-solving efficiency (see Table 5.2). As previously identified, this test evaluates four kinds of neurocognitive abilities based on the PASS (Planning, Attention, Simultaneous, and Successive) theory of cognitive processing. All four neurocognitive abilities combine to yield an overall or composite measure of cognitive functioning. Standard scores between 90 and 110 are considered to be in the average range.

Composite Score:

Nelson's overall CAS2 composite score was 89, which was in the below average range of functioning and at the 23rd percentile compared to peers. His individual cognitive processing ability scores were as follows.

Planning:

Nelson's Planning processing score reflects his ability to make decisions about how best to complete the tests, use strategies, monitor the effectiveness of

Table 5.2 Nelson's CAS2 Scoring

PASS Scales	Scaled Score	Percentile	Ability Range
CAS2 Planning: The ability to apply a strategy and self-monitor performance while working toward a solution	94	34	Average
CAS2 Attention: The ability to selectively focus on a stimulus while inhibiting responses from competing stimuli	98	45	Average
CAS2 Simultaneous Processing: The ability to reason and problem-solve by integrating separate elements into a conceptual whole, often involving visual-spatial tasks	74	4	Very low
CAS2 Successive Processing: The ability to put information into a serial order or particular sequence	90	25	Average
CAS2 Total Composite Score	89	23	Below average

strategies, change the plan when needed, and work efficiently. He earned a Planning score of 94, which was in the average range of functioning and at the 34th percentile compared to peers. He approached many problem-solving tasks with a specific search strategy (e.g., worked from bottom to top or left to right) based on the demands of the task. Nelson exhibited good Planning strategies and organizational skills, worked very diligently throughout the test, and focused his attention well to the task at hand. There were no weaknesses apparent.

Attention:
Nelson's Attention score reflects his ability to focus his thinking and resist distractions. He earned an Attention score of 98, which was in the Average range of functioning and at the 45th percentile compared to peers. He had little difficulty with response inhibition and was able to curb his impulses and refrain from naming or reading items when instructed to state a conflicting response instead. There were no weaknesses observed.

Simultaneous:
Nelson's Simultaneous score reflects the ability to integrate separate elements into a conceptual whole and often requires strong visual-spatial problem-solving skills. His Simultaneous processing score of 74 was a significant weakness and in the very low range of functioning at the 4th percentile compared to peers. Nelson worked very slowly and deliberately on these tasks

and often struggled with more difficult items. Lower Simultaneous processing can directly hinder a variety of academic skills such as spelling (difficulty conjuring up a visual spatial image of the printed word form), reading fluency and speed (difficulty automatically recognizing words as a conceptual whole), and mathematics (visualizing numbers).

Successive:

Nelson's score on the Successive processing scale reflects his ability to repeat information such as words or sentences in order and understanding verbal statements when the meaning was dependent on the sequence of the words. Nelson's overall Successive score was 90, which in the average range of functioning and at the 25th percentile compared to peers. This score suggests adequate ability to remember information in order and sequencing symbols, both of which are important for academic tasks such as decoding words when reading, sounding out words when spelling, memorizing basic math facts, and math computation skills. There were no significant weaknesses observed.

Cognitive Summary:

Nelson demonstrated adequate general cognitive abilities, with most PASS processing scores within the average range. However, a relative weakness was noted on the Simultaneous processing scale. Lower scores in this area can hinder mathematical problem-solving, visualizing words when spelling, and reading fluency skills.

Academic Measures:

Nelson was administered the Kaufman Test of Educational Achievement, Third Edition (KTEA-III) to assess his reading, math, spelling, and written language skills. His academic achievement scores in reading were as shown in Table 5.3 (mean = 100).

Nelson's overall reading composite score was 81 ± 6, which was in the Below Average range of functioning and at the 10th percentile compared to peers. He struggled with most aspects of the reading process and was very inconsistent with his overall word-identification skills (Letter Word Identification). A relative strength was Nelson's ability to apply decoding skills to unfamiliar words in print (Nonsense Word Decoding). In summary, Nelson was a slower-paced and dysfluent oral reader with inconsistent text-comprehension skills (Reading Comprehension) as well.

Nelson's overall math composite score was 90 ± 6, which was in the average range of functioning and at the 25th percentile compared to peers (see Table 5.4). He demonstrated an adequate conceptual understanding of

Table 5.3 Nelson's Scores on the KTEA-III Reading Subtests

Reading	Age Norms	Percentile	Range
Letter Word Recognition: The student reads isolated letters and words of gradually increasing difficulty.	81 ± 5	10 53	Below average
Nonsense Word Decoding: The student applies phonics and decoding skills to made-up words of increasing difficulty.	90 ± 5	25	Average
Reading Comprehension: The student reads a word and points to its corresponding picture or reads a simple instruction and responds by performing the action.	83 ± 10	13	Below average
Silent Reading Fluency: The student is required to read as many statements as possible in 2 minutes and must respond either "yes" or "no" as to whether each statement is valid.	80 ± 11	9	Below average
KTEA-III Reading Composite Score	81 ± 6	10	Below average

Table 5.4 Nelson's Scores on the KTEA-III Math Subtests

Math	Age Norms	Percentile	Range
Math Concepts and Applications: The student responds orally to applied math problems involving number concepts, time, money, measurement, and data analysis.	96 ± 6	39	Average
Math Computation: The student solves math equations in the response booklet including addition and subtraction.	87 ± 10	19	Below average
Math Fluency: This is a timed task requiring the student to solve as many single-digit addition, subtraction, multiplication, and division problems in a minute.	89 ± 11	23	Below average
KTEA-III Math Composite Score	90 ± 6	25	Average

mathematics (Math Concepts and Applications) and was able to read and interpret a graph, recognize a number pattern, solve problems involving elapsed time, and make change from a dollar. However, his automaticity for basic number facts (Math Fluency) was a little slower paced, and he occasionally misread math operational signs. Last, Nelson's math-calculation skills were a bit inconsistent (Math Computation), because he was able to add and subtract

Table 5.5 Nelson's Scores on the KTEA-III Writing Subtests

Writing	Age Norms	Percentile	Range
Written Expression: The student completes a series of writing tasks in the context of a storybook format. Tasks include writing from dictation, adding punctuation and capitalization, combining sentences, filling in the blank, and essay writing.	91 ± 10	27	Average
Spelling: The student is required to spell words of increasing difficulty dictated by the examiner.	86 ± 5	18	Below average
Writing Fluency: The student has 5 minutes to write as many sentences as possible describing various pictures.	88 ± 14	21	Below average
KTEA-III Written Language	87 ± 6	19	Below average

two-digit equations but often lost his place when borrowing or regrouping and was unable to solve long division or two-digit multiplication equations.

Nelson's written language composite score was 87 ± 6, which was in the below average range and at the 19th percentile compared to peers (see Table 5.5). He was right-handed with an adequate tripod grasp. Nelson worked very diligently when writing, and was extremely focused and on-task during extended writing tasks. Nevertheless, he often made careless miscues such as omitting ending punctuation, omitting articles and short words (e.g., *is, and, of,* etc.), and did not always capitalize the first words of sentence during a structured writing task (Written Expression). In addition, there were noted grammatical errors in his sentence structures, and his spelling skills were a bit inconsistent, though phonetically readable.

Academic Summary:
Nelson's overall reading and written language skills were not commensurate with grade-level expectations. He had adequate decoding skills but was a slower-paced and dysfluent oral reader with inconsistent passage comprehension skills. There were also noted spelling miscues, though his efforts were phonetically readable, and he tended to make numerous grammatical errors when writing.

Academic Processing:
Nelson was administered the Feifer Assessment of Reading (FAR), a comprehensive reading test designed to examine the underlying cognitive and linguistic processes that support proficient reading skills. See Table 5.6 for the obtained scores (mean = 100).

Table 5.6 Nelson's Scores on the Feifer Assessment of Reading (FAR)

FAR Index	Standard Score (95% CI)	Percentile	Qualitative Descriptor
Phonological Index	90 (±5)	25	Average
Fluency Index	73 (±7)	3	Moderately below average
Mixed Index	81 (±5)	10	Below average
Comprehension Index	97 (±8)	42	Average
FAR Total Index	84 (±5)	14	Below average

FAR Total Index:

Nelson obtained a FAR total index score of 84 ± 5, which is in the below average range of functioning and at the 14th percentile compared to peers. The following reading indices were obtained (mean = 100).

Phonological Index:

Nelson's Phonological Index score was 90 ± 5, which was in the average range and at the 25th percentile compared to peers. His overall phonemic skills were emerging, because he was able to blend, segment, and manipulate sounds in words. Nelson also had little difficulty when applying decoding skills to familiar and unfamiliar words in print, though he worked a little slowly when reading an isolated list of decodable words.

Fluency Index:

Nelson's Fluency Index was a significant weakness, because he scored 73 ± 7, which was in the moderately below average range and at the 3rd percentile compared to peers. He worked slowly when rapidly identifying objects and letters, demonstrated poor text orthography skills, and had difficultly reading an isolated list of phonologically irregular words (e.g., *yacht, onion, debt,* etc.). Lower scores on rapid naming and text orthography tasks often stem from poor Simultaneous processing and an inability to visualize the entire printed word form as a unique whole. This can lead to inconsistent spelling as well as slower print-identification skills when reading.

Comprehension Index:

Nelson's Comprehension Index score was 97 ± 8, which was in the average range and at the 42nd percentile compared to peers. His overall vocabulary and language-development skills were a significant strength. In addition, his verbal memory skills were also well developed, suggesting that Nelson had strong language and working memory skills to facilitate text comprehension. Last, his well-developed Planning and Attention abilities enabled him to remember specific details in the stories, though weaknesses with Simultaneous processing seemed to hinder his ability to understand the big picture and comprehend more abstract questions about the story.

FAR Summary:
Nelson's poor reading fluency skills stemmed from limitations with text orthography, which involves rapidly processing the entire printed word form. Limitations with text orthography are primarily because of poor Simultaneous processing. Weaknesses with Simultaneous processing seemed to hinder his ability to comprehend more abstract elements of the text, though his strong Planning and Attention did help facilitate remembering more detailed aspects of the story. Nelson's slower reading speed, difficulty reading phonetically irregular words, and poor Simultaneous processing were consistent with the profile of a student with surface dyslexia.

Summary:
In summary, Nelson's cognitive ability scores were mostly average with the exception of a significant weakness observed with his Simultaneous processing scale of the CAS2. This suggested he had considerable difficulty integrating separate elements of a problem into a conceptual whole. His poor Simultaneous processing ability is significantly hindering reading and written language skills. For instance, his spelling efforts were phonetically readable, but because of his inability to visualize the printed word form, they were often incorrect. In terms of his reading, his poor Simultaneous processing skills manifested through limitations with text orthography. This involves processing the entire printed word form rapidly and automatically, with limitations often leading to an overreliance on Successive processing, or sound-by-sound reading, and poor fluency skills. In addition, limitations with Simultaneous processing also hindered his ability to comprehend more abstract elements of the text. Nelson presented the academic and cognitive processing profile of a student with Surface Dyslexia. The following visual depiction of Nelson's processing strengths and weaknesses are noted in Figure 5.5 by way of the Discrepancy/Consistency Method.

Recommendations for School
1. Nelson would benefit from a targeted reading fluency intervention in order to increase text automatic recognition and fluency (e.g., Read Naturally, Great Leaps, RAVE-O, etc.).
2. Nelson's orthographic processing skills were somewhat weak. Color-coding letter-various syllable and sound subtypes, particularly vowel diphthongs

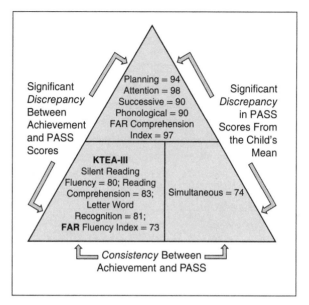

Figure 5.5 Nelson's Discrepancy/Consistency Method of SLD Results

in phonetically irregular words, may be very helpful (e.g., *caution, dangerous,* etc.).

3. Nelson may benefit from targeted writing activities to help reinforce letter and word recognition skills. Specific activities such as identifying which of three sight words is spelled correctly (e.g., *wuz, whas, or was*) may help to develop automaticity recognizing vowel patterns in words.

4. Nelson should benefit from using graphic organizers, story maps, and other prewriting activities to assist him when organizing his thoughts when writing. In addition, he should have access to a word bank of words to assist him with spelling as well.

5. Nelson might benefit from having access to a Franklin Word Speller and other technology devices and to assist with his overall spelling skills.

6. In order to improve Simultaneous processing and facilitate text-visualization skills, have Nelson practice spelling words with white space in between each syllable in the word. Next, frame each letter in a box similar to the letter size. For example, the word *fascinate* would be written as fas cin ate. The visual space draws attention to the different word parts and the boxes provide organizational cues. A similar method

that encourages children to put information into groups is found in Naglieri and Pickering's (2010) "Chunking for Spelling" intervention handout.

7. Nelson's writing mechanics remain an area of concern, though he has good Planning and Attention skills. He may benefit from learning the COPS strategy, a directional proofreading strategy in which Nelson rereads his work four times prior to completion. The first time he proofreads his passage to make sure he *capitalizes* the first word of each sentence, the second time is to make sure each paragraph is *organized* correctly, the third time is to check for *punctuation* errors, and the fourth time for *spelling* miscues.

Recommendations for Home

1. Nelson should be encouraged to read a minimum of 20 minutes per day after school in order to develop more text familiarity and enhanced fluency skills.

2. Nelson's parents may want to consider having a tutor work with him at home in order to improve his overall reading fluency skills.

3. Nelson's parents may want to consider using a reading fluency program at home (e.g., Great Leaps).

4. Nelson's parents may find the instructional methods described in the book *Helping Children Learn* (Naglieri & Pickering, 2010) to be useful. Especially appropriate are, for example, the handouts "Segmenting Words for Reading/Decoding," "Spelling, Word Sorts for Improving Spelling," and "Mnemonics for Spelling."

Student Feedback:

It is strongly recommended that the clinician provide direct feedback to help Nelson better understand his unique strengths and weaknesses as a learner. The initial goal is to change Nelson's attitude toward school and himself by exploring further his mind-set about his own abilities. This can be facilitated using the "Measure of Mindset" checklist shown in Figure 5.2. Next, it is important to help Nelson know that his PASS strengths can be used to manage the PASS weakness in Simultaneous processing. This can be accomplished with the aid of the handouts that are intended for students in *Helping Children Learn* (Naglieri & Pickering, 2010) and that describe each of the four PASS abilities. The overarching goal is to change Nelson's view of himself by providing reassurance that with knowledge of strengths and needs, success is possible. Therefore, the clinician and his parents should engage in a demystification process whereby the reason for academic failure is described and, most important, how PASS strengths can be used to overcome the weaknesses. The following discussion illustrates how this might happen:

Nelson, it was such a pleasure to work with you and discover all of your learning strengths. Believe me ... there were a ton. You have a remarkable ability to approach learning with a plan in mind, and you stay attentive and focused to your assignment until the very end. I did notice that when you read, you sometimes focus a little too much on decoding the words and not letting your natural reading skills take over. You do a great job pronouncing each word, so we want to work with you on increasing your speed and fluency just a bit. One of the ways we are going to do this is by having you read a little more frequently at home each day. I also noticed that you give such a great effort when writing, but sometimes it can be hard to spell new words. One of the tricks to being a good speller is to close your eyes and see if you can see the word in your head. We have a few activities that should help you see words in your mind a little more clearly and that should really help with spelling. Nelson, the rest of your academic skills look really good, and given your wonderful attitude and great effort you put forth each day, you will be a very successful student. It was really great to work with you.

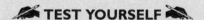

TEST YOURSELF

1. **Which of the following is the type of reading disability characterized by an overreliance on sound patterns, poor fluency and speed, and difficulty reading phonologically irregular words?**
   a. Mixed dyslexia
   b. Surface dyslexia
   c. Phonological dyslexia
   d. Comprehension dyslexia

2. **Which of the following are the main PASS processes involved with reading comprehension skills?**
   a. Executive Functioning and Vocabulary
   b. Successive and Simultaneous
   c. Planning and Attention
   d. Visual-Spatial Skills and Organization

3. **Which of the following statements is true for the Feifer Assessment of Reading (FAR)?**

   a. It can be paired with the CAS2 to determine the presence of a learning disorder.
   b. It can tease out four subtypes of reading disorders.
   c. It can be used by teachers, psychologists, and educational diagnosticians.
   d. All of the above are true.

4. **Which of the following is *not* one of the main four subtypes of dyslexia?**

   a. Dysphonetic dyslexia
   b. Surface dyslexia
   c. Dissimilar dyslexia
   d. Mixed dyslexia

5. **Which reading program is recommended for a 6-year-old student with poor successive processing and weak decoding skills?**

   a. Fundations
   b. Curriculum-Based Measurement
   c. Read 180
   d. Alphabet Scanning

Answers: 1. b; 2. c; 3. d; 4. c; 5. a

Six

STRENGTHS AND WEAKNESSES OF CAS2

Many important changes were made to the second edition of the CAS. This chapter provides a summary of the strengths and weaknesses of the CAS2 (English and Spanish), CAS2: Brief, and the CAS2: Rating Scale. The CAS2 has several strengths, perhaps most salient is the expansion from one test (e.g., the CAS) to three tests and a rating scale all designed to measure the four neurocognitive scales call PASS. These ways to assess PASS meet three different needs: CAS2 for comprehensive assessment, CAS2: Brief for reevaluations and screening, and CAS2: Rating Scale for evaluating classroom behaviors that reflect PASS. Having several measures of PASS is a substantial advantage for the practitioner when choosing the most efficient test for the task and as a means of establishing validity. Other important modifications of the CAS include changing the subtest formats to improve reliability, adding a new visual Successive processing scale subtest, new standardizations, and adding new supplemental scales (Working Memory, Executive Function, Verbal, Nonverbal, Visual-Auditory Comparison, and Speed/Fluency).

One of the most important consistencies between the CAS and the CAS2 is the PASS theory. We have shown in the first chapter of this book and elsewhere (Naglieri, 2015; Otero, 2015) that there is considerable evidence of the reliability and validity of the PASS neurocognitive theory. The four constructs are highly correlated with achievement and effective for eligibility determination, nondiscriminatory assessment, and intervention planning.

Even though the CAS2, CAS2: Brief, and CAS2: Rating Scale have weaknesses, similar to other tests, we see these related more to the specificity of the measure. For example, CAS2: Rating Scale is not intended for eligibility determination but could be used as part of the process when combined with the CAS2.

In this chapter we provide more details of the strengths and weaknesses of the CAS2, CAS2: Brief, and CAS2: Rating Scale. Sometimes the weakness is only a weakness from a particular perspective with which we do not agree, making it a strength from our perspective. In those instances we will label the topic as a strength or weakness. These will be organized into the following categories: theoretical, specific learning disability eligibility, practical issues, and nondiscriminatory assessment.

THEORETICAL

Weakness or Strength: Assessment of Intelligence Has Been Dominated by Traditional IQ Tests for Many Years but the CAS2 Measures the PASS Neurocognitive Theory of Human Learning

The field of ability testing has been dominated by traditional IQ tests such as the Wechsler since the verbal, nonverbal, quantitative approach was first introduced in 1917 by the US Army (see Naglieri, 2011). This means that any alternative is destined to meet with opposition if for no other reason than the historical momentum of 100 years of doing something in a particular way. The greatest weakness of any new approach to understanding human learning, including the PASS theory as measured by the CAS2, is to overcome the inertia of traditional IQ. This begs the question, "Why should CAS2 be considered?"

The brain-based neurocognitive PASS theory as measured by the CAS2 is an approach to understanding learning that will help professionals in several important ways. First, it will identify a disorder in basic psychological processing, which is central to identification of those with a specific learning disability. Second, it is not confounded by knowledge, so it assesses diverse populations fairly. Third, PASS has considerable relevance to instruction in general and academic interventions in particular. Finally, the CAS2 will answer the question "*Why* does the student fail?"—a critical question to answer for eligibility determination and instructional planning. Given these advantages, how can CAS2 be introduced into everyday practice?

We have found that practitioners who use the CAS2 in addition to their traditional battery find that it adds considerable value. Teachers ask for information about PASS, students understand their PASS strengths and weaknesses, and parents come away from meetings with a clearer view of their child and what is needed. So we suggest that traditional IQ tests could be used because it is expected, but use CAS2 to more fully understand the individual's needs and strengths. It will not take long for everyone to see that the brain-based neurocognitive PASS theory as measured by the CAS2 is an approach that offers much more than traditional IQ testing.

Strength: The PASS Theory as Measured by the CAS2 Excludes Verbal and Quantitative Subtests

Sometimes our colleagues have suggested that a weakness of the PASS theory and the CAS2 is the omission of verbal and quantitative subtests because these tests are considered an essential part of an ability test. We have several reactions to this question. First, CAS2 was designed to measure PASS neurocognitive processes, not traditional IQ. We fully understand that traditional IQ tests have included verbal and quantitative test questions, but we reject the use of subtests that demand lots of knowledge. This is not a new idea, as illustrated by the Yoakum and Yerkes' (1920) position that test questions that do not rely on knowledge are necessary "in order that injustice by reason of relative unfamiliarity with English may be avoided" (p. 19). Simply put, we see no reason that a person's ability to think (PASS) should be measured in a way that demands verbal and math skills, especially because opportunity to learn plays a critical role in one's fund of knowledge. Is this logic consistent with research data? Yes.

Let's begin with the first point—our view that verbal and quantitative test questions are not needed. In Chapter 1 of this book we showed that when compared to traditional IQ tests, as well more contemporary tests such as the KABC-II, the CAS scores correlated the strongest with achievement test scores. This means that the PASS cognitive processes are as effective for explaining the variability in achievement test scores as tests that include measures of verbal knowledge, even though the CAS and CAS2 do not include academically laden subtests. This simply means that the PASS scales provide a way to measure a students' foundation for learning.

The second point is even more important because it relates to social justice and IDEA. The federal law clearly states that assessments used to evaluate a student must be selected and administered so as not to be discriminatory on a racial or cultural basis. When race and ethnic differences are examined across all ability tests (Naglieri, 2015), we find that, as researchers have suggested, neuropsychologically oriented tests are more appropriate for diverse populations (Fagan, 2000; Naglieri 2005). This is consistent with suggestions by Fagan (2000) and Suzuki and Valencia (1997) that measures of cognitive processes that do not rely on tests with language and quantitative content are more appropriate for assessment of culturally and linguistically diverse populations. As described in Chapter 1 and elsewhere in this book, the PASS theory yields the smallest difference across race and ethnic groups.

The exclusion of verbal and quantitative test questions and the emphasis on measuring thinking (PASS), not knowledge, clearly distinguish the CAS2 from traditional IQ tests.

Strength or Weakness: The CAS2 and IQ Tests

One of the strengths of the CAS2 is that it is certainly not a traditional IQ test. There are several important reasons for this. First, CAS2 was designed to measure the four basic psychological neurocognitive processes called PASS. It is the only test that was originally designed and continues to be based on a specific theory of human neurocognitive functioning without being constrained by previous notions of what should be included. The theory of brain functioning articulated by A. R. Luria preceded the test and was used to guide the development of scales and subtests as well as the interpretation of the scores the tests yield. Second, the PASS constructs are measured using tests that require very little knowledge. This means that subtests that require definition of words, word analogies, and math word problems, for example, were not included because they are too influenced by educational opportunities. Despite the fact that knowledge acquisition is dependent on PASS, subtests that require knowledge are not efficient measures of PASS. Third, the very purpose of the CAS and the CAS2 was to provide a neurocognitive measure that could be used to understand children's learning. Traditional IQ tests with their verbal, nonverbal, and quantitative content, all of which are based on the Army Mental Tests (Naglieri, 2015), were not developed for that purpose. So the strength of the CAS2 is that it was never intended to be an IQ test. Some may say this is a weakness, but we see it as a strength.

If CAS2 is not a traditional IQ test, is it an intelligence test? It could be said that the PASS theory is a very different approach to defining the elusive concept of intelligence. We reject the description of intelligence as what IQ tests measure. In fact, we believe that traditional IQ is fundamentally flawed by its inclusion of test questions that demand knowledge. We suggest that there is nothing inherently wrong with terms such as *intelligence, ability,* and *cognition.* We also suggest that PASS could be viewed as a better way to define and measure the concept called *intelligence* if it reflects an understanding of how the brain functions. After all, our accomplishments as a species on this planet are based on our amazing brain!

Strength: The Subtests Within the Successive Scale Is Now Varied by Modality

One of the weaknesses of the CAS Successive processing scale was that all the subtests were verbal and orally presented. This issue was addressed in the CAS2 by eliminating the Speech Rate subtest and adding a Visual Digit Span subtest. The addition of this subtest also provided the opportunity to compare a student's scores on a visual and auditory task from the same PASS neurocognitive scale—Successive. The visual-auditory comparison is accomplished by comparing the Word Series and Visual Digit Span subtests scaled scores.

SPECIFIC LEARNING DISABILITY ELIGIBILITY

Strength: Using CAS2 for Pattern of Strengths and Weaknesses Method to Specific Learning Disabilities Determination

Identifications of students with an SLD under the pattern of strengths and weaknesses (PSW) method can be accomplished using the Discrepancy/Consistency Method (DCM) of analyzing PASS scores described in Chapter 3, "Interpretation," in this book and elsewhere (see Naglieri, 2011). This is a significant strength for the CAS2 because the federal definition of SLD is "a disorder in one or more of the basic psychological processes," which can be represented by the PASS scores. As noted by Hale, Kaufman, Naglieri, and Kavale (2006), establishing a disorder in the basic psychology processes is *essential* for determining SLD so that the legal definition is aligned with the procedural methods used for eligibility determination.

Practitioners have the responsibility to determine which tests to use that best operationalize "basic psychological processes" because a definition is not provided in the law. There are several reasons why we recommend PASS as measured by the CAS2. First, because the CAS2 is specifically designed to measure basic psychological (neurocognitive) processes, this test is very well suited for the purpose of SLD eligibility. Second, PASS is a well-validated theory that has been shown to be sensitive to the specific processing weaknesses children with SLD have (Huang, Bardos, & D'Amato, 2010; Naglieri & Otero, 2011). Third, research has shown that the CAS and CAS2 meet the nondiscriminatory requirement of IDEA (Naglieri, 2015; Otero, 2015). Fourth, research has shown that information about PASS has relevance to intervention (Iseman & Naglieri, 2011; Naglieri & Pickering, 2010).

Perhaps the most important reason why PASS scores should be used in the PSW model is that these four processes are easy to explain to teachers, parents, and the students, especially when using the intervention handouts that are provided by Naglieri and Pickering (2010) in English and Spanish.

Strength: Communicating PASS Scores to Teachers, Parents, and the Students Is Easy

We all have experienced the challenge of explaining the meaning of standard scores, percentile ranks, and the sometimes obscure scales included in ability tests.

A strength of the PASS theory is that these four neurocognitive concepts are not hard to explain, so easy in fact that there are handouts for the examinees by Naglieri and Pickering (2010) in English and Spanish. In simplest terms, they clarify the four PASS processes:

- Planning is thinking about how to do things.
- Attention is focusing one's thinking while resisting distractions.
- Simultaneous is thinking about how things go together to make a whole.
- Successive is thinking in a sequence.

Strength: Empirical Support to Use PASS Scores

One of the strengths of the PASS theory is that, when subject to factor analysis (Canivez, 2011), more variance is associated with the PASS scales than to the overall general factor. This means that there is empirical support for the interpretation of PASS scale scores, for example, when using a PSW approach to eligibility determination. What makes this a particularly important strength is that this is in contrast to findings for traditional IQ tests such as the WISC-IV and Stanford-Binet V (Canivez, 2011).

Research included in the CAS2 manuals shows support for the PASS structure when the three CAS2 measures were studied using confirmatory factor analysis. When the results were compiled across several different methods of fit indices (see Table 5.16 in the CAS2 interpretive manual), the findings indicated that the four-factor PASS model was the best fit. The same was true for analysis of the CAS2: Brief and the CAS2: Rating Scale. Thus, across three different tools for measuring PASS, three different samples, and three different methods (subtests, item clusters, and individual items), the CAS2, CAS2: Brief, and CAS2: Rating Scale data support the organization of the PASS scales.

PRACTICAL ISSUES

Strength or Weakness: The CAS2 Has a Full Scale

The inclusion of a Full Scale, or Total Scale, score on any test is a strength and a weakness. For the CAS2, as well as the CAS2: Brief and CAS2: Rating Scale, this composite score will be a *good overall description* when the PASS scores are similar and a *misleading description when* the four PASS scores are different. The strength of the Full Scale is reflected in the fact that this score has higher reliability than the separate PASS scores, and in some situations it can be a good overall description of a person's neurocognitive functioning.

In that case the CAS2 online scoring and report writing program includes this statement:

> There was no significant variation among the separate PASS scales of the CAS. This indicates that the examinee performed similarly when using Planning, Attention, Simultaneous, and Successive cognitive processes. This also means that the Full Scale is a good description of overall performance on the CAS2.

By contrast, if there is significant PASS score variation then it is important to state that the Full Scale is *not* a good overall description. The CAS2 online report writer provides such a statement:

> Because there was significant variation among the PASS scales, the Full Scale will sometimes be higher and other times lower than the four PASS scales in this test.

The next important point to make is to identify which PASS scale was found to be a weakness relative to the student's average PASS score *and* if the score is also significantly below the norm (i.e., a cognitive weakness). Such a finding has important implications for diagnosis, eligibility determination, and therapeutic and educational programming. Strengths should be similarly described.

It is also important to note that the Full Scale score is not used in the DCM when making eligibility decisions. The reason is simple. The DCM approach is based on having significant variability among the PASS scores; therefore, the Full Scale will be higher and lower than the PASS scores and, therefore, not a good summary score.

Strength: Supplemental Scales in the CAS2

One of the most important tasks when completing a comprehensive assessment is integration of results across tests, rating scales, and behavioral observations. This task is made difficult when PASS is used because the correspondence of these neurocognitive constructs to those used in other measures may not always be immediately obvious. The supplemental scales were designed to provide a way to connect the CAS2 scores to other test results. For example, having an executive function score on the CAS2 allows the practitioner to relate that score obtained from the performance of a student with the executive function score obtained from a behavior rating scale. Similarly, the working memory score obtained from the CAS2 could be compared to a similar score from another test. These and other comparisons are facilitated by the inclusion of supplemental scores on the CAS2. For more information, see Chapter 3 of this book.

Strength: The CAS2 Has Three Administration Times

The CAS2: Brief was developed to provide a 20-minute examination of PASS that can be used for reevaluations, screening (e.g., as part of gifted identification), and instructional decision making. The 8-subtest version of the CAS2 takes about 40 minutes to administer and the full 12-subtest version takes about 60 minutes. These three ways to measure PASS can be selected depending on the purpose of the testing.

Strength and Weakness: The CAS2: Rating Scale Is Not a Substitute for the CAS2: Brief or the CAS2

The CAS2: Rating Scale is not intended to be used instead of the CAS2: Brief or the CAS2. The CAS2: Rating Scale was designed to be used at any level of service delivery, from Tier I to Tier III, to measure classroom behaviors corresponding to the four PASS concepts for two purposes. First, it gives the professional who administers the CAS2 or the CAS2: Brief information about observable classroom behaviors, and second, it helps teachers better understand what PASS scores mean. Thus, the CAS2: Rating Scale provides important information that can be used in conjunction with that obtained from the CAS2 or the CAS2: Brief. In addition, the CAS2: Rating Scale could be used by teachers to better understand the learning strengths and weaknesses of their students.

Strength: Online Scoring and Interpretative Report

The process of scoring and generating an interpretive report has always been a time-consuming task. Today's tests are best scored using some type of computer-based method that includes generation of a narrative report. The CAS2 online scoring and report system converts CAS2 subtest raw scores into standard scores, percentile ranks, and descriptive categories and the PASS and Full Scale composite scores. The system also determines if there is significant subtest or PASS scale variability. The narrative report, which is provided as a Word or pdf document, includes all the CAS2 subtests and PASS and Full Scale as well as the supplemental scales, completed sections of the record form, and intervention options.

NONDISCRIMINATORY ASSESSMENT

Strength: PASS Yields the Smallest Differences Between Races

The need for tests that are appropriate for diverse populations has become progressively more important as the characteristics of the US population have changed, and recent federal law (e.g., IDEA 2004) stipulates that assessments must be selected and administered so as to be nondiscriminatory on a racial or cultural basis. The extent to which test scores differ by race and ethnicity has been an important topic in psychology since these tools were developed in the early 1900s. Fagan (2000), Naglieri (2005), and Suzuki and Valencia (1997) have suggested that using tests based on neuropsychological constructs are particularly appropriate for assessment of culturally and linguistically diverse populations.

Researchers have traditionally found a mean difference of about 12 to 15 points between African Americans and Whites on measures of IQ that include verbal, quantitative, and nonverbal tests (Kaufman & Lichtenberger, 2006). Recently, Naglieri (2015) summarized the research across several measures of ability and found the CAS2 to yield the smallest difference between African Americans and Whites—a difference of only 4 standard score points. This has been a strength of the CAS and now the CAS2, as well as the CAS2: Brief and the CAS2: Rating Scale.

Strength: Bilingual Spanish-Speaking Students Were Included in the CAS2 Normative Group

The percentage of Hispanic students in the standardization samples for the CAS2, CAS2: Brief, and the CAS2: Rating Scale closely matches the percentage of Hispanics in the United States (20%). Of those Hispanic students the majority (approximately 70%) came from homes with parents who were bilingual or spoke a language other than English at home. This issue of language for the CAS2 is less relevant than for traditional IQ tests for several reasons:

1. When administering the CAS2 and CAS2: Brief there is ample opportunity to provide an explanation of the demands of the test in any language necessary. This is the examiner's opportunity to ensure that the student understands the demands of the item (see Chapter 2 in this book and the respective administration and scoring manuals).
2. Researchers have found that as a group Hispanic children earn PASS scores that are very similar to non-Hispanics (Naglieri, Rojahn, & Matto, 2007). When the CAS was administered in English and Spanish there was a very small difference in the Full Scale scores, and the decisions made about PASS profiles were nearly identical for both versions of the test (Naglieri, Otero, DeLauder, & Matto, 2007; Otero, Gonzales, & Naglieri, 2012).
3. The CAS2, Spanish Edition (Naglieri, Moreno, & Otero, 2017) provides administration and scoring as well as a record form for administration in Spanish. This version of the CAS2 was carefully developed to maximize the likelihood that PASS neurocognitive scores for Spanish-speaking children and adolescents can be accurately obtained.

Strength: The CAS2 May Be the Only Test of Neurocognitive Abilities That Was Developed From the Ground Up Based on a Theory of How the Brain Works

There is a substantial body of literature supporting the neurocognitive correlates of PASS and brain function (see Naglieri & Otero, 2011). Luria's theoretical account of dynamic brain function is perhaps one of the most complete (Lewandowski & Scott, 2008). Luria conceptualized a functional organization of the brain based on structure, syndromes and impairments arising in brain-based disorders, and clinical methods of assessment. Cognition and behavior result from an interaction of brain activity across several areas. Luria's (1980) research on the functional aspects of brain structures formed the basis for the development of the Planning, Attention, Simultaneous, Successive (PASS) processing theory, initially described by Das, Naglieri, and Kirby (1994) and later operationalized by Naglieri and Das (1997) in the CAS. Cognitive functions, such as attention and executive functions, for example, are composed of flexible and interactive subcomponents that are mediated by equally flexible, interactive, neural networks (Luria, 1966, 1980a, 1980b). These cognitive functions could be conceptualized as three separate but connected functional units that provide four basic psychological processes (PASS).

Strength: Ease of Administration, Scoring, and Interpretation

There are several practical advantages of the CAS2 and CAS2: Brief. First, these tests are easy to administer and score. Second, the CAS2 and CAS2: Brief are composed of tasks that students enjoy. This is achieved by having tasks that most children and adolescents find engaging and because the tasks do not demand knowledge that students who have a history of school difficulties will likely struggle with. Third, the CAS2: Brief directions for administration are on the examiner's record form, making administration of this short test easier. Fourth, all directions on both tests follow a similar pattern: at first the examiner demonstrates the task, then the examiner and the student complete a sample item, then the student completes an item independently. The gradual transmission of responsibility to solve the item includes opportunities for the examiner to provide additional help as needed. The places for which this help is permitted are clearly indicated in the administration directions. This means that the examiner is free to help the student understand the demands of the task in whatever way or language is appropriate (see the test manuals for more details). This level of flexibility, which is embedded in the standardized instructions, is unique among tests of this type and helps ensure that the best most reliable measure of PASS is obtained. Fifth, the tests are easy to score. There is no need for scoring rules to determine if the score is a 0, 1, or 2, for example. Scoring is simple if completed manually or instantly with the online scoring and reporting system. Finally, interpretation of the CAS2 and the CAS2: Brief is based on PASS theory so there is little need for examiners to search for ways to interpret the four scores. The manual provides ample description of what the test measures in a clear and unambiguous manner. This simplifies communication to teachers, parents, and the students and increases the likelihood that interventions will be on target and effective.

🐂 TEST YOURSELF 🐂

1. **The CAS2 now has three versions.**
   a. True
   b. False
2. **The three versions of the CAS2 are based on what theory?**
   a. PASS neurocognitive theory
   b. CHC
   c. Verbal/nonverbal
   d. All of the above
3. **The CAS2 yields which of the following scales?**
   a. PASS and Full Scale
   b. Working Memory
   c. Executive Function
   d. Verbal
   e. Nonverbal
   f. All of the above
4. **The CAS2 yields PASS scores based on**
   a. 8 subtests
   b. 12 subtests
   c. 16 subtests
   d. 8 and 12 subtests
5. **The CAS2 yields the smallest differences by race and ethnicity.**
   a. True
   b. False
6. **The CAS2: Spanish is based on the PASS theory.**
   a. True
   b. False

Answers: 1. a; 2. a; 3. b; 4. d; 5. a; 6. a

Seven

CLINICAL APPLICATIONS OF THE CAS2

I n this chapter we provide a brief summary for each of several types of special populations followed by cases that illustrate various issues related to the assessment of these students with special needs. Our goal was not to present examples of a specific way to write a comprehensive report but rather to show a variety of ways in which to describe the performance of children and adolescents on the CAS2, CAS2: Brief, and CAS2: Rating Scale, as well as other test results. The reports presented here are typically not a complete rendering of all the data—because our goal is not to illustrate what a comprehensive report is but rather to illustrate how three CAS2 scales may be described and related to other measures. All the cases are real and are intended to show how information can be interpreted and in some cases how the diagnostic process may unfold. The cases are written in several different formats: Sometimes the text will be similar to that included in a comprehensive report; other times the text will be more of a discussion. Our goal here is simply to illustrate various ways of understanding and communicating about the results obtained within the context of PASS.

SPECIFIC LEARNING DISABILITIES

Students can experience academic difficulties for many reasons, including poor instruction, lack of motivation, hearing and visual problems, lack of exposure to books and reading, instructional methods that are not best for a student's particular style of learning, overall limited intellectual ability, and a specific deficit in a basic psychological process. Students who have a disorder in one or more of the basic psychological processes that underlie academic success or failure are best identified via a comprehensive assessment. We believe this should include the CAS2 combined with documented academic failure despite adequate instruction and a consideration of other exclusionary factors. Such a student would meet the criteria for an SLD as defined by the 2004 reauthorization of the Individuals with Disabilities Education Improvement Act (IDEA).

Children with learning disabilities constitute the largest group of students who receive special educational services. In fact, according to the National Center for Educational Statistics (2013), during the 2012–2013 school year, of the 6.4 million students (see Figure 7.1) being served under IDEA, 2.3 million had an SLD designation, and this group represented 3.5% of all students with disabilities. Clearly, accurate identification of these students is a critically important task for school psychologists. It is, therefore, vital that we identify these individuals in a way that is accurate *and* consistent with the federal definition of SLD (see Hale, Kaufman, Naglieri, & Kavale, 2006).

One of the greatest advantages of the CAS2 is that it can detect a disorder in one or more of the basic psychology processes (see Chapter 1 in this book), which provides evidence that can be used for eligibility determination of a specific learning disability as defined in IDEA 2004:

Specific learning disability means a *disorder in one or more of the basic psychological processes* [emphasis added] involved in understanding or in using language, spoken or written, which may manifest itself in the imperfect ability to listen, think, speak, read, write, spell, or do mathematical calculations. Such term includes such conditions as perceptual disabilities, brain injury, minimal brain dysfunction, dyslexia, and developmental aphasia.... Such term [SLD] does not include a learning problem that is primarily the result of visual, hearing, or motor disabilities, of mental retardation, of emotional disturbance, or of environmental, cultural, or economic disadvantage. (p. 46)

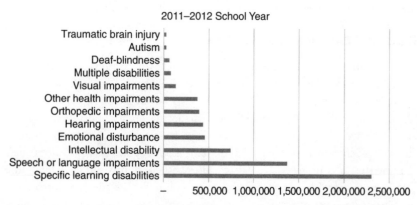

Figure 7.1 Children 3 to 21 Years Old Served Under IDEA Part B by Type of Disability 2012–2013

It is clear that the identification of a disorder in one or more of the basic psychological processes, which can be easily determined with the CAS2, in addition to documented academic failure despite adequate instruction, is *essential* for SLD eligibility determination (Fuchs & Young, 2006; Hale, Kaufman, Naglieri, & Kavale, 2006). The PASS profile provides a way to detect a pattern of strengths and weaknesses (PSW) in processing, which is exactly what the Discrepancy/Consistency Method (DCM) described in Chapter 3, "Interpretation," provides, that is, a procedure for connecting the disorder in basic psychological processing that provides a PSW in cognition as defined by PASS with a PSW in academics. Most important, detection of a disorder in a basic psychological process answers the critical question of *why* a student struggles in school. Equally important, cognitive and academic processing deficits and strengths form the basis of instruction that is tailored to the unique needs of the learner as described in Chapter 5, "Intervention."

≡ *Rapid Reference 7.1*

PASS scores can be used to detect a PSW for identification of an SLD using the Discrepancy/Consistency Method.

Although no longer required under IDEA, students with an SLD can be identified on the basis of a discrepancy between ability (IQ) and achievement test scores (Reynolds, 1990). In those states in which a discrepancy is required for identification, the CAS2 discrepancy between a high PASS processing score and low achievement can be used to meet this need. Use of the CAS2 Full Scale score is not recommended because that score will not be representative of the separate PASS scores when significant variability of PASS scores was found. Significant differences among the PASS scores indicate that the Full Scale will be misleading. Of course, the consistency (a cognitive weakness that is consistent with the level of achievement) provides the answer to the question, "Why does the student fail?" (See Chapter 5 in this book.)

We are suggesting that significant variability of the CAS2 PASS scores can be used to identify a PSW in basic psychological processes (see Chapter 3, "Interpretation"). The kinds of profiles that could be detected were studied by Huang, Bardos, and D'Amato (2010).

DON'T FORGET 7.1

A cognitive weakness in any of the PASS scale scores is evidence of a "disorder in one or more of the basic psychological processes."

DON'T FORGET 7.2

It is unusual for a student to have a cognitive weakness in more than one PASS scale, but it does happen. Usually the two that are low are Planning and Successive or Attention and Planning.

They conducted a profile analysis study on more than 2,000 students and found 10 core profiles for regular and 12 core profiles from students with learning problems. What is most noteworthy about their study was that they found groups of students with a weakness in Planning, Attention, Simultaneous, or Successive as well as some with two weaknesses (Planning and Successive). This gives additional support, as discussed in Chapter 1 of this book, that the CAS2 is well suited to uncover a profile of cognitive processing strengths and weaknesses. The CAS2 also yields small differences between race and ethnic groups and has intervention implications (Naglieri & Otero, 2011)—an essential requirement of SLD assessment under IDEA.

The Case of Allen

Allen is a 13-year-old seventh grader who was evaluated as part of a comprehensive appraisal of his educational needs and at the request of his parents because of their concern about continuing problems with written language and spelling. Although he typically gets average grades, Allen has struggled with the mechanics of writing and reading comprehension since second grade. Allen was able to produce good ideas on paper but has had poor spelling, organization of content, and mechanics of writing, such as capitalizations, punctuations, and so forth. The teachers' reports indicated he was also becoming frustrated with his performance in language arts and has lost confidence in his ability to do the work.

Allen reported that he likes to read but found it difficult to organize his writing. Much of his cognitive resources were allocated to spelling correctly, and he found it difficult to keep track of the ideas he wanted to write about and remember to apply the proper writing mechanics. At home Allen's father, who helped him study for spelling tests, reported that Allen tends to inconsistently spell words correctly. Allen can spell words correctly on a test but often spells the same word incorrectly later that day when writing the same word in a sentence. Allen also frequently confused letters and numbers such as *b* and *d, p* and *q,* and 6 and 9, and 5 and 3. He also reads similarly spelled words incorrectly. For example, he will read *vicious* as *vicarious, cleanse* as *clean,* and *suite* as *suit.* Allen reported that sometimes he says certain words within his sentences out of order. Importantly, Allen reported that tasks that required him to work with information in a specific linear order were confusing.

Allen was previously evaluated at the request of his fourth-grade teacher by members of his school's multidisciplinary team. He attained a Wechsler Intelligence for Children IV Verbal Reasoning score of 91, Perceptual Reasoning score of 86, Working Memory score of 83, a Processing Speed score of 88, and a Full Scale score of 84. Academic achievement scores from the Wechsler Individual Achievement Test III are as follows: Word Reading: 68, Reading Comprehension: 84, Pseudoword Decoding: 78, Numerical Operations: 79, Math Reasoning: 79, Written Expression: 78, and Listening Comprehension: 89. On select subtests of the Clinical Evaluation of Language fundamentals he demonstrated below average performances on Recalling Sentences, Concepts and Following Directions, and Number Repetition Forward. He attained average scores on Word Definitions and Understanding Paragraphs subtests.

Selected Assessment Results
Allen earned a CAS2: Full Scale score of 87, which is within the below average classification and is a percentile rank of 19. This means that his performance is equal to or greater than that of 19% of children his age in the standardization group. There is a 90% probability that Allen's true Full Scale score falls within the range of 83 to 92. Because there was significant variation among the four PASS scales, the Full Scale will sometimes be higher and other times lower than the four scales in this test. The Simultaneous scale was found to be high in relation to his average PASS score. This finding has important instructional implications. The Successive scale was found to be a significant cognitive weakness. This means that Allen's Successive score was a weakness both in relation to his average PASS score and when compared to his peers. This cognitive weakness has important implications for diagnosis, eligibility determination, and therapeutic and educational programming.

Allen earned a Simultaneous scale score of 106, which was significantly above his average PASS score. This scale measures his ability to work with information that is organized into groups and form a cohesive whole and understand how shapes as well as words and verbal concepts are interrelated. Allen's Simultaneous score is within the average classification and is a percentile rank of 66. This indicates that Allen did as well as or better than 66% of children his age in the standardization group. This relatively high score has educational implications because it suggests that this strength could be used to enhance learning through the use of instruction that emphasizes visual-spatial organization of numbers, words, ideas, or images.

Allen's Successive score was significantly lower than his average PASS score and below the average range. This means that Allen performed particularly poorly on tests that required repetition of words or numbers in order and an understanding of verbal statements when the meaning was dependent on the sequence of the words. Allen earned a CAS2 Successive scale score of 73, which is within the poor classification and is a percentile rank of 4. The percentile rank indicates that Allen did as well as or better than 4% of others his age in the standardization group. This cognitive weakness has important implications for diagnosis, eligibility determination, and educational and therapeutic programming. Children who are weak on the Successive scale often have problems with tasks that required sequencing, such as motor movements, sound blending, reading decoding, sequencing of words within sentences and sentences within paragraphs, and following step-by-step directions.

Allen's profile of high Simultaneous processing and weak Successive processing was consistent with his performance on a number of academic tasks. For example, Allen did exceptionally well on a task that required him to listen to information and answer big-picture questions. Allen earned a high standard score (102) on a test of listening comprehension. On a similar task that required him to describe pictures, paying particular attention to organizing his sentences and his choice of words, Allen generally responded with accurate information, but he expressed his concepts using words in grammatically incorrect order, which lowered his score (Oral Expression subtest score of 89). This difference between these scores can be understood more clearly when this variation is related to his strength in Simultaneous processing and weakness in Successive processing (see Table 7.1).

Allen's Successive processing weakness and Simultaneous processing strength have influenced the scores he earned on the reading tasks. His reliance on his strong Simultaneous processing ability leads him to look at the whole word rather than carefully examine the sequence of letters for proper decoding. For example, he earned a standard score of 73 when reading from a list of words on Letter and Word Recognition. This was apparent from the types of errors Allen made. When reading, he omitted letters and often used words more familiar to him that looked

Table 7.1 Allen's CAS Standard Scores and Comparisons of Each PASS Score to His Mean (From CAS2 Online Scoring and Report)

	Score		Sig/NS	Strength/Weakness	% in Sample
Planning	93	2.5	NS		76.8
Simultaneous	106	15.5	Sig		10.8
Attention	90	−0.5	NS		96.3
Successive	73	−17.5	Sig	W	8.3
PASS Average	90.5				

or sounded similar to the target word. For instance, he said *clean* when reading *cleanse*. He started by reading words as a whole but as they became more difficult he slowed down and attempted to sound them out. In some instances, however, Allen omitted letters such as *s*. He periodically added sounds such as /s/ or /ed/ to the ends of words. Conversely, Allen was able to use the context of a story to figure out the meaning of unfamiliar words and answer questions about what he had read by determining meaning from the context of the passage.

Some of Allen's lowest scores were on written tasks that required a lot of Successive processing. For example, it is very important to put letters in the proper order during a spelling test, but this was difficult for Allen, and he earned a standard score of 79 because of letter-sequencing problems. Other written tasks that also involve Successive processing were similarly problematic. He earned a standard score of 84 on a test of written expression, which required him to fill in blanks and write descriptions and responses to pictures and stories. At times words within a sentence were in the wrong order, his ideas were good, but the successive demands required for writing interfered with his performance. Throughout his written response Allen also had several letter transpositions or letter confusion (*d* for *b*, *q* for *p*, and *b* for *p*, for example).

Allen also performed poorly when sounding out pseudowords, and he earned a standard score of 75 on the Nonsense Word Decoding subtest. Allen's low score illustrates the impact a cognitive weakness in Successive processing can have on this important reading task. Sounding out unfamiliar or nonsensical words requires letters and sounds to be interpreted in the order they are presented as well as the sequential correspondence of sounds with letter combinations. When asked to decode at faster speeds his errors increased and his score went down.

Allen earned a Planning scale score of 93, which measures his ability to solve problems using strategies, self-monitor the success of the strategies, modify or change solutions when needed, and efficiently complete tasks. His Planning score is within the average classification and is a percentile rank of 32. This indicates that Allen did as well as or better than 32% of children his age in the standardization group. There is a 90% probability that Allen's true Planning score is within the range of 87 to 100. Similarly, Allen's Attention score of 90 falls in the average range, which is a percentile rank of 26. This means that he performed as well as or better than 26% of the children in the standardization group. There is a 90% probability that Allen's true Attention score is within the range of 84 to 98. This score reflects his ability to focus his attention and resist distractions.

Allen's scores on the CAS and reading fit the Discrepancy/Consistency Method described previously in Chapter 3 of this book and shown in Figure 7.2. He has a cognitive weakness in Successive processing (standard score of 73), which is

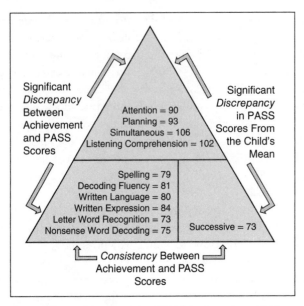

Figure 7.2 Allen's Scores Illustrate the PSW Approach to SLD Determination Using the Discrepancy/Consistency Method

significantly lower than his average PASS score and substantially below average. This provides evidence of intra-individual variability in his levels of psychological processing abilities. This is accompanied by a weakness in reading evidenced by scores in the 70s and 80s. Said another way, there is a consistency between his cognitive ability and academic weaknesses (Successive and reading). Moreover, there is a discrepancy between his low reading scores and his other cognitive processing scores (e.g., Simultaneous, Planning, and Attention are all in the average or higher range). Finally, his weaknesses in processing and achievement are substantially below average. Allen's scores provide evidence of a disorder in basic psychological processes and reading failure that have apparently not been adequately managed in the regular classroom environment. In this case, special instruction was necessary.

Intervention

The results of Allen's evaluation provided an opportunity to better understand his disorder in basic psychological processes and strengths. Shortly thereafter he was given interventions for spelling and writing in an effort to improve his weak spelling and written language skills. Allen attended nine 1-hour sessions three times a week over the course of approximately 3 weeks. During this time

Table 7.2 Pre- and Post-Intervention Achievement Raw Scores, Standard Scores, Differences, and Effect Sizes for Allen

	Pre-Intervention		Post-Intervention			
	Raw Score	Standard Score	Raw Score	Standard Score	Pre-Post Difference	Effect Size
Written Language Composite	162	80	200	100	20	1.3
Written Expression	165	84	189	117	36	2.2
Spelling	15	79	20	83	2	0.3
Nonsense Word Decoding	4	75	14	97	11	1.5
Word Recognition Fluency	17	81	23	97	2	1.1
Decoding Fluency	3	81	16	97	16	1.1
Spontaneous Writing Composite	—	80	—	100	10	1.3
Average of All Subtests	—	80.0	—	98.7	13.9	1.2

Note: Effect size was calculated by comparing the standard score means and dividing that difference by the normative SD of 15.

Allen received individualized instruction and completed four tasks from the PASS Reading Enhancement Program (PREP; Das, 2000). The PREP tasks focused on improving the use of Successive processing strategies. In addition to the individual lessons, Allen completed several homework assignments as a way of practicing the various rules and skills being taught. Table 7.2 provides Allen's scores on language- and spelling-related standardized subtests before and after the intervention. Allen answered more problems correctly on almost every subtest, significant improvements were apparent, and sizable effect sizes were found for most of the standard scores.

The PREP remedial reading program provided a way to improve Allen's use of cognitive processing strategies within an academic context, particularly Successive processing, which is so important for reading. Only those PREP tasks that focus on Successive processing were used because Allen has a Successive processing cognitive weakness. PREP tasks involve a process training component and a curriculum-related component. The processing instruction for Allen encouraged the application of Successive strategies and provided him with the opportunity to come up with his own strategies that work best. Allen described the PREP tasks as helpful and enjoyable. In fact, on days PREP tasks were not used he specifically requested them. These tasks enabled Allen to practice processing information in a specific linear order and relate to sequencing and tracking.

Allen showed significant improvement in Written Expression. His score increased by 36 points from a standard score of 81 to 117. He more frequently used appropriate words and phrases when completing written tasks. This was likely because he proofed his writing and corrected several errors without prompting. This suggests that the lessons on proofreading had a positive impact. Furthermore, though spelling does not contribute to the Written Expression score, Allen misspelled several more words on the pretest than he did on the posttest.

Allen's score on the Written Language Composite also improved significantly—his score increased by 20 points (from 80 to 100). Allen's standard scores on the TOWL-3 Spontaneous Writing Composite also increased by 10 standard score points. Examination of Allen's story showed particular improvement in the content and composition of his story (Story Construction). His composition was more interesting and described the setting and characters more thoroughly. Allen's score on the Story Construction portion of the pretest fell at the 37th percentile and on the posttest fell at the 84th percentile.

Although Allen's standard score showed modest improvement on the Spelling subtest he did show much improvement on more complex words after intervention. On the pretest Allen discontinued on item 29 but on the posttest Allen discontinued on item 43. He answered 14 more items on the posttest and spelled eight more words correctly. This improvement was not, however, sufficient enough in relation to the rate of improvement for other children his age to yield a large change in standard scores. Further instruction in spelling is, therefore, needed.

Allen's decoding skills improved as represented by his posttest score on Nonsense Word Decoding. Although his standard score increased by 11 points, his raw scored more than doubled from his pretest to posttest. On the pretest Allen earned a standard score of 86 and on the posttest he earned a standard score of 97, which yielded a large effect size. The lesson on letter combinations proved useful in this area. Allen read the pseudowords more fluidly, recognizing letter combinations rather than sounding out each individual letter. Specifically, he recognized (and did not pronounce) silent letters that he previously verbalized (e.g., he did not make a *G* sound when seeing a *gn* letter combination as in *foreign*).

Allen demonstrated a significant difference of 16 points in Decoding Fluency. He increased his standard score from an 81 on the pretest to a 97 on the posttest. Although the rapidity of his word recognition fluency improved slightly, the increase was not statistically significant. Fluency was not addressed during the intervention and no lessons were specifically focused on improving fluency, yet he demonstrated a large effect size on the Decoding Fluency subtest.

Several intervention lessons from Helping Children Learn (Naglieri & Pickering, 2010) were directly related to development of written language skills. This included instruction in letter combinations, spelling patterns, phonological awareness, decoding, and proofreading. Allen learned that certain letter combinations often make similar sounds within a word. He also learned a number of memory strategies (mnemonics) to help him avoid some of his more frequent errors. Some of the letter patterns and combinations Allen learned include the sound generally produced from an /oi/ letter combination (e.g., *boil, coin, point, voice, noise*); the sound generally produced from an /ou/ letter combination (e.g., *found, proud, announce, doubt*); and silent letters (e.g., *k(n)* as in *know* and *knife*, *gh* as in *night* and *fight*, *g(n)* as in *sign* and *reign*, *(m)b* as in *lamb, bomb*, and so forth). Some of the mnemonics involved rhymes such as "Use *i* before *e* except after *c* or when sounding like *a* in *neighbor* or *weigh*." Using these phrases employs Simultaneous processing; thus, we use his strength to overcome his weakness in Successive processing. Our goal is to use his strengths and work with his weakness.

Allen completed pre-quizzes before learning new rules and took similar quizzes after he expressed an understanding of the material. To avoid practice effects Allen did not spell the same words on post-quizzes. Instead he spelled different words that encompassed the same rule or skill. In order to spend more time on instruction and less on quizzing, some quizzes were given in a multiple-choice format. On each pre- and posttest Allen showed notable improvement (see Table 7.2).

Summary of Intervention Results

The combination of individual instruction and the Successive processing training appears to have led to significant improvements in written language scores. Overall, participation in the intervention helped improve many of Allen's academic skills. He made the significant improvements in Written Expression and on the Written Language Composite. He also made notable gains in Decoding Fluency, Nonsense Word Decoding, and Spontaneous Writing (particularly content of plot and descriptions of details). Comparisons of raw scores on classroom tests and standard scores that control for natural gains attributed to his increase in age (from 8 years 1 month to 8 years 8 months) provided a thorough examination of his performance. The significant improvements and sizable effect sizes suggest that the combination of individual instruction and PREP tasks helped Allen become a more competent writer, helped increase his skills in writing-related areas, and improved his self-confidence. Selection of these methods (PREP for the Successive weakness) and mnemonics (using his strength in Simultaneous processing) proved to be an effective intervention plan.

The Case of Clark: Is He SLD or ADHD?

Clark is an 8-year-old second-grade male who was seen was seen in connection with an evaluation to assess his educational needs. He was recently diagnosed with ADHD by his physician and is currently taking 10 mg of Vyvanse in the mornings. Prior to being on medication he was observed as more inattentive. After medication he is reported to have improved somewhat but still fidgety and seems to be always doing something with his hands. His mother reported that his focus and memory continue to be an issue. She also reported that even though Clark received tutoring last summer and has been receiving Title I reading intervention three times a week all school year she remains concerned about Clark's reading comprehension.

During the present evaluation, Clark was friendly, cooperative, and put forth excellent effort across, though he reported being tired. Clark demonstrated appropriate emotion and mood throughout the session. His memory for recent events was intact and his sustained attention when listening to directions was adequate. Clark did pick at or bite his nails continuously for the three hours of testing and attempts to help him limit this behavior were ineffective. On tests that required him to respond using paper and pencil, Clark tended to initiate tasks prematurely, inconsistently self-monitored and self-corrected.

Selected Tests Results
- Cognitive Assessment System 2
- Kaufman Test of Educational Achievement, Third Edition
- Comprehensive Executive Function Inventory

> **DON'T FORGET 7.3**
> ....
> The Executive Function Supplemental scale on the CAS2 is composed of one Planning subtest and one Attention subtest. When the Planning and Attention scales on the CAS2 are different, as in the case of Clark, the Supplemental scale of Executive Function will be misleading. Focus should be on the importance of the difference between Planning and Attention.

Clark earned a CAS2 Full Scale score of 87, which is within the below average classification and is a percentile rank of 19. This means that his performance is equal to or greater than that of 19% of children his age in the standardization group. There is a 90% probability that Clark's true Full Scale score falls within the range of 83 to 92. Because there was significant variation among the four PASS scales, the Full Scale will sometimes be higher and other times lower than the four scales in this test. The Planning scale was found to be a strength in relation to his average PASS score and his Attention was found to be a weakness. These finding have important instructional implications.

Clark earned a Planning scale score of 98, which was significantly higher than his average PASS score. This scale measures his ability to use strategies when solving problems, check to see if the strategies are effective, modify or change solutions when needed, and efficiently complete tasks. Clark's Planning score is within the average classification and is a percentile rank of 45. This indicates that Clark did as well as or better than 45% of children his age in the standardization group. There is a 90% probability that Clark's true Planning score is within the range of 91 to 105. This cognitive strength has implications for educational programming because being relatively strong in Planning suggests that the youth may do well when given the opportunity to use strategies to solve problems and modify plans to improve efficiency.

Clark's Simultaneous score measures his ability to work with information that is organized into groups and form a cohesive whole. This scale also requires an understanding of how shapes as well as words and verbal concepts are interrelated. Clark earned a Simultaneous scale score of 89, which is within the below average classification and is a percentile rank of 24. This means that Clark did as well as or better than 24% of the children in the standardization group. There is a 90% probability that Clark's true Simultaneous score is within the range of 84 to 96.

Clark's Successive score reflects his ability to repeat information, such as words or sentences, in order and an understanding of verbal statements when the meaning was dependent on the sequence of the words. Clark earned a Successive scale score of 91, which is within the average classification and is a percentile rank of 27. This means that Clark did as well as or better than 27% of the children in the standardization group. There is a 90% probability that Clark's true Successive score is within the range of 85 to 98.

Clark's Attention score was significantly lower than his average PASS score and below the average range. This means that he performed particularly poorly on tests that required focused thinking and resistance to distraction when given many stimuli to look at. Clark earned an Attention scale score of 81, which is within the below average classification and is a percentile rank of 10. This means that Clark did as well as or better than only 10% of the children in the standardization group. There is a 90% probability that Clark's true Attention score is within the range of 77 to 92. This cognitive weakness as well as his cognitive strength in Planning are associated with his academic failure and success.

In general, application of math facts is associated with Planning. This means that we would expect a student like Clark to have average scores on math and Planning, which is the case. He received a Math Concepts and Applications standard score of 97 and a Math Computation standard score of 95, both of which fall in the average range. The skills required in these subtests require that he *apply* knowledge of mathematical principles to real-life situations (e.g., using basic math skills to solve problems involving time and money, measurement, data investigations, and higher math concepts). By contrast, he earned low scores on those KTEA-II subtests that required knowledge *and* especially demanded focused attention and resistance to distraction.

Clark struggled with academic tasks that demand Attention as measured on the CAS2. For example, he earned a Spelling standard score of 77 (which affected his Written Expression standard score of 84), a Reading Comprehension standard score of 79, and a Phonological Processing subtest score of 79. His difficulty with attention affects his spelling because he does not focus on the sequence of letters and instead uses a whole-word approach. It is noteworthy that his Letter and Word Recognition subtest standard score of 96 falls in the average range and that most of the words included in this subtest are irregular to ensure that the subtest measures more word recognition than decoding. His Reading Comprehension score is low because of the items that demand recall of literal facts, which he missed when he reads. Finally, his Phonological Processing score is low because managing the sequence of sounds is a task that requires focus and a lot of resistance to the distraction of the nontarget sounds.

Clark also received a particularly low score on the Attention scale of the Comprehensive Executive Function Inventory (CEFI) completed by his father. His CEFI Attention scale standard score was 58, which falls in the well below average range and is ranked at the 1st percentile, meaning that he scored as well as or better than only 1% of the children his age in the standardization group. This means that his father noted considerable problems with day-to-day behaviors related to focus of attention. By contrast, Clark's Emotion Regulation score on the CEFI was 95 (average range), which reflects his control and management of emotions, including staying calm when handling small problems and reacting with the right level of emotion. All of these regulation behaviors are associated with Planning on the CAS2 (see Figure 7.3).

☰ *Rapid Reference 7.2*

....

Clark's results fit the PSW approach for SLD eligibility determination, as illustrated in Figure 7.4.

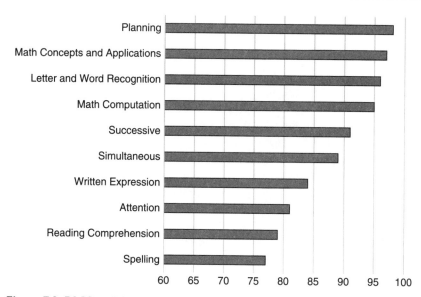

Figure 7.3 PASS and Achievement Test Scores for Clark

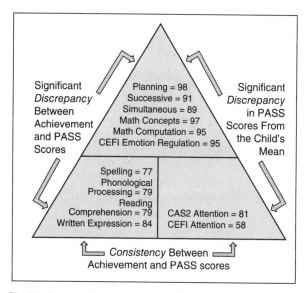

Figure 7.4 Clark's Scores Illustrate the PSW Approach to SLD Determination Using the Discrepancy/Consistency Method

Summary

The results of this analysis strongly suggest that Clark has a disorder in the basic psychological process of Attention as measured by the CAS2, which is consistent with a low Attention scale score on the CEFI and corresponds to specific areas of academic failure. His struggles with reading comprehension (especially literal recall), spelling, and its impact on written language are also related to his difficulty with focus of attention and resistance to distraction. The Attention weakness is in contrast to his strength in Planning, which is associated with high scores in math concepts and applications, reading words aloud from a list, and math computation. These finding suggest that teachers should use Clark's strength in Planning, that is, the use of strategies, to overcome difficulties related to Attention. The following recommendations are offered.

Interventions

It is very important that Clark be informed of his strength in using strategies (Planning) and how his good ability to think about how to do things can help him overcome his challenges when focused thinking and resisting distractions (Attention) are required. This will be especially important when he is reading (particularly literal questions) and writing. The informational handouts "How to Be Smart: Attention" and "How to Be Smart: Planning" from *Helping Children Learn* (Naglieri & Pickering, 2010) should be given to Clark when the results of this evaluation are explained to him. Special attention should be given to his mind-set about his own abilities, and emphasis should be placed on the view that he can do better if he thinks smart. The method described in the "Overcoming Problems with Inattention" sheet from that book should be used to guide his thinking about attending so that he can feel empowered to manage his attention. These same recommendations should be shared with his parents and teachers.

Practical Instructional Modifications

Improving Attention

- Break lessons and assignments into segments so that Clark can complete them.
- Simplify instructions and present them in segments that Clark can manage.
- Establish a cue that the teacher or parent always uses to help Clark recognize when attention is lost.
- Teach Clark to systematically and carefully look at materials before responding (e.g., look at all the options before choosing an answer).
- Decrease the amount of distracting information in the environment.
- Use materials that are interesting to Clark.

- Teach Clark to check work using calculators, spell checkers, and other helpful items.
- Encourage Clark to slow down and look carefully at how words are spelled, for example.

Making Instructions Easier to Process
- Make sure you have Clark's attention.
- Provide oral and written instructions.
- Give one instruction at a time and then repeat the instructions to Clark, if necessary.
- Have Clark repeat back the instructions to confirm that he understands what to do.

Structuring the Environment to Improve Attention
- Be clear and concise when discussing behavior changes with Clark. Avoid lengthy discussions of problematic behaviors.
- Develop a strategy and an action plan for how Clark can increase positive attention from others.
- Seat Clark at the front of the class near the teacher.
- Avoid open concept classroom layouts. A more enclosed, traditional classroom environment reduces distractions.
- Modify Clark's schedule so that more demanding classes are taught earlier in the day.
- Schedule activities and courses in a way that maximizes Clark's attention by alternating tasks that require a lot of attention (instruction classes) with other activities (physical activity) and breaks. It is best if the schedule is predictable so that Clark has consistency.
- Suggest strategies for reducing distractions and sensory stimulation, such as using headphones or earplugs.
- Provide only those materials that are necessary for the task and model this practice so that Clark will learn to focus and use only what is needed to complete his work.
- Assign a job or task during large-group activities or when Clark needs to be patient for his turn to keep him engaged throughout the activity.
- Decrease workload (e.g., break tasks up into smaller, more manageable parts) so that it aligns with Clark's attention level and abilities. Increase workload as Clark gains a greater attention span.
- Reduce the length of assignments to emphasize quality over quantity of work.

- Accommodate regular breaks during tasks that allow Clark to get out of his seat and move around.
- Allow extra time on assignments, quizzes, and tests.
- Consider restructuring tests to a format that best suits Clark's abilities (e.g., multiple-choice will reduce writing demand; some children do better giving answers orally, whereas other children like to use a word processor to type out their responses).
- Provide an unlimited amount of time to finish tests and provide breaks as necessary.
- Teach meditation, yoga, martial arts, or tai-chi, all of which require Clark to focus his attention.

Help Classroom Focus
- Have a peer assist in note-taking.
- Have the teacher ask questions to encourage participation.
- Enlist Clark to help present the lesson.
- Cue Clark to stay on task with a private signal—a gentle tap on the shoulder.
- Schedule a 5-minute period for Clark to check over work before turning in assignments.

When Observed to Daydream in class
- Have the teacher use clear verbal signals, such as "Freeze," "This is important," or "One, two, three … eyes on me."
- Allow Clark to earn the right to daydream for 5 to 10 minutes by completing the assignment
- Use a flashlight or a laser pointer to illuminate objects or words to pay attention to.
- Illustrate vocabulary words and science concepts with small drawings or stick figures.

Settle Fidgety, Restless Behaviors
- If Clark taps his foot or pencil nervously in class or gets up out of his seat a lot, offer these suggestions:
  ◦ Allow him to run errands, to hand out papers to other students, clean off bookshelves, or to stand at times while working.
  ◦ Give Clark a fidget toy in class to increase concentration.
  ◦ Slot in short exercise breaks between assignments.
  ◦ Give Clark a standing desk or an air-filled rubber disk to sit on so he can wiggle around.

Commentary on the SLD Examples

The case of Clark illustrates how a child with a disability could be provided services to improve performance in the classroom. The exact logistics of eligibility determination will vary from state to state. For example, some state or local forms need to be completed using terminology that is not consistent with PASS constructs. Oftentimes these forms require designation of a disorder based on terms such as *visual* or *auditory processing, dyslexia* or *dyscalculia, verbal* or *nonverbal,* and so forth. We recognize the challenges this presents to the practitioner; however, we suggest that the concepts of PASS can be used to meet the requirements of IDEA (finding a disorder in one or more of the basic psychological processes). Determining which box to check in an eligibility form is less important than explaining exactly what the processing issue is. We suggest that if the categories are, for example, visual and auditory, they would most likely correspond to Simultaneous and Successive scales, respectively. Dyslexia would likely correspond to a cognitive weakness on the Successive scale, Dyscalculia to Planning. See Chapter 5, "Interventions," for more examples of SLD.

ATTENTION-DEFICIT/HYPERACTIVITY DISORDER

The American Psychiatric Association's *Diagnostic and Statistical Manual of Mental Disorders, Fifth Edition* (*DSM-5*) describes attention-deficit/hyperactivity disorder (ADHD) as a pattern of inattention and/or hyperactivity-impulsivity that interferes with functioning. These two types are summarized as follows (see *DSM-5* for actual diagnostic criteria).

Inattention is identified if the correct number of symptoms are found, for example, more than five symptoms of inattention for children up to age 16 (more than four at age 17 and older). The symptoms of inattention must have been present for at least 6 months and be inappropriate for the developmental level. The symptoms include difficulties such as failure to attend to details, sustain attention over time, make careless mistakes, not listen or follow through on instructions, failure to complete work, disorganization, tendency to avoid work or give up easily, and being forgetful.

The hyperactivity-impulsivity category requires more than five symptoms for children up to age 16 (more than four at age 17 and older). The symptoms of inattention must have been present for at least 6 months and have been disruptive and inappropriate. This includes symptoms such as being fidgety, out of seat in class, much movement when it is not appropriate, excessive talking, difficulty with impulse control, and frequent interruptions.

The diagnosis of ADHD also requires that symptoms were present before age 12, symptoms are present in two or more settings, and they interfere with functioning interpersonally, at school, or at work. Additionally, another mental disorder should not better explain the symptoms.

≡ Rapid Reference 7.3

Three Diagnostic Categories of ADHD

1. Combined Presentation: Inattention and Hyperactivity-Impulsivity
2. Predominantly Inattentive
3. Predominantly Hyperactive-Impulsive

It is important to note that ADHD diagnosis also requires that symptoms are having an adverse impact on performance socially or at school or work. This means that the disorder is causing impairment in everyday functioning. The same requirement can be found under the IDEA: The child must have a disability and must need special education and related services to reduce the impact of the disability. Typically, eligibility is accomplished using the Other Health Impaired category in IDEA. The definition of ADHD (see Rapid Reference 7.4) requires that the disorder adversely affects a student's performance in school. One way to quantify the impact of a disability is the Rating Scale of Impairment (Goldstein & Naglieri, 2016). This scale evaluates functional impairment across six scales: School/Work, Social, Mobility, Domestic, Family, and Self-Care.

We suggest that ADHD could also be designated as a specific learning disability when (1) a disorder in one or more of the basic psychological processes (e.g., a cognitive weakness in Planning or Attention) is found and (2) academic failure is present.

As summarized in Chapter 1 of this book, researchers have reported a relationship between the symptoms of ADHD and PASS. Naglieri and Das (1997) first reported that children with ADHD earned significantly lower scores on the Planning scale of the CAS. This was followed by other studies by Dehn (2000); Naglieri, Goldstein, Iseman, and Schwebach (2003); and Iseman and Naglieri (2011); all of which have shown that as a group children and adolescents with an ADHD diagnosis are poor in Planning. This is very consistent with views of

ADHD as proposed by, for example, Barkley (1997), who describes the disorder as a "delay in the development of response inhibition … [and an] inefficiency in the neuropsychological functions that we believe inhibit responding" (p. vii) and a "profound disturbance in self-regulation and organization of behavior across time" (p. vii). These symptoms are often described as executive functions and associated with the prefrontal regions of the brain (Goldberg, 2009; Hynd, Voeller, Hern, & Marshall, 1991).

≡ Rapid Reference 7.4

IDEA Regulations: Part 300 / A / 300.8 / c / 9

(9) Other health impairment means having limited strength, vitality, or alertness, including a heightened alertness to environmental stimuli, that results in limited alertness with respect to the educational environment, that—

  (i) Is due to chronic or acute health problems such as asthma, attention deficit disorder or attention deficit hyperactivity disorder, diabetes, epilepsy, a heart condition, hemophilia, lead poisoning, leukemia, nephritis, rheumatic fever, sickle cell anemia, and Tourette syndrome; and

  (ii) Adversely affects a child's educational performance.

From the PASS theory this description implies that students with hyperactive-impulsive ADHD have difficulty with Planning (self-regulation, inhibition of responses, control of behavior) as measured on the CAS2. By contrast, the Attention scale is expected to be low for those with the inattentive type of ADHD because of their difficulty with sustaining attention and resisting distraction. This PASS pattern was reported by Taddei and Venditti (2010), who found that when diagnosed with ADHD hyperactive-impulsive, the profile revealed a weakness in Planning, but when the diagnosis was ADHD inattentive, the weakness was in Attention on the CAS. The following case studies illustrate how CAS2 can be used as part of an evaluation of individuals referred for possible ADHD.

The Case of Anthony

Anthony was referred for evaluation because of parent concerns with attention and overactivity. Additionally, the parent reported concerns about Anthony's frustration and self-esteem when he is unable to complete a task. The purpose of the evaluation is to find out the nature of Anthony's difficulties for the purposes of educational planning and suggesting interventions.

Relevant Background Information
Anthony is an 8-year-old, right-handed male of Mexican descent (mother's side) who is currently completing third grade at H. E. School. He lives at home with his biological mother, Ms. M. Anthony was conceived through in vitro fertilization through an unknown sperm donor and no information is known about Anthony's biological father. Currently, only Spanish is spoken within the home. Although Anthony is fluent in Spanish, Ms. M reported that English is his dominant language because he has been exposed to English socially and since preschool. Early and developmental history is generally unremarkable. Ms. M reported no complications with her pregnancy or delivery with Anthony, although Anthony experienced jaundice after birth and was put under a lamp for several hours. Anthony weighed 7 lbs 9 oz at birth, and Ms. M said she and Anthony bonded well and latched on without incident.

From 6 months to age 4 Ms. M reported that Anthony demonstrated temper tantrums, colic, and variable poor eye contact. She stated that Anthony would settle down "just fine" in the evening. Developmental milestones were reportedly met within normal limits, with the exception of speech/language. Ms. M reported that Anthony said "mama" around the age of 15 months, put two words together around 2 years old, and put four to five words together to relate an experience around 4 to 5 years old. When Anthony was 2 years old a pediatrician referred him to the early intervention program because of concerns regarding expressive language development. A speech/language evaluation indicated "reduced expressive/receptive language skills." Additional evaluation results indicated possible difficulties with attention, distractibility, overactivity, gross/fine motor, and nonverbal cognition. According to Ms. M, Anthony received early intervention services for approximately 1 year for occupational and speech/language therapy and benefited from interventions. At age 4, he suffered a concussion because of a fall from a bounce house and hitting his head on the concrete floor; although there was no loss of consciousness he vomited immediately afterward. Anthony was taken to the hospital, medically cleared, and released the same day. No additional information was provided about this incident from Ms. M. History is negative for known additional concussions, psychotropic medication, and chronic illness. Anthony has seasonal allergies and asthma for which he takes albuterol as needed. Anthony has passed recent vision and hearing screenings and is reported to be generally healthy.

Educational History

Anthony's parent reported in the interview that he attended local daycare at the age of 2. At age of 3, he moved to Mexico to live with his grandmother and attended preschool and kindergarten there. Ms. M reported that the separation was difficult for both her and Anthony, yet she was able to visit multiple times on a relatively regular basis. Anthony moved back to the United States at age 5 and attended a private school for first and second grade. Anthony, now a third grader, began attending H. E. Elementary public school at the beginning of the current school year. Teachers have described Anthony as bright and enthusiastic, but they had concerns regarding his initiation of play with other children, sometimes becoming upset and occasionally crying if he makes mistakes and is given constructive criticism by a teacher, difficulty sustaining his attention on adult-directed tasks, and as "needing to be in constant movement and fidget with things." Anthony has occasional difficulties when changes occur in the typical school routines, meaning that he sometimes demonstrates inflexibility in adapting or being ready for new topics and following through with changes in class activities. However, teachers reported that Anthony is generally a wonderful student and is academically successful. Ms. M requested this evaluation because of concerns regarding Anthony's problems with attention, overactivity, and occasional emotional regulation at school.

Procedures for Evaluation

- Review of records
- Observations
- Kaufman Test of Educational Achievement, Second Edition (KTEA-III)
- Cognitive Assessment System, Second Edition (CAS2)
- Kaufman Assessment Battery for Children, Second Edition (KABC-II)
- NEPSY Second Edition (NEPSY-II): Selected subtests
- The Test of Everyday Attention for Children (TEA-Ch)
- Behavior Assessment Scale for Children, Second Edition (BASC-2)
- Vineland Adaptive Behavior Scales, Second Edition: Parent and teacher reports
- Clinical Evaluation of Language Fundamentals, Fourth Edition (CELF-4)

Behavioral Observations

Anthony attended assessment sessions in an enthusiastic and cooperative manner. He was appropriately dressed and appeared well-groomed. No concerns were noted with fine or gross motor skills, gait, or posture. Anthony demonstrated good eye contact and was able to follow all instructions and directions provided. He appeared adequately alert and oriented throughout sessions. Anthony cheerfully participated in reciprocal conversation, asking and answering questions appropriately relevant to the conversation. Although Anthony initially asked worrisome questions about missing class and his teachers knowing where he was, he adjusted quickly to the testing situation and appeared excited, especially when provided the option to play games during breaks.

Off-task behavior such as looking around the room, attempting to look through test materials, fidgetiness, and interrupting the flow of the assessment by asking questions were observed throughout the evaluation. When redirected, Anthony remained on-task for short periods. He was repeatedly told to "hold his questions for later" or that he could make a comment after first completing the designated task. His off-task and distracted behavior seemed to have affected his performance during various tasks (specifically, tasks requiring sustained attention, such as a listening comprehension measure and measures of attention). Anthony often asked if he answered questions correctly, if tasks were "for a grade," and if he was doing as well as other students who have taken the tests.

Classroom Observations

Anthony was observed in the general education setting in various classes and across different days and times of day. Overall, Anthony demonstrated generally age-appropriate performance as long as he was in movement. When just sitting and required to listen and follow lecture-like instruction he would look around the room, in his desk, and find items to look at and manipulate. In gym class, Anthony would fidget while listening to instructions from the teacher. The students were instructed to walk when they heard slower music and run when they heard faster music. Anthony did not alter between walking and running. He only ran and only momentarily would adjust his speed when directed to. During the daily morning meeting time in his homeroom, Anthony sat in a circle with the other students. He took his turn greeting the student next to him with a handshake and eye contact, saying, "Good morning." During independent work time, Anthony only partially completed a writing work sheet quietly at his desk. Within a period of about 15 minutes, Anthony raised his hand to ask questions nine times. Each time, his question was about how to complete the work sheet. Anthony had difficulty completing the work sheet, in spite of the teacher providing repetition of instruction and encouraging him to continue working.

General Intelligence

Anthony's cognitive scores varied considerably and the findings are revealing (see Tables 7.3 through 7.11). On the KABC-II, Anthony's cognitive scores show variability with Planning and Simultaneous processing within the average range. His General Knowledge score was average and Learning was above average. The Sequential processing score was a significant weakness in relation to his own performance and to the normative group on which the test is based.

Specifically, Anthony's weakness could be described as on a measure of short-term memory (Sequential processing). This indicates that Anthony has difficulty taking in and holding information in short-term storage, then manipulating and using it within a few seconds. On a measure of long-term storage and retrieval (Learning), Anthony demonstrated above-average skills. This means that Anthony can easily store newly learned information, if given time to encode it, and can retrieve this information later on, especially when taught explicitly and given the opportunity to practice.

On tasks of visual processing and visual-spatial skills (Simultaneous processing), Anthony showed solid abilities, falling within the average range, because he

Table 7.3 KABC-II Scores for Anthony

Scale	Standard Score	Classification
Sequential/*Gsm*	80	Below Average
Number Recall	6	
Word Order	7	
Planning	88	Average
Story Completion	7	
Pattern Reasoning	9	
Simultaneous/*Gv*	113	Average
Rover	11	
Triangles	13	
Learning/*Glr*	117	Above average
Atlantis	15	
Rebus	11	
Knowledge/*Gc*	97	Average
Verbal Knowledge	10	
Riddles	9	

Table 7.4 NEPSY Scores for Anthony

NEPSY		
Subtest	Standard Score	Classification
Affect Recognition	12	At expected levels
Auditory Attention Combined Scaled Score	12	At expected level
Response Set Total Correct	9	At expected levels
Response Set Combined Scaled Score	11	At expected levels
Memory for Faces	13	At expected levels
Theory of Mind	9	At expected levels

Table 7.5 TEA-Ch Scores for Anthony

Measure	Age-Scaled Score
Sky Search	8
Time per target	3
Attention Score	2
Score!	4
Creature Counting	6
Map Mission	7
Score DT	7
Opposite Worlds	5

Table 7.6 CAS2 Scores for Anthony

Scale	Standard Score	Classification
Planning	79	Poor
Planned Codes	7	
Planned Connections	6	
Attention	76	Poor
Expressive Attention	7	
Number Detection	5	
Simultaneous	108	Average
Matrices	12	
Verbal Spatial Relations	11	
Successive	109	Average
Word Order	10	
Sentence Repetition	13	
Supplementary Scores		
Executive Function	79	Poor
EF+WM	94	Average

Table 7.7 KTEA-III Scores for Anthony

Subtest	Standard Score	Classification
Reading Composite	96	Average
Letter and Word Recognition	100	Average
Reading Comprehension	93	Average
Nonsense Word Decoding	90	Average
Word Recognition Fluency	96	Average
Decoding Fluency	87	Average
Reading Vocabulary	108	Average
Letter Naming Facility	84	Below average
Object Naming Facility	91	Average
Listening Comprehension	68	Low
Math Composite	96	Average
Math Concepts and Applications	96	Average
Math Computation	100	Average
Written Language Composite	99	Average
Written Expression	100	Average
Spelling	101	Average

Table 7.8 CELF-4 Scores for Anthony

Subtest Scaled Score	Receptive	Expressive	Language Content	Language Structure
Concepts and Following Directions	6	—	6	—
Word Structure	—	12	—	12
Recalling Sentences	—	5	—	5
Formulating Sentences	—	6	—	6
Word Classes	11	—	10	—
Sentence Structure	7	—	—	7
Expressive Vocabulary	—	—	5	—
Standard Score	88	87	82	85
Percentile Rank	21	19	12	16

displayed good decision making, problem-solving, and organization on nonverbal tasks. When required to solve novel problems using inductive and deductive (Riddles) verbal reasoning Anthony demonstrated average range abilities, meaning that he can apply critical thinking skills to problems (such as making predictions or drawing conclusions) similar to same-age peers. On a measure of acquired knowledge, Anthony demonstrated a solid foundation of commonly known, factual information.

Table 7.9 Vineland-II Scores for Anthony

	Parent Ratings		Teacher Ratings	
	Score	Adaptive Level	Score	Adaptive Level
Communication	90	Average	80	Moderately low
Receptive	14	Average	11	Moderately low
Expressive	12	Average	11	Moderately low
Written	14	Average	13	Adequate
Daily Living Skills	85	Average	88	Adequate
Personal	13	Average	16	Adequate
Domestic	13	Average	—	
Academic	—		13	Adequate
Community	12	Average	—	
School Community	—		11	Moderately low
Socialization	87	Average	67	Mild deficit
Interpersonal Relationships	13	Average	8	Low
Play and Leisure Time	10	Average	9	Low
Coping Skills	15	Average	10	Moderately low
Adaptive Behavior Composite	85	Below average		

Table 7.10 BASC-3 Teacher Ratings for Anthony

BASC-3: Teacher	Teacher 1*	Teacher 2	Teacher 3*
Composites			
Externalizing Problems	64	43	45
Internalizing Problems	60	58	59
School Problems	58	53	63
Behavioral Symptom Index	60	54	55
Adaptive Skills	58	60	62
Scales			
Hyperactivity	70	66	64
Aggression	57	43	43
Conduct Problems	52	42	42
Anxiety	65	62	68
Depression	53	48	55
Somatization	50	53	47
Attention Problems	67	65	76
Learning Problems	58	50	58
Atypicality	60	61	55
Withdrawal	60	56	49
Adaptability	41	43	39
Social Skills	43	42	34
Leadership	42	37	35
Study Skills	46	43	43
Functional Communication	47	51	47

Table 7.11 BASC-3 Parent Ratings for Anthony

BASC-3: Parent Report	T-Scores
Composites	
Externalizing Problems	66
Internalizing Problems	56
Behavioral Symptom Index	49
Adaptive Skills	48
Scale Scores	
Hyperactivity	75
Aggression	42
Conduct Problems	40
Anxiety	50
Depression	53
Somatization	59
Atypicality	46
Withdrawal	56
Attention Problems	71
Adaptability	50
Social Skills	50
Leadership	49
Activities of Daily Living	49
Functional Communication	45

His cognitive processing on the CAS2 demonstrates similarities and differences when compared to the KABC-II. Looking at Anthony's performance at the macro level, he attained a similar score on Simultaneous processing on both tests, suggesting Anthony can synthesize stimuli simultaneously (holistically) to produce the appropriate solution. At a micro level, however, there are some notable differences in the tasks that should be mentioned. The tasks on the KABC-II can be considered primarily visual-spatial (Triangles) as well as understanding addition and subtraction of numbers as they relate to distance to a target (Rover). On the CAS2, Simultaneous processing is theoretically defined as the ability to work with information that is organized into a group and form a cohesive whole that enables understanding how shapes, patterns, as well as words and verbal concepts are interrelated. Thus, one important difference is that simultaneous processing as conceptualized and operationalized on the CAS2 can be measured by items requiring verbal-spatial analysis (Verbal-Spatial Relations) and pattern analysis (Matrices).

Anthony performed within the average range on Planning on the KABC-II and within the poor classification on the CAS2. This discrepancy in performance can be explained by the key differences in the tasks that make up each test's Planning scale. The KABC-II subtests that purport to measure Planning teach the task and place constraints on the examinee to complete the task in a rather circumscribed manner. On the CAS2, however, the examinee is allowed to develop a strategy for how to best complete the task. This maximizes the likelihood that a strategy is generated and, the efficiency of the particular strategy evaluated and whether or not the selected strategy is common in relation to peers. Anthony's poor Planning performance on the CAS2 is in line with the referral question, rating scales results, and observations.

Anthony performed below average on the sequential processing scale of the KABC-II, suggesting underdeveloped short-term memory skills. On the CAS2 Successive processing scale Anthony performed within the average range. The KABC-II sequential processing tasks require the examiner to repeat a string of numbers or touch pictures in the order heard. These tasks are said to be measures of short-term memory. The tasks Anthony completed on the CAS2 required him to repeat words heard of increasing length in order and to understand a verbal statement based only on the syntax of the words. The recall of numbers, words, and pictures require the examinee to simply maintain information in order, whereas the CAS2 Sentence Questions subtest requires more complex processing.

Attention is not measured on the KABC-II. The inclusion of an Attention scale on the CAS2 is the unique contribution over existing cognitive tests and represents how well Anthony is able to use this cognitive process to focus, sustain, and shift his attention as he resists distractions. Anthony's poor performance on the Attention scale is consistent with the referral question, other performance measures, rating scales, and observations.

Auditory Processing

Auditory processing refers to the ability to take in sound and interpret that information, such as understanding directions, making sense of verbally presented information, and acting on that information. These processes enabled Anthony to comprehend and problem-solve with information that is presented verbally. Assessment results show that Anthony is able to discriminate sounds and perceive auditory information. Testing and classroom observations showed that Anthony does not always understand and comprehend information, such as following directions. Similarly, assessment of Anthony's listening comprehension was affected by off-task behaviors, inattention, and difficulty maintaining information in memory.

Visual Processing

Visual processing is the ability to use sight to compare features of an item, to distinguish one object for another, and to visualize how to rotate objects. Anthony is able to perceive the environment around him, including his classroom surroundings and the board, with ease. Anthony can visually organize his materials and his writing. Additionally, Anthony successfully completed several tasks requiring complex visual manipulation and problem-solving and mental imagery (i.e., Matrices and Triangles). Tasks requiring problem-solving within the visual-motor domain and the use of strategy generation and cognitive shifting (i.e., Planned Codes, Planned Connections, and Number Detection) significantly challenged him, however.

Sensory-Motor

Sensory-motor abilities refer to gross motor skills, such as balance, gait, and understanding where the body is in space. More complex skills, such as playing sports and other physical activities, would be included in this area in addition to fine motor skills, such as grasping smaller objects, handwriting, and typing. According to current observations and informal motor assessments, there are no concerns regarding Anthony's sensory-motor functioning. Additionally, Anthony's fine and gross motor skills are intact.

Language

Language abilities refer to understanding the language of others and expressing thoughts and understanding of the world. Language also incorporates the ability to not only express needs but also express the need to communicate (pragmatic speech) and the intent to connect with another. We would expect Anthony, at his age, to be able to understand the speech of all other individuals in school and to be able to express his concerns, needs, and wants in a fluent and socially appropriate manner orally. These aspects of cognitive ability are easily influenced by factors such as experience, education, and cultural opportunities.

Based on formal and informal measures, Anthony demonstrated age-appropriate receptive and expressive language skills. When Anthony is not distracted, he is able to follow most directions, answer simple questions in relation to a story and conversation, and understand age-appropriate vocabulary. Per parent and teacher reports he often needs questions repeated and questions need to be simplified. In addition, Anthony is able to use age-appropriate vocabulary and generate grammatically correct sentences. Although Anthony showed slight errors with language construction and sentence structure, these mistakes are believed to be related to Anthony's bilingualism, because he would sometimes confuse the order of verbs or adjectives within a sentence (common errors made by students who are bilingual or ELL).

Additionally, although Anthony exhibited isolated areas of mild weaknesses because of decreased attention, such as difficulty sequencing events when retelling a story and staying on topic, he seems able to grasp the big picture or main idea of what he listens to when visual aids are available. This observation is consistent with his good Simultaneous processing as measured on the CAS2 and the KABC-II.

Attention

Attention is the basic ability needed for all mature complex problem-solving and learning. Attention begins in infancy as the child orients to different objects and people in the environment (orient/focus attention) and then lengthens to sustaining involvement with an event for longer and longer periods of time (sustained attention) while resisting distractions. Attention abilities are also involved when the child has to switch from one thing to another (shifting attention) and so begin the abilities to decide what and who to pay attention to (selective attention). Attention in someone Anthony's age is demonstrated in the classroom by the student being able to demonstrate adequate sustained attention during lessons, sustain effort on classroom tasks, and keep track of what he should be doing.

Assessment results indicate challenges with his attention across several measures of attention and within normal limits on others. Anthony demonstrated adequate performance on tests of auditory attention on the NEPSY-II. On the TEA-Ch Anthony's performance was varied on tasks measuring sustained attention and switching his attention from one aspect of a task to another, but his selective attention was uncompromised. Performance on the CAS2 demonstrated poor performance on the Attention scale and consistency across subtests. Behavior rating scale data across parent and teacher ratings were significant for difficulties sustaining and shifting his attention.

Executive Function (EF)

Particular aspects of Anthony's EF was assessed using several performance measures. The Planning scale measured his ability to use strategies when solving problems, checking to see if the strategies are effective, modifying or changing his behavior or solutions when needed, and efficiently completing tasks. Anthony scored within the poor classification. The EF scale of the CAS2 was also well below average. These findings are consistent with observations, rating scale data, the reason for referral, and represent an ecologically valid picture of his EF. Anthony's EF challenges are represented by difficulty completing tasks correctly, staying focused enough to monitoring his progress, reacting impulsively, and not having a repertoire of ways to approach problems. Although the Planning scale of the KABC-II was average, it is this examiner's contention that the scale is not measuring the same Planning construct as the CAS2.

Memory

Developmentally, memory processes begin with procedural memory and build to semantic memory with long-term storage and retrieval with automaticity in strategy generation. Memory abilities can range from simple short-term tasks, such as remembering a phone number, to more complex tasks, such as taking in information from class and storing it for long-term use. Anthony demonstrated slight weaknesses in short-term memory, although his weaker performance was likely affected by decreased attention during memory tasks because of intrusive worrisome behavior and questions about his performance. Anthony showed strong abilities for long-term memory storage and retrieval. It was evident that Anthony excels in remembering and storing newly learned information, especially when taught explicitly and given the opportunity for practice.

Social-Emotional Functioning

Developmentally, we expect young children to form attachments with others, seek out relationships, and practice and explore emotional regulation. As children grow, the social emotional skills become more sophisticated to enjoying humor, demonstrating strong social skills, and tolerating ambiguity. Social-emotional rating scales were completed by three teachers in addition to a parent rating scale completed by Ms. M. It should be noted that Teacher 1 and Teacher 3 may have rated Anthony in an overly negative light. Additionally, Teacher 1's responses were inconsistent at times, suggesting that these ratings should be interpreted with caution.

Ms. M's parent responses indicated only two areas of some concern for Anthony: attention and hyperactivity. Per teacher reports, the area of externalizing problems was rated as being of the highest concern. All three teachers reported significant concerns in the areas of attention, hyperactivity, whereas concerns of anxiousness were considered "at risk." Teacher ratings also indicate that Anthony frequently acts in strange or unusual ways. This is consistent with teacher comments of Anthony acting silly and making off-task comments that do not make sense in some situations, meaning his responses are impulsive and irrelevant to whatever is asked or discussed in class. Other areas that showed slight concern were adaptability (adapting to changes in environment or routine), social skills, leadership, study skills, and functional communication. Considering these concerns in light of current observational data, it appears that Anthony's greatest social-emotional weakness are related to externalizing problems, specifically hyperactivity, attention, as evidenced by intrusive comments and questions; needing constant movement; and difficulty sustaining his attention to tasks. Some degree of anxiety is noted and judged to be related to his awareness of his struggles: Anthony strives to be a good student, but can be thrown off-track as he becomes upset when he is unsure of academic expectations, has difficulty keeping track of what he needs to do to complete tasks, or feels that he has made the same mistake repeatedly.

Social Cognition

On various measures of social cognition, which is how Anthony thinks and understands social interactions, concepts, and the perception of others, he demonstrated strong skills overall. Anthony showed the ability to successfully recognize affect and understand mood by examining facial expressions, remembering faces, and understanding the perspective of others within context and specific situations. These results indicate that there are no apparent problems with Anthony's ability to apply social knowledge within the school setting.

Academic Skills

Anthony's achievement levels in reading, writing, math, and listening comprehension were assessed and compared to a national sample of same-age peers and criterion for what children his age should be exposed to and have obtained with adequate mastery. Overall, Anthony performed solidly within the average range in the areas of reading, writing, and math. In reading, Anthony was able to decode new words, read words fluently, and comprehend what he had read similarly to his same-age peers. In the area of math, Anthony successfully solved age-appropriate computation and applied math problems. In the area of writing, Anthony showed the ability to adequately spell words and generally express his thoughts through writing with age-appropriate mechanics, grammar, and sentence structure. On a listening comprehension test, Anthony's score fell within the low range and was likely negatively influenced by his limited sustained attention during the test.

Adaptive Functioning

At Anthony's age, it would be expected that he is able to functionally communicate his wants and needs, participate in reciprocal conversation, socialize with other students, and seek out friendships and play with peers. Adaptive rating scales completed by Ms. M indicated that Anthony is functioning comparably to same-age peers in the areas of communication, daily living skills, and socialization. A rating scale completed by Anthony's general education teacher indicated some concerns in the areas of receptive/expressive language (moderately low), daily living skills at school (moderately low), interpersonal relationships and play and leisure time (low). Within these areas, the teacher reflected concerns consistent with previous teacher reports about Anthony's slight struggles listening to and following directions, initiating friendships and conversations with peers in appropriate ways, and playing and socializing with other students. These observations, however, seem to be related to him being a new student at this school rather than behavior that is a chronic problem. Overall, Anthony may benefit from accommodations that help him attend to and understand directions and possibly a social peer group that will help him make new friends and practice social skills and interactions.

Summary

Assessment results indicate that Anthony's cognitive strengths and weaknesses vary depending on the test used. The results of the KABC-II suggest good overall intelligence with the exception of a slight weakness in short-term memory that was likely affected by his lack of attention during testing. Results of the CAS2 indicate significant weaknesses on the Planning and Attention scales. Anthony's profile is what would be expected of a child diagnosed with attention-deficit/hyperactivity disorder combined type.

He has appropriate auditory, visual, and sensory motor skills. Anthony demonstrated generally age-appropriate receptive and expressive language skills overall, with mild weaknesses noted in language construction and sentence structure, which were likely related to Anthony's bilingual abilities. According to assessment results, teacher reports, and observational data, Anthony demonstrates difficulty regulating his attention and motor behaviors. Additionally, some of Anthony's problems with attention, self-control, and anxiety collectively contribute some of his difficulties with social and functional abilities, such as adjusting to changes in routine, accepting teacher criticism, and coping with mistakes made or not understanding work expectations.

Recommendations

The first step is to help Anthony understand the nature of his Attention problems (from Naglieri & Pickering, 2010):

1. Concepts such as Attention, resistance to distraction, and control of Attention
2. Recognition of how attention affects daily functioning
3. Recognition that the deficit can be overcome
4. Basic elements of the control program

Second, teachers and parents can help Anthony improve his motivation and persistence:

1. Promote success via small steps.
2. Ensure success at school and at home.
   a. Allow oral responses to tests.
   b. Circumvent reading whenever possible.
3. Teach rules for approaching tasks.
   a. Help Anthony to define tasks accurately.
   b. Assess Anthony's knowledge of problems.
   c. Encourage Anthony to consider all possible solutions.
   d. Teach Anthony to use a correct test strategy (Pressley & Woloshyn, 1995).
4. Discourage passivity and encourage independence.
   a. Provide only as much assistance as is needed.
   b. Reduce the use of teacher solutions only.
   c. Require Anthony to take responsibility for correcting his own work.
   d. Help Anthony to become more self-reliant.
5. Encourage Anthony to avoid the following:
   a. Excessive talking
   b. Working fast with little accuracy
   c. Giving up too easily
   d. Turning in sloppy disorganized papers

Third, teachers and parents should give Anthony specific problem-solving strategies.

1. Model and teach strategies that improve attention and concentration.
2. Help Anthony to recognize when he is under- or overattentive.

This instruction benefits students who have problems maintaining attention or who are overactive. These strategies may be particularly helpful for children who demonstrate low scores in Attention and children who show weaknesses in Attention along with problems with Planning. Because a student who has a Planning weakness may have a particularly difficult time monitoring and controlling his or her actions, these strategies may be useful to provide structure and help the student follow specific plans to increase his or her self-control and focus of attention.

To encourage positive self-control, Anthony can be directly taught to pay attention to and think about his behavior, followed by a sequential plan to determine his best options for responding given the context. Detailed information for this intervention can be found in Naglieri and Pickering (2010).

Additional Suggestions

- Anthony may benefit from participating in social groups that focus on appropriate conversational skills, recalling the events from a story, and staying on-topic.
- Consider social work services or counseling within the school to target anxiety and worrisome thoughts and behavior.
- Practice coping skills when faced with challenging tasks or provided with constructive criticism.
- Consider peer buddy group or "lunch bunch" group to practice social skills (i.e., initiating conversation, cooperative play) and help Anthony build friendships despite being a new student this school year.
- Provide preferential seating next to a model peer to whom Anthony can ask questions or watch to know exactly how to follow instructions.
- Provide written instructions simultaneously with visual instructions.
- Provide verbal reminders and checks for understanding.
- Provide a model or example of work expectations.
- Use peer buddies or a small group within classroom to enhance Anthony's understanding of material gone over and social cooperation.
- Provide a schedule on Anthony's desk to help with daily routines and expected activities.
- To help with negative self-statements or frustration, emphasize what Anthony does well and provide specific praise.
- Allow Anthony to reflect on his strengths and have him write down three things he did well at the end of each day; allow his mother to reinforce these strengths with positive feedback or rewards.
- Consider a classwide activity of providing compliments from peer to peer at the end of each day.

AUTISM

Autism spectrum disorder (ASD) is defined by diagnostic criteria that include deficits in social communication and social interaction and restricted, repetitive patterns of behavior, interests, or activities. ASD is now defined by the American Psychiatric Association (APA) (2013) and by the World Health Organization (WHO) (2014) as a disorder that includes other disorders that were previously considered separate. Initial signs and symptoms are typically apparent in the early developmental period; however, social deficits and behavioral patterns might not be recognized as symptoms of ASD until a child is unable to meet social, educational, or other important life-stage demands that are expected during school years. Functional limitations vary among individuals with ASD and might develop over time (Christensen et al., 2016).

Young children with autism have significant social-communication delays in symbolic play and joint attention. The ability of very young children to engage others and communicate socially using nonverbal cues such as pointing, smiling, or making eye contact is critical to social and language development. Studies show that children who engage their parent or caregiver in sharing communications, such as pointing to things of interest or directing another's attention to objects, learn language faster (Kasari, Gulsrud, Wong, Kwon, & Locke, 2010; Pickard & Ingersoll, 2015). These skills, which are examples of joint attention, are impaired in young children with autism.

A deficit in joint attention distinguishes children with autism from typically developing children as well as from children with intellectual disabilities (Mundy, Sigman, Ungerer, & Sherman, 1986). Furthermore, symbolic play, which is dependent on joint attention, is significantly associated with later social (Sigman et al., 1999); cognitive (Mundy, Gwaltney, & Henderson, 2010; Stanley & Konstantareas, 2007); and communication development (Kasari et al., 2010).

There are many behaviors that clinicians observe as signs of poor attention, such as lack of eye contact, not responding to his or her name being called, not smiling when engaging in play or when smiled at, not visually following objects or gestures when things are pointed to, and being overly focused visually on items, toys, or parts of toys without disengaging attention to play functionally with the object or sharing interest with another person.

The attention difficulties seen in children with ASD often look similar to those of children with ADHD. Although autism and ADHD are distinct disorders, individuals with these different diagnoses do share difficulties in listening, following instructions, organization, interrupting, social impairments, and especially self-regulation (Deprey & Ozonoff, 2009). Whereas individuals with ADHD and autism have attention problems, there is a marked difference in the nature of their ability to attend. Those with ADHD have problems attending and resisting distractions by external stimuli in contrast to individuals with autism, who have been described as having "difficulties in disengaging and shifting attention" (Klinger, O'Kelley, & Mussey, 2009, p. 214). The cognitive processing and behavioral differences regarding attention for these two groups were recently studied.

The suggestion that individuals with autism and ADHD have a cognitive difference in their ability to attend was the focus of a research study presented in the *Autism Spectrum Rating Scale Manual* (ASRS; Goldstein & Naglieri, 2010). The study provided scores on the ASRS and CAS for 92 children and adolescents. The results for the four PASS scores and the separate ASRS scales

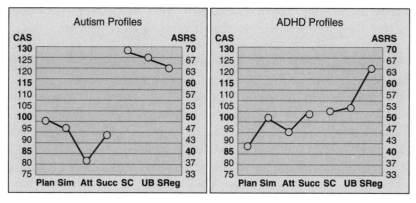

Figure 7.5 Different Profiles for Those With Autism and ADHD

of Social/Communication (SC), Unusual Behaviors (UB), and Self-Regulation (SR) are summarized in Figure 7.5 for individuals with autism and for those with ADHD (data from the *ASRS Manual* and Chapter 1 of this text). The mean scores for the CAS Planning, Simultaneous, and Successive scales were each in the average classification of ability, but this sample of individuals with autism earned a low score on the Attention scale. This supports the statement by Klinger et al. (2009) that there is a cognitive component to autism that is described as difficulties in disengaging and shifting attention. This is in contrast to those with ADHD, who have a self-regulation problem as noted by Barkley (1997). These findings suggest that when making a differential diagnosis, the cognitive and behavioral aspects of ADHD and autism can be better understood by obtaining information from these two measures.

The Case of Betty

Betty is a 5-year-old female who previously received early intervention services for speech and language and continued to receive services as a preschooler until the end of the current school year. She is very difficult to understand and uses gibberish and some gesturing to communicate her wants. Betty's mother requested an evaluation to assist in her educational planning because she will be attending kindergarten at a local private school in the coming academic year.

According to Betty's mother, Betty was diagnosed with autism spectrum disorder at age 3. She was described as "stubborn, active, and curious about many things" but prefers playing with technology, such as an iPad or her parent's cell phone. Although she has a variety of toys, she shows little interest in these in favor of technology. Betty occasionally wiggles her fingers in front of her face and stares at them. Her eye contact tends to be variable and when she does look at you she often does so by "looking out the side of her eyes." When attempts are made to introduce other items, toys, or people, she either shows disinterest or yells in protest. She will follow one-step directions that are already within her repertoire of routine activities. Betty's ability to follow two-step directions is emerging but reported as inconsistently executed. Her parents have made several attempts to expose her to a variety of social interactions with other children outside of the home, such as by going to the playground or having play dates with another child from her preschool. Betty shows marginal interest in playing with others, sharing toys, or being interested in what others are doing.

During Betty's evaluation she did not respond to her name. When given a variety of objects or toys, she did not imitate the function of objects. She did not point to objects named that had been placed in front of her or pictured in a book. She did look toward the items but did so by moving her head in one direction and then by moving her eyes. Betty made spontaneous and often unintelligible utterances when she heard the sound of the fire truck passing down the street or heard a sudden noise in the environment. Betty followed simple directions given to her when supplemented with gestures. Although she preferred to wander around the room for a long time, she was conditioned to sit at a table and work with the examiner using a variety of "first this, then that" methods. For example, the brief use of a cell phone was permitted as a reinforcement for appropriate behavior. This method allowed her to remain on task and complete the test items presented to her.

Betty's mother and preschool teacher were given rating scales to complete, and Betty was given the CAS2 (see Table 7.12). Consistent with her existing diagnosis, the behavior rating scales indicate that Betty has behavioral characteristics that are similar to the behaviors of children diagnosed with autism spectrum disorder and symptoms directly related to the *DSM-5* diagnostic criteria for ASD. Overall Betty has difficulty using appropriate verbal and nonverbal communication for social contact, engages in unusual behaviors, has difficulty relating to children, has difficulty relating to adults, has difficulty providing appropriate emotional responses to people in social situations, uses language in an atypical manner, engages in stereotypical behaviors, has difficulty tolerating changes in routine, overreacts to sensory stimulation, and has problems with inattention. Behaviors related to difficulties with peer socialization, adult socialization, and social-emotional reciprocity were rated as very elevated. The Attention/Self-regulation scale was slightly elevated.

Table 7.12 PASS Composite Index Scores

Scale	PLAN	SIM	ATT	SUC
PASS Composite Index scores	94	100	73	82
Percentile rank	34	50	4	12

This last finding is of interest for several of reasons. First, many of the difficulties involve sustained or shifting attention. Second, the in-session observations are consistent with the reported concerns. Last, the willingness and capacity to successfully engage in activities that develop and maintain relationships with other children or adults and the ability to provide an appropriate emotional response to another person in a social situation *all* require attention. The fact is that Betty's attention deficit may be more of a problem than what was picked up on behavior ratings is suggested by her CAS2 results.

Betty attained CAS2 scores that reflect good Planning and Simultaneous processing. This finding suggests she can size up a novel task and figure out how to complete it as subtle changes in demand characteristics change. Additionally, she shows good ability to tackle visual-spatial and verbal-spatial aspects of a task that demand understanding patterns and relationships (see Table 7.13).

Betty's CAS2 results demonstrate a significant neurocognitive processing weakness in Attention, suggesting difficulties with modulating different aspects of her Attention resources. This is a weakness in relation to her own performance and in relation to her same-age peers in the standardization group. Her poor Attention is consistent with many of the behavioral observations made by her mother, behaviors noted on parent and teacher ratings and consistent with the data presented by Goldstein and Naglieri (2010). Betty's Successive processing, although not a significant weakness, is a normative weakness and is below average. Her performance suggests she has some difficulty keeping information in order, such as remembering the sequence of sounds, words, ideas, and actions

Table 7.13 PASS Scale Comparisons

	Index Score	*d* value	Sig NS	Strength/Weakness	% in sample
Planning	94	6.7	NS		45.9
Simultaneous	100	12.7	Sig		20.5
Attention	73	−14.3	Sig	W	13.7
Successive	82	−5.3	NS		66.0
PASS mean	87.3				

exactly in the order in which presented. Betty's performance on the Word Series and Sentence Repetition subtest of the CAS2 would certainly reflect this difficulty and certainly adds to understanding why she has difficulty following multiple-step directions and articulating sounds in speech.

Comments on This Case

One of the key goals in any assessment is to obtain a comprehensive understanding of a person. In order to achieve that goal, we include many data-gathering procedures. The case of Betty illustrates how information from behavioral and cognitive measures helps us go beyond the diagnostic criteria. Knowing that a student has difficulty in shifting attention and in working with information in a sequence provides valuable insight to parents and teachers as well as direction for the kinds of interventions that are needed. For example, because Betty is good at seeing the big picture (Simultaneous processing) and in using strategies (Planning), these strengths can be leveraged to help her manage tasks that demand sequencing and shifting of attention. Thus, a clearer understanding of a person's cognitive and behavioral attributes is the first step in the process of intervention planning.

TRAUMATIC BRAIN INJURY

Traumatic brain injury (TBI) is an acquired injury resulting from sudden trauma causing damage to the brain (Hayden, Jandial, Duenas, Mahajan, & Levy, 2007; McGinley, Master, & Zonfrillo, 2015). Although several diagnostic systems exist (e.g., ICD-10; American Academy of Neurology), the US Department of Defense and Department of Veterans Affairs (2010) provide one of the most comprehensive and updated criteria for classification purposes associated with such injuries. Using this system TBIs are classified as mild, moderate, or severe depending on the Glasgow Coma Scale (GCS) score, length of loss of consciousness (LOC), and length of posttraumatic amnesia (PTA). Traumatic brain injuries can also be classified as closed or open. In general, a closed head injury is a trauma in which the brain is injured as a result of a blow to the head or a sudden, violent motion that causes the brain to knock against the skull. Closed-head injury accounts for the majority of child TBI instances (Catroppa, Anderson, Beauchamp, & Yeates, 2016).

Among children and adolescents, approximately one in four TBI incidents in those under the age of 15 is the result of unintentional blunt-force trauma. More than half of TBIs among children up to the age of 14 were caused by falls (CDC National Center for Injury Prevention and Control, 2015). In recent years, much attention has been given to sports-related TBI (Halstead & Walter, 2010).

Concussions are frequent causes of TBI in older children, teenagers, and young adults. The rate of emergency visits for sports- or recreation-related injuries with a diagnosis of TBI rose by 57% among those 19 years of age or younger (CDC, 2011, as cited in CDC National Center for Injury Prevention and Control, 2015). However, it is important to note that many people who experience a concussion might not seek medical attention.

The *DSM-5* (APA, 2013) includes TBI under the neurocognitive disorders (NCDs) classification. NCDs include a range of cognitive difficulties and accompanying impact on academic, social, or occupational functioning. The diagnostic criteria for any of the NCDs are all based on key cognitive domains along with defined guidelines for clinical thresholds. Those key cognitive areas that are affected and their descriptions include the following:

Attention—Deficits in sustained attention, divided attention, selective attention, and speed of cognitive processing

Executive function—Deficits in executive function, also frequently identified as executive dysfunction, which may include difficulties with planning, problem-solving, decision making, error correction, inhibition, and cognitive flexibility

Learning and memory—Learning and memory deficits ranging from difficulty with implicit and immediate memory to very-long-term memory impairment for autobiographical information

Language—Language deficits including expressive and receptive communication difficulties; deficits may include various aphasias, such as word-finding problems, lack of fluency, and improper use of grammar and syntax

Perceptual-motor—Any difficulty in sensory perception or sensory processing that may be included under the realm of a perceptual-motor deficit; problems with visual perception, inability to initiate or complete motor responses (visuo-construction and apraxias), and inability to name or recognize objects (agnoses)

Social cognition—Difficulties in social cognition are one of the newer areas of understanding. Social cognition includes the ability to recognize emotions properly and theory of mind, which is the ability to consider another person's mental state or point of view.

By the *DSM-5* definition, NCDs because of TBI involve impairment to at least one of the six key cognitive domains. The more cognitive impairments are typically part of the key domains of attention, executive functioning, learning and memory, and language. Children with cognitive impairments because of TBI may have difficulty with multitasking (or shifting cognitive sets), planning and organizing their daily schedules and homework, or retaining and recalling information for their math test. Children with deficits in the language domain may complain of difficulty with reading, comprehension, solving math story problems, or spelling. Some students identified by teachers as "lazy" or "not living up to her potential" might have suffered a mild concussion falling off the swing set or see-saw in preschool or kindergarten.

Research has demonstrated that children with milder injuries are likely to recover well, with few residual problems. With increasing severity, recovery is less complete. Those with severe injury are at risk for ongoing difficulties across a range of areas, such as motor dysfunction, communication difficulties, poor attention and information processing, reduced memory, executive dysfunction, and social and emotional disorders (Hessen, Nestvold, & Anderson, 2007; Jaffe, Polissar, Fay, & Liao, 1995; Yeates, Swift, Taylor, Wade, et al., 2004). Additionally, functional outcomes are affected with evidence of low academic achievement, reduced vocational opportunities, and poor adaptive skills.

Some researchers have identified patterns in IQ scores among children with TBI. For example, processing speed and perceptual organization from the WISC-III tend to be the most sensitive to TBI at the acute and long-term assessment levels (Ewing-Cobbs, Barnes, & Fletcher, 2003). Only children with severe TBI have had Full Scale scores that were significantly lower than those with mild TBI or typical controls (Catroppa & Anderson, 2007). Donders and Janke (2008) reported low WISC-IV processing speed index scores for children with mild to severe TBI but that the WISC-IV should be supplemented with other measures. Children with moderate to severe TBI performed poorly on all of the WISC-V scales (Wechsler, 2014), indicating general cognitive difficulties with only slight variation across the five scales.

Researchers have found that children with TBI suffer from two important cognitive limitations. First is an impairment in attention, which is one of the most common effects of TBI. This is especially problematic in cases of severe head injury in which the impairment may last for at least 10 years (Draper & Ponsford, 2008). Second, significant executive dysfunction is common, especially in the first year after injury, with greater dysfunction reported for children with more severe TBI (Sesma, Slomine, Ding, & McCarthy, 2008). These findings are consistent with the results for the first edition of the CAS. Gutentag, Naglieri, and Yeates (1998) studied children who had sustained a TBI with closed head injuries of moderate to severe magnitude, as defined by the number of days of impaired consciousness following their injuries. Each TBI child was matched to a control subject selected from the CAS standardization sample based on age, gender, race, and geographic region. The results of the study showed that the deficits that children with TBI displayed in Planning and Attention were detected with the CAS. Similarly, McCrea (2007) described the results of the CAS for a case study involving significant head injury. A year and a half after the TBI, frontal executive dysfunction (low Planning and Attention) were found. The results suggest that those with TBI will likely have significant deficits in Planning and Attention and that these deficits are not likely detected nor are they measured with traditional measures ability.

The Case of Michael

The following report is an abbreviated version of a more extensive report for purpose of illustrating the use of the CAS2. Extensive information was also omitted in order to protect the identity of the child and family, but sufficient detail is provided regarding the reason for referral assessment procedures and results to illustrate the usefulness of the CAS2 as part of larger assessment of a student having suffered repeated concussions yet medically cleared over a period of 15 months.

Michael is a 10-year-old male who had repeated concussions when he was 8 years old. He suffered his first injury on his eighth birthday when he fell from his skateboard. The second incident was 6 months later when he was hit with a baseball during a Little League game. Two months after he fell from a tree house in his back yard from a height of approximately 10 to 12 feet. Michael's mother Mrs. C indicated that he had lost consciousness for 5 to 10 minutes on the first injury but did not lose consciousness on the following occasions. She stated that he was quite "dazed and disoriented" for the second incident and did have a couple of episodes of vomiting. There was no report of headaches, dizziness, fatigue, and loss of consciousness or vomiting for the most recent episode. Michael's mother indicated that she had taken him to the hospital for the first and the second injuries. Each time he was given a physical exam, screened neurologically, and discharged the same afternoon. For both incidences he suffered from fatigue, sporadic headaches, and some vomiting. The vomiting subsided the same day of injury but the fatigue and headaches persisted for several weeks. She did not take him for a medical examination on the third occasion as he "got up right away and seemed okay."

Michael has struggled academically since his injuries. His teachers reported difficulties with sustained attention, initiation, persistence, and fatigue. Michael was able to read, spell, and write short sentences but struggled with discerning essential from nonessential details in math word problems. His teachers described him as tiring easily, having difficulty concentrating, not completing work on a timely basis, and having particular difficulty with math calculation and math word problems. His teachers have been particularly concerned because previous to his injuries Michael had been a good student and did not have academic or behavioral issues. Michael's mother indicated that at home he forgets to do his chores, he misplaces his personal belongings, homework completion takes twice as long as it previously did, and he plays fewer video games than he used to because the games are harder for him to master and he does not enjoy playing them as much. After Michael's fist accident his mother requested an evaluation because she was concerned of the possibility that, although medically cleared, Michael might have some cognitive impairment that would affect his learning. As a consequence of the evaluation Michael was provided with a 504 plan with accommodations for his fatigue, attention difficulties, and struggles in math.

Michael's difficulties in math persisted into the fifth grade and worsened as the demands of the curriculum increased. There were continued concerns about Michael's attention and difficulty getting work completed. Michael had been treated with a low-dose stimulant medication for 8 months, and he had taken his medication the morning of this evaluation. The medication has helped Michael by increasing his level of alertness throughout the morning and becoming somewhat less fatigued. The results of the CAS2 from immediately after his last injury and approximately 18 months later are revealing.

Evaluation results for Michael at ages 8 and 10 show a marked change in the relationships among the PASS scores (see Figures 7.6 and 7.7). At age 8 there was little variability among the PASS scores; all were low and only ranged from 72 to 82. There were no cognitive strengths or weaknesses relative to his overall PASS average of 76.8. By contrast, at age 10 there was a significant strength in Simultaneous and a significant weakness in Planning with a low score in Attention that was not significantly lower than his average PASS score of 89.5 but is considerably below the average range. The current PASS profile is consistent with his academic achievement test scores.

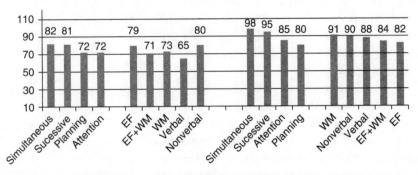

Figure 7.6 Evaluation Results for Michael at Ages 8 and 10

Michael's scores on several measures of academic skills form a pattern that is consistent with his weaknesses in Planning (and poor score in Attention) and strength in Simultaneous (and good score on Successive), as seen in Figure 7.6. His strength in Simultaneous processing is consistent with his scores on Letter and Word Recognition (he uses a Simultaneous–whole word approach), and he can decode using good Successive processing when necessary, as shown on the Spelling and the Nonsense Word Decoding subtests. His cognitive weakness in Planning underlies his low scores in Math Calculation, Reading Comprehension, and Math Applications. When the Planning weakness is combined with poor Attention the result is considerable problems in Michael's ability to acquire information to the extent needed to be fluent. He can perform well when using Simultaneous and Successive processing, but he needs ample time to work (very hard) to be successful.

Discussion of Results

The case of Michael illustrates how the PASS scores from the CAS2 can be used to assess the possible effects of TBI across a 2-year interval and relate these scores to academic achievement scores. Although there was some improvement in Michael's Planning and Attention scores from one administration to the other, these scales are quite weak and are consistent with the behaviors noted by his teacher and parent. These results and his CAS2 EF score of 82 indicate that he

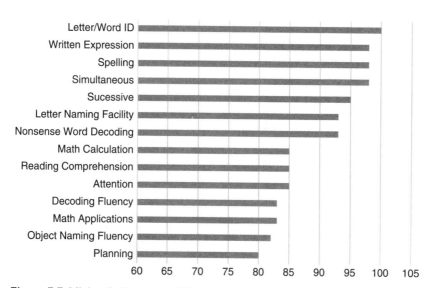

Figure 7.7 Michael's Neurocognitive and Academic Achievement Results at Age 10

is quite limited in what can also be described as EF. Michael's Simultaneous and Successive processing have also improved and are now well within the average range. This suggests adequate recovery of neurocognitive functions that relate to how Michael takes in, manages, and organizes information.

GIFTED AND TALENTED STUDENTS

The identification of gifted and talented students has its controversies involving definitions, criteria for eligibility, and educational programming, similar to other types of special populations who receive appropriate services in the schools (Naglieri, 2008a). This is mostly related to the fact that there is no universally accepted definition of gifted and talented, which explains why nearly every state in the United States has its own definition. Of course state and federal guidelines provide direction to school administrators who wish to identify and educate gifted and talented students, as does the National Association for Gifted Children (NAGC), which provides the following definition:

> Gifted individuals are those who demonstrate outstanding levels of aptitude (defined as an exceptional ability to reason and learn) or competence (documented performance or achievement in top 10% or rarer) in one or more domains. Domains include any structured area of activity with its own symbol system (e.g., mathematics, music, language) and/or set of sensorimotor skills (e.g., painting, dance, sports). (NAGC, 2010) http://www.nagc.org/resources-publications/resources/definitions-giftedness

The Federal Definition of Gifted and Talented included in the No Child Left Behind Act reads:

> The term "gifted and talented," when used with respect to students, children, or youth, means students, children, or youth who give evidence of high achievement capability in such areas as intellectual, creative, artistic, or leadership capacity, or in specific academic fields, and who need services or activities not ordinarily provided by the school in order to fully develop those capabilities. (No Child Left Behind Act, P.L. 107-110 (Title IX, Part A, Definition 22) (2002); 20 USC 7801(22) (2004))

These definitions are also similar to the most widely accepted views presented by Gagné and Renzulli. Gagné (1985) proposed a definition with a clear distinction between giftedness and talent. In his view giftedness refers to natural abilities (called *aptitudes* or *gifts*) in at least one aspect of ability to an extent that a student is among the top 10% of his or her peer group. Talent indicates the superior mastery of knowledge and skills, also in the upper 10% of age peers. His approach includes five aptitude domains: intellectual, creative, socio-affective, sensorimotor, and others such as extrasensory perception. This view places the origin of giftedness in a biological context and the talent in an environmental one.

Renzulli's (1978) definition includes the gifted and talented perspective but adds other attributes. He suggests that gifted behavior occurs when there is an interaction among three basic clusters of human traits. This includes above-average general or specific abilities, high levels of task commitment (e.g., motivation), and high levels of creativity. Gifted and talented students possess or are capable of developing this group of traits and applying them to any potentially useful area of performance.

What is apparent in all these definitions is the view that gifted and talented students are those who have a natural ability to perform above the 89th percentile or those who have the *potential* to perform at such a high level. Given that the definition of gifted is based on finding high-ability students, the critical question becomes, "using which IQ test?" Traditional IQ tests are a mixture of ability (those sections that do not require knowledge) and talents (those sections that do require knowledge). Of course, the underlying purpose of this text is to evaluate ability more exactly, which means that the knowledge-based questions in traditional IQ tests should be avoided because they are so highly related to educational opportunity.

Naglieri, Brulles, and Lansdowne (2008) proposed that gifted students with very high ability could be identified with tests that do not include verbal and quantitative measures, whereas talented students could be identified by measures of academic achievement. This means that students who are gifted (high in ability) and not *currently* achieving at high levels in school would not be selected if eligibility demanded "academic giftedness" as described by Giessman, Gambrell, and Stebbins (2013, p. 108). We propose that talented students should receive the appropriate level of education in a gifted program. Those gifted students who show potential to achieve at a very high level should also be provided the appropriate level of education in a gifted program.

The conceptualization of gifted and talented has important implications for professionals who are responsible for identifying *all* gifted students, especially diverse populations who have been traditionally underrepresented (Naglieri et al., 2008). Although achieving equitable representation of Black and Hispanic students in gifted education programs is a multidimensional issue (Castellano & Frasier, 2010; Ford, 2010, 2013; Frasier, Garcia, & Passow, 1995), Ford (2013) and Naglieri and Ford (2003) state that traditional ability tests with their verbal and quantitative content are the main obstacle to inclusion of Black and Hispanic students in gifted programs. How much of a problem does this present?

Representation by Race and Ethnicity

Black and Hispanic students have been and remain considerably underrepresented in gifted education (Baldwin, 2004; Castellano & Frasier, 2010; Ford, 2013; Ford, Grantham, & Whiting, 2008; Frasier et al., 1995; Office for Civil Rights (OCR), 2004, 2006, 2009, 2011, 2012). According to the OCR Data Collection in 2012, Black students were underrepresented by 50% in gifted education and Hispanic students by 40%. Every year of data collected between 2004 and 2012 indicate that Black students are the most underrepresented racial group, followed by Hispanic students. How many students do these numbers represent?

According to the National Center for Educational Statistics (http://nces.ed .gov/fastfacts/display.asp?id=3), there were approximately 50.1 million public school students entering prekindergarten through grade 12 in fall 2015. White students accounted for 24.7 million. The remaining 25.4 million were composed of 7.7 million Black students, 13.1 million Hispanic students, 2.6 million Asian/Pacific Islander students, 0.5 million American Indian/Alaska Native students, and 1.5 million students of two or more races. These numbers allow for the calculation of the numbers of Black and Hispanic students who could have been identified as gifted if the top 8% were selected (92nd percentile). The calculations provided in Rapid Reference 7.5 show that nearly three-quarters of a million students of color in schools during the 2015–2016 academic year could have been identified as gifted and were not.

The need to identify and serve more Hispanic and Black students for gifted programming is not just an important issue for those of us who work within the educational environment; it is a critical social justice issue that has considerable implications for our country. That is, when an increasingly large percentage of our school population (namely, Black and Hispanic students) is not identified as gifted and those students are in need of intellectual and academic challenge, our schools lose nationally and internationally. The United States cannot afford to exclude these students, especially because they represent more than half of our public school population (Domenech, Sherman, & Brown, 2016).

≡ Rapid Reference 7.5

Number and Percentage of Students in US Public Schools Grades K–12 in 2015

Race/Ethnicity	% in US	N	8% G and T	N Missed
White	49	24,700,000	1,976,000	
Black	15	7,700,000	616,000	308,000
Hispanic	26	13,100,000	1,048,000	419,200
Other	9	4,600,000	368,000	
Total	100	50,100,000	4,008,000	727,200

Note: N Missed is based on 50% of Black and 40% of Hispanics. G and T is *gifted and talented*.

What Are the Barriers to Identification?

There is ample evidence that gifted Black and Hispanic students can be identified using a test that does not include verbal and quantitative content (i.e., the Naglieri Nonverbal Ability Test (NNAT/NNAT2/NNAT3; Naglieri, 1997, 2008b, 2016b). For example, Naglieri and Ronning (2000) found small differences in mean NNAT scores between White–African American, White-Hispanic, and White-Asian groups matched on geographic region, socioeconomic status, ethnicity, and public/private school ($N = 22,620$). Naglieri and Ford (2003) reported similar rates of identification as gifted across these groups using the NNAT. Naglieri, Booth, and Winsler (2004) found that the NNAT mean score for Hispanic children with limited English proficiency was very similar to the mean for Hispanic children who were proficient in English skills. However, significant differences were found between these groups on measures of vocabulary, reading comprehension, and listening comprehension. The implication of that study was that language-based tests pose an obstacle to gifted placement for students with limited English language skills.

The use of language-based measures of ability was the focus of a recent trial. The case of *McFadden v. Board of Education for Illinois School District U-46* (2013; 984 F.Supp.2d 882) involved Hispanic parents' concerns that their students were significantly underrepresented in gifted education classes. Over 40% of the students in the Elgin School District (U-46) were Hispanic, but only 2% of the students in the district's mainstream elementary school gifted program were Hispanic. The district required students who were in ELL programs to obtain high scores on a measure of ability that demands knowledge of English and quantitative skills (e.g., the CogAT6; Lohman & Hagen, 2001) even if they had a very high score on a nonverbal measure of ability (the NNAT2). The Court ruled that the use of tests that demanded knowledge of English contributed to the underrepresentation of Hispanic students in gifted education. Judge Gettleman ruled that

> gifted children for whom English is a second language would likely score lower on a [verbal] test than the nonverbal, culturally neutral Naglieri Nonverbal Ability Test, which plaintiffs' expert testified identified gifted students without a bias towards those students with higher English verbal skills. (p. 24)

This case illustrates that although including a nonverbal test alone will not solve the problem of underrepresentation, it could, if used correctly, increase access for Hispanic students as well as Black students (Ford, 2013).

Implications for Use of CAS2 and CAS2: Brief

There are two important reasons why the CAS2 and the CAS2: Brief can be used for identification of gifted students. First, in other sections of this book we have shown that these two measures are very useful for fair assessment of diverse groups of students. That is, the CAS2 and CAS2: Brief yield small differences across race and ethnicity as shown in the tests' manuals and summarized by Naglieri (2015). In addition, because the content of CAS2 and CAS2: Brief is knowledge reduced and the administration formats allow for instructions to be explained in any language, we have seen that PASS tests work well across languages and countries (see Naglieri, Taddei, & Williams, 2013; Otero, Gonzales, & Naglieri, 2012). For these reasons, when individual assessment for identification of gifted students is being conducted we recommend that the CAS2 or CAS2: Brief be used so that a more equitable approach to eligibility determination may be obtained. By measuring neurocognitive abilities without the emphasis on language and knowledge, many of the 727,000 students currently in public schools today would be considered eligible for gifted services.

INTELLECTUAL DISABILITY

There are several definitions of intellectual disability used in the field of psychology and medicine. All share the requirement that cognitive ability is significantly below average and there are concomitant deficits in adaptive behaviors. According to the American Association of Intellectual and Developmental Disabilities (AAIDD), intellectual disability (ID) is a disability characterized by significant limitations in intellectual functioning and adaptive behavior, which covers many everyday social and practical skills. This disability originates before the age of 18 (Schalock et al., 2010). Generally, according to AAIDD (2010), test scores of cognitive ability below 70 or as high as 75 indicate a limitation in intellectual functioning. Persons with intellectual disabilities also have limitations in adaptive behavior—the collection of conceptual, social, and practical skills that are learned and performed in everyday life.

According to the *DSM-5* (APA, 2013), ID is defined as a disorder with onset during the developmental period that includes intellectual and adaptive functioning deficits in conceptual, social, and practical domains. A diagnosis of intellectual developmental disorder requires that three criteria be met (see Rapid Reference 7.6).

≡ Rapid Reference 7.6

1. Deficits in intellectual functions confirmed by clinical assessment and individualized, standardized testing (functions such as reasoning, problem-solving, abstract thinking, academic learning, learning from experienced)
2. Marked deficits in adaptive functioning that lead to inability to meet developmental and sociocultural standards for personal independence and social responsibility (e.g., communication, social participation, independent living)
3. Onset of intellectual and adaptive deficits during the developmental period (childhood and adolescence; many consider 18 years of age the cutoff point, although not specified in the *DSM-5*)

The *DSM-5* is meant to parallel the WHO's international classification of diseases (ICD), and though the current edition of the ICD uses the term *intellectual disability*, the next version of ICD will use the term *intellectual developmental disorder*. This is why the *DSM-5* uses the current term *intellectual disability* with the future term (*intellectual developmental disorder*) in parentheses. Intellectual disability is classified on the basis of the severity of intellectual impairment, but this classification is no longer dependent on an IQ score in the *DSM-5*. Instead, the specifiers related to mild, moderate, severe, and profound refer to level of intensity of services required because of adaptive functioning deficits.

Intellectual disability, as defined by the IDEA, is "significantly sub average general intellectual functioning, existing concurrently with deficits in adaptive behavior and manifested during the developmental period, that adversely affects a child's educational performance." There are two key components within this definition: a student's IQ and his or her capability to function independently, usually referred to as functional impairment or adaptive behavior (Regulations: Part 300 / A / 300.8 / c / 6).

There are other disorders, such as autism spectrum disorder, that present with symptoms similar to ID or that may co-occur with ID. Historically there have been large numbers of individuals with ASD who also have comorbid ID. Some may not have intellectual impairments but continue to have significant deficits in social pragmatic communication (Brue & Wilmshurst, 2016). However, many children with ID are socially engaging. Their social difficulties are mostly because of immaturity and innocence. The *DSM-5* cautions that IQ scores for children with ASD may be lowered because of problems with social communication or behavioral issues rather than intellectual deficits (APA, 2013, p. 40). Thus, differentiating between the ID and ASD is of importance in clinical practice. As we have shown in this chapter and elsewhere, children diagnosed with ASD have distinct PASS profiles, and although they may present as if they are intellectually disabled, they are not. This finding may enable a clinician to separate any diagnostic conundrum regarding diagnostic conclusions.

There are advantages of using the PASS theory when evaluating a person for ID. First, it provides assessment that requires minimal acquired knowledge. This ensures that the individual will not fail the test for lack of facts typically obtained from school (e.g., vocabulary, arithmetic, and general information). This issue was studied by Naglieri and Rojahn (2001), who found that Wechsler Full Scale IQ scores underestimated in comparison to CAS2 Full Scale standard scores for African American children with mental retardation. Second, it is especially important that Planning and Attention are measured because, as suggested by Das, Naglieri, and Kirby (1994), Planning is related to some aspects of adaptive functioning. This has resulted in cases in which children earn low IQs and experience academic failure but do function adequately outside of school. From the PASS perspective, that means children with low achievement and perhaps low Simultaneous processing but adequate Planning and Attention can do poorly academically but well out of school.

The Case of Jenny

Jenny's academic record in kindergarten, first, and the start of second grade indicated she was not grasping basic concepts, was significantly behind peers in basic reading and math, had difficulty following multistep directions, and needed directions and instruction repeated to her. There were no behavior problems noted. Her first-grade teacher offered extra support in class and after school in order to help Jenny along; she also received Title I instruction and speech and language services two to three times a week depending on staff availability. At the start of second grade she was referred by the student support team for comprehensive evaluation. She was found eligible for special education services under the ID category and was placed in a modified learning program classroom. Results of intelligence testing and adaptive behavior scales are shown in Table 7.14.

At the time of the previous evaluation the data seem to support placement in special education. However, some of Jenny's adaptive behaviors appear to be considerably better developed than her cognitive abilities. Furthermore, school records suggest that the team did not consider her particular immigration history, previous birth history, or educational, cultural, or language factors that might have had impact on any of these initial results.

By fourth grade, Jenny showed notable improvements in vocabulary, language structure, and usage. Her classroom teacher noted that although she was 2 years behind in reading, she can read, does basic math calculations, and can solve short math word problems. She could write sentences in response to pictures and write a three-sentence paragraph of something of interest to her with variable attention to

Table 7.14 Stanford-Binet Intelligence Scales, Fifth Edition (SB-V) and Vineland II Adaptive Behaviors Scales

Stanford-Binet Intelligence Scales, Fifth Edition (SB-V)	Score	Classification
Full Scale	48	Delayed
Nonverbal IQ	66	Below average
Verbal IQ	49	Below average
Fluid Reasoning	65	Below average
Knowledge	50	Delayed
Quantitative Reasoning	68	Below average
Visual Spatial	58	Delayed
Working Memory	45	Delayed

Vineland II Adaptive Behaviors Scales	Teacher 1	Teacher 2
Domain	**Score**	**Score**
Communication	65	67
Daily Living	70	75
Socialization	78	76
Composite Score	72	75

proper mechanics of writing. She had poor penmanship, but no other fine or gross motor concerns were noted. Jenny was described as having difficulty initiating tasks and as appearing unmotivated. She did, however, have adequate personal hygiene, kept her belongings organized, and typically was liked by other students. Perhaps the most revealing comment made by Jenny's teacher was that she felt Jenny was perhaps at a higher skill level than her peers.

Upon reevaluation, Jenny's test results using the CAS2 showed her cognitive abilities were not consistent with her current special educational programming placement. She demonstrated average Simultaneous processing score of 92, with slightly lower scores on Planning (83) and Attention (81). Her Successive processing score was very low (64). The Full Scale score in a case like this should be considered an imperfect reflection of her abilities because it is an aggregate of very different scores. Her adaptive behavior scores (see Table 7.15) are more in line with her PASS neurocognitive abilities and suggest overall higher functioning in communication and socialization domains compared to previous ratings, a likely result of the supports she had received since her last evaluation.

This case illustrates several important points. First, the use of tests of cognitive ability that have verbal and quantitative test questions really test knowledge more than ability, especially for a child with a background such as Jenny. This is potentially discriminatory and not consistent with conducting fair assessments. Second, based on these results the team realized, as suspected by the classroom teacher, that Jenny has greater skills than other children in her current classroom and therefore was in a more restrictive environment than was warranted. Last, given her PASS profile it is likely that Jenny will continue to improve in some areas but also have academic struggles. Measuring PASS not only minimized the impact of lack of cultural and academic experiences but also it provided a pattern of results that are informative for instructional interventions. In Jenny's case her stronger Simultaneous processing ability can be leveraged to suggest a variety of interventions to the teacher to address reading, math, and writing.

Table 7.15 Vineland Adaptive Behavior Scale II

Standard Scores	Parent	Teacher
Communication	82	85
Daily Living Skills	79	82
Socialization	83	84
Adaptive Behavior Composite	78	83

From the book *Helping Children Learn* (Naglieri & Pickering, 2010), interventions such as the following can be suggested:

- Summarization Strategy for Reading Comprehension
- Word Families for Reading/Decoding
- Word Sorts for Improving Spelling
- Teaching Vocabulary Using Visual Cues
- Cuisenaire Rods and Math

The Case of Adolfo

Adolfo is a Hispanic fourth grader and has a history of attention difficulties. He has been receiving several types of support in reading and math. He is an English language learner who can converse in English and Spanish and whose parents speak only Spanish. He speaks Spanish at home and mostly English at school. The results of Adolfo's yearly language proficiency testing indicate he is still developing cognitive-academic English language skills His teacher describes him as a hard worker, likes to try new things, and enjoys volunteering for different classroom chores and activities within the school building. He enjoys being in school and is happy, inquisitive, and a hard worker. Based on district-wide testing, Adolfo's teacher indicated his overall reading skills are below grade level. Reading Comprehension and Fluency are below the 10th percentile. His math calculation skills are judged as within average limits but math reasoning is at the 8th percentile. Socially, he is described as outgoing, well-liked, and as having many friends in and out of school. He plays on a soccer team as a goalie. His coach placed him in this position because he had difficulty following strategic directions given to him when he played other positions on the field.

Adolfo was described as having difficulty following all that is said in a conversation, often having difficulty keeping up with classroom lectures, and looking as if he does not understand when given lengthy directions. Difficulties on math reasoning tasks were reported as stemming from his difficulty keeping all elements of the word problem in memory in order to decide how to go about solving the problem. His basic reading skills, although weak, have been slowly improving. Reading comprehension continues to be an area of significant difficulty for Adolfo.

Adolfo's teacher has attempted to assist him in math and reading by giving tasks that are shorter in length, of lower difficulty level, and fewer in number. He also receives small-group instruction for 15 to 20 minutes a day from a classroom aid. Adolfo told the school psychologist that he enjoys the extra attention but gets frustrated when he sees others getting all their work done while he sees himself as just starting. He typically has to take work home to complete and never is able to complete it entirely. He has an older brother who helps him with his work but not consistently. Both his parents have very limited educational experience, work many hours, and are not home to provide further support. Adolfo has been showing signs of becoming anxious about his performance in school. He has begun to have somatic complaints, and as of late, he looks for approval while working on reading and math tasks. Although he does not refuse to engage in schoolwork, he has been seen to procrastinate starting a task, be more vigilant of the clock for lunch and recess periods, and more distractible than usual.

Previous IQ testing when Adolfo was a third grader by a monolingual school psychologist indicated very low Verbal Comprehension (63), Visual Spatial was low average (84), Fluid Reasoning low average (86), very low Working memory (65), and low average Processing speed (81). Adolfo's Full Scale on WISC-V was within the lower extreme (65) (see Figure 7.8). A previous speech and language evaluation indicated low average receptive and expressive language skills. Based on these results, he did not meet the school district's eligibility criteria for speech-language impairment. Fine and gross motor skills were reported as age appropriate by the classroom and physical education teachers.

Standardized academic achievement testing in English and Spanish is consistent with the reports from the classroom teacher. Adolfo's results in English reveal scores are low average in basic reading skills and basic writing skills. His score is very low in reading comprehension and math reasoning. Test results in Spanish

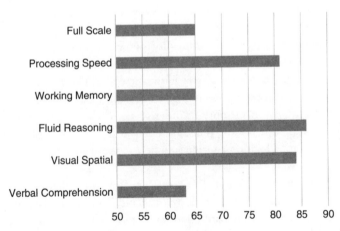

Figure 7.8 IQ Scores for Adolfo

suggest his math reasoning is in the low range and his scores are very low in reading comprehension. Basic writing skills are low average.

Adolfo's cognitive processes were evaluated by a bilingual psychologist using the CAS2. He was friendly, cooperative, and put forth his best effort during the evaluation. He was well-oriented, displaying a good range of affect and adequate episodic memory. Attention and concentration were variable depending on the complexity of question or task demands. Of note was the need to repeat instructions and check for understanding across several subtests. Adolfo was noted to have difficulty processing multi-component questions, displayed difficulty keeping information in sequential order, and sustaining adequate focus when tasks required an increase level of analysis and cognitive shifting. Occasionally, Adolfo was distracted by noise in the hallway. Considerable difficulties in cognitive processing as represented by the CAS2 Attention (77) and Successive (66) processing scales were revealed. These results indicate that he has considerable difficulty with focus of attention and resisting distractions and with working with any information in a specific sequence. These two cognitive weaknesses have a direct impact on his poor academic achievement in reading and math reasoning.

In Adolf's case, his difficulties with Attention and Successive processing are at the root of his poor academic performances in reading comprehension and math reasoning. For example, because of his limited ability to attend and work with information arranged in a specific sequence, Adolfo has difficulty keeping details of what he reads in order and maintaining an appropriate level of sustained attention. On math reasoning tasks, in order to solve the problems, he was required to listen to the problem, recognize the procedure to be followed, and then perform relatively simple calculations. Because many of the problems include extraneous information, Adolfo needed to decide not only the appropriate mathematical operations to use but also what information to include in the calculation. His ability to comprehend connected discourse while reading performance is limited on tasks requiring his cognitive skills to use syntactic and semantic cues in comprehending written discourse as it is being read.

The CAS2 results further showed that Adolfo has scores in the average range in Planning (94) and Simultaneous (90) processing, with academic strengths in basic reading skills and math calculations (see Figure 7.9). These findings are very important because they indicate that Adolfo is best when he is asked to understand how things and ideas fit together to make an organized whole (Simultaneous processing) and that he is also good at figuring out how to solve problems, control his actions, and determine if his solution is working or not (Planning processing). These two strengths are the key to successful instruction, especially when the results of his difficulties with sequencing and attending are being managed.

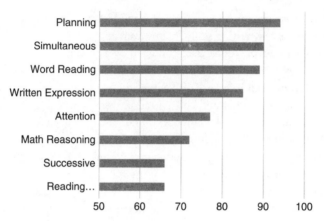

Figure 7.9 Adolfo's PASS and Achievement Scores

Reflections on This Case

Because of the complex nature of Adolfo's processing weaknesses, several interventions from *Helping Children Learn* (Naglieri & Pickering, 2010) were suggested based on Adolfo's cognitive processing strengths and weaknesses. His teacher was very receptive and willing to try anything in order to further help Adolfo in attaining academic success. Teaching Adolfo about Attention using the handout "Teaching Students About Attention" was the first step (Naglieri & Pickering, 2010, p. 58), followed by other handouts: "Improving Attention" (p. 76) and "Overcoming Problems with Inattention" (p. 67). These handouts assist the teacher in understanding what Attention is, how it works, and gave Adolfo options for how to manage his level of Attention. For Adolfo, this allowed him to feel a sense of self-efficacy and to feel successful in light of his cognitive weakness.

Adolfo's poor Successive processing was addressed using other handouts: "Teaching Students About Successive Processing" (p. 62), "More Strategies for Math Word Problems" (p. 120), "Seven-Step Strategy for Math Word Problems" (p. 177), and "Improving Reading Skills Online" (p. 92). These handouts helped Adolfo to recognize that often information is organized in a sequence and that maintaining information in order is the key to understanding and learning. Additionally, developing systematic strategies while mentally keeping information in order will aid Adolfo in the successful completion of word problems. Finally, Adolfo can work on improving his reading comprehension skills using online games that are engaging and require multiple cognitive processes.

The Case of Eric

Eric is 8 years old and in the second grade at a local public school. He experiences moderate delays in cognitive ability, functional academics, and functional communication. These delays are sufficiently severe that Eric would likely qualify for a classification of ID. In 2014, Eric experienced cognitive delays and functional communication deficits, but his academic skills were in the below to low average range. He also had just entered kindergarten and other indicators at that time (e.g., standardized achievement test scores, parental input, socialization skills) suggested that the classification of ID be deferred.

Eric was born 8 weeks premature and weighed less than 5 pounds. He spent 10 days in neonatal intensive care, was jaundiced, had difficulty breathing, and was delayed in latching on. Jaundice is a factor that occurs in approximately 60% of births (Shapiro, 2003). Moderate elevations in bilirubin are associated with a general at-risk factor for cognitive, perceptual, motor, and auditory disorders (Koziol, Beljan, John, & Barker, 2016) and places neonates at risk for subsequent academic learning difficulties (Johnson & Bhutani, 2011; Shapiro & Popelka, 2011; Soorani-Lunsing, Woltil, & Hadders-Algra, 2001). Later, Eric was discharged from the hospital as medically stable and no further reports of medical issues were reported. Eric experienced delays in walking and talking. He did not say his first word until 13 months of age and walked at 16 months, was toilet trained at 3.6 years, and had some degree of hypotonia (a state of low muscle tone and reduced muscle strength).

Currently, Eric struggles with most academic content. His teacher noted that he can recognize only a few letters of the alphabet, struggles with counting up through 100, and has difficulty verbally expressing himself. When counting he gets confused, loses his place, and skips numbers. The school learning support teacher-diagnostician administered the Woodcock-Johnson IV Tests of Achievement (WJ-IV), and results were in the delayed range across all academic areas. His language skills are low for his age, and he especially struggles with oral expression. Eric's apparent delays in cognitive ability, functional academics, and functional communication were sufficiently severe that an evaluation was indicated. Among other instruments, information from the CAS2 and the Adaptive Behavior Assessment System, Third Edition (ABAS-3) was obtained. Eric's PASS scores are uniformly low with no significant strengths or weaknesses (see Table 7.16). The scores ranged from a low of 60 (Successive) followed by Simultaneous (62) and Attention (63) with a high of 72 (Planning). His Full Scale score was 57.

Scores from the ABAS-3 obtained by interview with Eric's current teacher and his mother demonstrate adaptive behaviors at school and home that fall within

Table 7.16 Analysis of the Variability in Eric's PASS Scale Scores

Scale	Score	Difference	Significant or Not
Planning	72	7.8	NS
Simultaneous	62	−2.3	NS
Attention	63	−1.3	NS
Successive	60	−4.3	NS
Child's Average	64.3		

Table 7.17 Adaptive Behavior Assessment System II (ABAS-III) Scores for Eric

Adaptive Scale	Teacher Score	Parent Score
Conceptual Composite	71	67
Social Composite	70	80
Practical Composite	63	60
General Adaptive Composite	65	65

the extremely low range (see Table 7.17). According to Eric's teacher's and his mother's observations, Eric is very low in all areas of Adaptive skill. These scores are also very consistent with his PASS scores and raters' observations of Eric.

Intervention Suggestions

Eric may benefit from opportunities to use strategies to solve problems and modify plans to improve efficiency.

1. Teach Eric specific skills sets for particular circumstances and then do not tell him what to do but ask him to "think" and "decide" what to do next.
2. Teach Eric decision-making rules for discriminating important from unimportant details.
3. Use strategies for remembering, such as elaborative rehearsal and clustering information together.
4. Use strategies such as chunking, backward shaping (teach the last part of a skill first), forward shaping, and role modeling.
5. Use mnemonics (words, sentences, pictures, devices, or techniques for improving or strengthening memory).

Eric's low score in Successive processing suggests that he would have significant challenges following multistep directions, keeping information in order, and difficulty following along with what is said or read to him, for example. Eric's ability to use successive processing may be improved in several ways:

- Memorizing songs and poems
- Following specific ordinal instructions
- Saying and writing out the steps to complete an activity
- Teaching him to organize things in steps as a strategy to complete tasks
- Using sequencing cards to teach the order of events

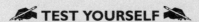

TEST YOURSELF

1. **The Discrepancy/Consistency Method is used to do which of the following?**
   a. Identify gifted students
   b. Operationalize the PSW approach to SLD
   c. Obtain an ability achievement discrepancy
   d. Detect the connection between a disorder in basic psychological process with academic weaknesses
   e. B and D

2. **Children with attention-deficit/hyperactivity disorder impulsive and combined types have poor scores in which of the following processes?**
   a. Planning and Successive
   b. Simultaneous and Successive
   c. Attention
   d. Planning and Attention

3. **Children with attention-deficit/hyperactivity disorder inattentive type have poor scores in which of the following processes?**
   a. Planning and Successive
   b. Simultaneous and Successive
   c. Attention
   d. Planning and Attention

4. **Using PASS theory for assessment of English language learners is particularly valuable because the CAS2 and CAS2: Brief do which of the following?**
   a. Require very little knowledge
   b. Enable the examiner to explain the task demands through instructions
   c. Are administered in a short amount of time
   d. A and B

5. **Using the CAS2 or CAS2: Brief for assessment of gifted students is particularly valuable because of which of the following reasons?**

   a. These measures are fair for diverse populations.
   b. Instructions enable the examiner to explain the task demands.
   c. The CAS2: Brief can be administered in a short amount of time.
   d. A and C

6. **Using the CAS2 for assessment of students with intellectual disability is particularly valuable because of which of the following reasons?**

   a. The test questions demand very little knowledge.
   b. The test yields small differences across race and ethnicity.
   c. PASS scores can be used to develop interventions.
   d. All of the above

Answers: 1. e; 2. d; 3. c; 4. d; 5. d; 6. d

CAS2 KTEA-3 COMPARISONS

Table A.1 Values Needed for Significance When Comparing the CAS2 Extended and Core Battery PASS and Full Scale Scores to All Scores From the KTEA-3

Subtests	CAS2 12-Subtest Extended Battery										CAS2 8-Subtest Core Battery									
		p = .05					*p* = .10					*p* = .05					*p* = .10			
	FS	Plan	Sim	Att	Suc	FS	Plan	Sim	Att	Suc	FS	Plan	Sim	Att	Suc	FS	Plan	Sim	Att	Suc
Letter and Word Recognition	7	10	9	11	10	6	8	8	9	8	9	11	9	12	11	7	9	8	10	9
Reading Comprehension	11	13	12	14	13	9	11	10	11	11	12	14	13	15	14	10	11	11	12	12
Nonsense Word Decoding	8	10	9	11	10	6	8	8	9	8	9	11	10	12	11	7	9	8	10	9
Phonological Processing	10	12	11	12	12	8	10	9	10	10	11	12	11	14	13	9	10	9	11	11
Word Recognition Fluency	12	14	13	14	14	10	11	11	12	11	13	14	13	15	15	11	12	11	13	12

(continued)

Table A.1 (continued)

| | CAS2 12-Subtest Extended Battery | | | | | | | | | | CAS2 8-Subtest Core Battery | | | | | | | | | |
| | $p = .05$ | | | | | $p = .10$ | | | | | $p = .05$ | | | | | $p = .10$ | | | | |
	FS	Plan	Sim	Att	Suc	FS	Plan	Sim	Att	Suc	FS	Plan	Sim	Att	Suc	FS	Plan	Sim	Att	Suc
Decoding Fluency	13	14	14	15	14	11	12	12	12	12	14	15	14	16	15	11	12	12	13	13
Silent Reading Fluency	13	15	14	15	15	11	12	12	13	12	14	15	14	16	16	12	13	12	14	13
Reading Vocabulary	9	11	11	12	11	8	9	9	10	9	10	12	11	13	12	9	10	9	11	10
Math Concepts and Applications	8	10	10	11	10	7	9	8	9	9	9	11	10	13	12	8	9	8	11	10
Math Computation	8	11	10	11	11	7	9	8	10	9	9	11	10	13	12	8	10	9	11	10
Math Fluency	11	12	12	13	12	9	10	10	11	10	11	13	12	14	14	10	11	10	12	11
Written Expression	13	14	14	15	14	11	12	11	12	12	13	15	14	16	15	11	12	12	13	13
Spelling	8	10	10	11	10	7	9	8	9	9	9	11	10	13	12	8	9	8	11	10
Writing Fluency	15	17	16	17	17	13	14	13	14	14	16	17	16	18	17	13	14	14	15	15
Listening Comprehension	12	14	13	15	14	10	12	11	12	12	13	15	14	16	15	11	12	12	13	13
Oral Expression	14	15	15	16	15	12	13	12	13	13	14	16	15	17	16	12	13	13	14	14
Associational Fluency	19	20	20	20	20	16	17	16	17	17	19	20	20	21	21	16	17	17	18	17
Object Naming Facility	17	18	17	18	18	14	15	15	15	15	17	18	18	19	19	14	15	15	16	16
Letter Naming Facility	18	19	18	19	19	16	16	15	16	16	18	19	19	20	19	16	16	15	17	16

Composites

Reading	8	10	10	11	10	7	9	8	9	9	9	11	10	13	12	8	9	8	11	10
Math	7	10	9	10	10	6	8	7	9	8	8	10	9	12	11	7	9	8	10	9
Written Language	9	11	10	12	11	7	9	9	10	9	10	12	11	13	12	8	10	9	11	10
Academic Skills	6	9	8	10	9	5	8	7	8	8	8	10	9	12	11	7	8	7	10	9
Battery																				
Sound-Symbol	8	10	9	11	10	6	8	8	9	8	9	11	10	12	11	7	9	8	10	10
Decoding Fluency	7	9	8	10	9	6	8	7	8	8	8	10	9	12	11	7	8	7	10	9
Reading Fluency	9	11	10	12	11	8	9	9	10	9	10	12	11	13	12	8	10	9	11	10
Reading Understanding	8	11	10	11	11	7	9	8	10	9	9	11	10	13	12	8	10	9	11	10
Oral Language	12	14	13	14	14	10	11	11	12	11	13	14	14	16	15	11	12	11	13	12
Oral Fluency	16	17	17	18	17	13	14	14	15	14	17	18	17	19	18	14	15	14	16	15
Comprehension	10	12	11	12	12	8	10	9	10	10	11	12	12	14	13	9	10	10	12	11
Expression	11	13	12	14	13	9	11	10	11	11	12	14	13	15	14	10	11	11	12	12
Orthographic Processing	10	12	11	13	12	8	10	9	11	10	11	13	12	14	13	9	10	10	12	11
Academic Fluency	10	12	11	13	12	8	10	9	11	10	11	13	12	14	13	9	11	10	12	11

Appendix B

CAS2 AND WIAT-III COMPARISONS

Table B.1 Values Needed for Significance When Comparing the CAS2 Extended and Core Battery PASS and Full Scale Scores to All Scores From the WIAT-III

	CAS2 12-Subtest Extended Battery										CAS2 8-Subtest Core Battery									
	$p = .05$					$p = .10$					$p = .05$					$p = .10$				
	FS	Plan	Sim	Att	Suc	FS	Plan	Sim	Att	Suc	FS	Plan	Sim	Att	Suc	FS	Plan	Sim	Att	Suc
Subtests																				
Listening Comprehension	13	15	14	15	15	11	12	12	13	12	14	15	15	16	16	12	13	12	14	13
Early Reading Skills	11	13	12	13	13	9	11	10	11	11	12	13	13	15	14	10	11	11	12	12
Reading Comprehension	12	14	13	15	14	10	12	11	12	12	13	15	14	16	15	11	12	11	13	12
Math Problem Solving	10	12	11	13	12	8	10	9	11	10	11	13	12	14	13	9	11	10	12	11
Alphabet Writing Fluency	17	18	18	19	18	14	15	15	16	15	18	19	18	20	19	15	16	15	16	16

(continued)

Table B.1 (continued)

	CAS2 12-Subtest Extended Battery										CAS2 8-Subtest Core Battery									
		$p = .05$				$p = .10$						$p = .05$				$p = .10$				
	FS	Plan	Sim	Att	Suc	FS	Plan	Sim	Att	Suc	FS	Plan	Sim	Att	Suc	FS	Plan	Sim	Att	Suc
Sentence Composition	12	13	13	14	13	10	11	11	12	11	12	14	13	15	14	10	12	11	13	12
Word Reading	7	10	9	10	10	6	8	7	9	8	8	10	9	12	11	7	9	8	10	9
Essay Composition	11	13	13	14	13	10	11	11	12	11	12	14	13	15	14	10	12	11	13	12
Essay Composition: Grammar and Mechanics	13	15	14	15	15	11	12	12	13	12	14	15	14	16	16	12	13	12	14	13
Pseudoword Decoding	7	10	9	11	10	6	8	7	9	8	8	11	9	12	11	7	9	8	10	9
Numerical Operations	9	11	11	12	11	8	10	9	10	10	10	12	11	13	13	9	10	9	11	10
Oral Expression	12	14	13	14	14	10	11	11	12	11	13	14	13	15	15	11	12	11	13	12
Oral Reading Fluency	9	11	11	12	11	8	9	9	10	9	10	12	11	13	12	9	10	9	11	10
Oral Reading Accuracy	13	15	14	15	15	11	12	12	13	12	14	15	15	17	16	12	13	12	14	13
Oral Reading Rate	10	12	11	12	12	8	10	9	10	10	10	12	11	14	13	9	10	9	11	11
Spelling	8	11	10	11	11	7	9	8	9	9	9	11	10	13	12	8	9	9	11	10

Math Fluency—Addition	13	14	14	15	14	13	12	13	12	11	12	12	11	14	15	16	11	12	12	13	13
Math Fluency—Subtraction	11	13	12	14	13	11	10	12	11	10	11	11	10	13	14	15	10	11	11	12	12
Math Fluency—Multiplication	11	13	12	13	13	10	10	12	11	10	10	11	10	12	13	14	10	11	10	12	11
Composites																					
Oral Language	10	12	12	13	12	9	10	11	11	10	11	10	11	12	13	14	9	11	10	12	11
Total Reading	7	9	9	10	9	6	7	9	8	8	8	8	8	9	10	12	7	9	8	10	9
Basic Reading	6	9	8	10	9	5	7	8	8	7	8	8	8	9	10	12	6	8	7	10	9
Reading Comprehension and Fluency	10	12	11	12	12	8	9	11	10	9	10	10	11	11	12	14	9	10	9	11	11
Written Expression	9	11	11	12	11	8	9	10	9	9	9	10	10	11	12	13	8	10	9	11	10
Mathematics	8	10	10	11	10	7	8	9	9	8	9	9	9	10	11	13	8	9	8	11	10
Math Fluency	9	11	10	12	11	7	9	10	9	9	10	10	10	11	12	13	8	10	7	11	10
Total Achievement	7	9	9	10	9	6	7	8	8	7	9	8	8	9	10	12	7	9	8	10	9

Appendix C

CAS2 AND WJ-IV ACHIEVEMENT COMPARISONS

Table C.1 Values Needed for Significance When Comparing the CAS2 Extended and Core Battery PASS and Full Scale Scores to All Scores From the WJ-IV

| | CAS2 12-Subtest Extended Battery | | | | | | | | | | CAS2 8-Subtest Core Battery | | | | | | | | | |
| | $p = .05$ | | | | | $p = .10$ | | | | | $p = .05$ | | | | | $p = .10$ | | | | |
	FS	Plan	Sim	Att	Suc	FS	Plan	Sim	Att	Suc	FS	Plan	Sim	Att	Suc	FS	Plan	Sim	Att	Suc
Subtests																				
Letter-Word Identification	9	11	10	12	11	7	9	9	10	9	10	12	11	13	12	8	10	9	11	10
Applied Problems	8	11	10	11	11	7	9	8	9	9	9	11	10	13	12	8	9	9	11	10
Spelling	8	11	10	11	11	7	9	8	9	9	9	11	10	13	12	8	9	9	11	10
Passage Comprehension	11	13	12	13	13	9	11	10	11	11	12	13	13	15	14	10	11	10	12	12
Calculation	9	11	11	12	11	8	9	9	10	9	10	12	11	13	13	9	10	9	11	10
Writing Samples	11	12	12	13	12	9	10	10	11	10	11	13	12	14	14	10	11	10	12	11
Word Attack	11	12	12	13	12	9	10	10	11	10	11	13	12	14	14	10	11	10	12	11

(continued)

Table C.1 (continued)

| | CAS2 12-Subtest Extended Battery | | | | | | | | | | CAS2 8-Subtest Core Battery | | | | | | | | | |
| | p = .05 | | | | | p = .10 | | | | | p = .05 | | | | | p = .10 | | | | |
	FS	Plan	Sim	Att	Suc	FS	Plan	Sim	Att	Suc	FS	Plan	Sim	Att	Suc	FS	Plan	Sim	Att	Suc
Oral Reading	8	10	9	11	10	7	8	8	9	8	9	11	10	12	11	7	9	8	10	10
Sentence Writing Fluency	9	11	10	12	11	7	9	9	10	9	10	12	11	13	12	8	10	9	11	10
Math Facts Fluency	8	10	9	11	10	7	8	8	9	8	9	11	10	12	11	7	9	8	10	10
Sentence Writing Fluency	14	16	15	16	16	12	13	13	13	13	15	16	15	17	16	12	13	13	14	14
Reading Recall	10	12	11	12	12	8	10	9	10	10	11	12	11	14	13	9	10	10	12	11
Number Matrices	10	12	11	12	12	8	10	9	10	10	11	12	11	14	13	9	10	10	12	11
Editing	10	12	11	13	12	9	10	10	11	10	11	13	12	14	13	9	11	10	12	11
Word Reading Fluency	10	12	11	13	12	9	10	10	11	10	11	13	12	14	13	9	11	10	12	11
Spelling of Sounds	11	13	13	14	13	10	11	10	11	11	12	14	13	15	14	10	11	11	13	12
Reading Vocabulary	11	13	13	14	13	10	11	10	11	11	12	14	13	15	14	10	11	11	13	12
Clusters																				
Reading	8	11	10	11	11	7	9	8	9	9	9	11	10	13	12	8	9	9	11	10
Broad Reading	7	10	9	11	10	6	8	7	9	8	8	11	9	12	11	7	9	8	10	9
Basic Reading Skills	8	11	10	11	11	7	9	8	9	9	9	11	10	13	12	8	9	9	11	10
Reading Comprehension	9	11	11	12	11	8	9	9	10	9	10	12	11	13	13	9	10	9	11	10
Reading Fluency	8	10	9	11	10	7	8	8	9	8	9	11	10	12	11	7	9	8	10	10

Measure																			
Reading Rate	8	10	9	11	10	7	8	9	8	9	8	9	11	10	12	11	7	9	8	10
Mathematics	8	10	9	11	10	7	8	9	8	9	8	9	11	10	12	11	7	9	8	10
Broad Mathematics	7	10	9	11	10	6	8	9	7	9	8	8	11	9	12	11	7	9	8	9
Math Calculation Skills	7	10	9	11	10	6	8	9	7	9	8	8	11	9	12	11	7	9	8	9
Math Problem Solving	8	11	10	11	10	7	8	9	8	9	9	9	11	10	13	12	8	9	9	10
Written Language	9	11	10	12	11	7	9	10	9	10	9	10	12	11	13	12	8	10	9	10
Broad Written Language	8	11	10	11	10	7	9	9	8	9	9	9	11	10	13	12	8	9	9	10
Basic Writing Skills	8	11	10	11	10	7	9	9	8	9	9	9	11	10	13	12	8	9	9	10
Written Expression	10	12	11	12	11	8	10	10	9	10	10	10	12	11	14	13	9	10	10	11
Academic Skills	7	10	9	11	10	6	8	9	7	9	8	8	11	9	12	11	7	9	8	9
Academic Fluency	7	10	9	11	10	6	8	9	7	9	8	8	11	9	12	11	7	9	8	9
Academic Applications	8	10	9	11	10	7	8	9	8	9	8	9	11	10	12	11	7	9	8	10
Academic Knowledge	8	11	10	11	11	7	9	9	8	9	9	9	11	10	13	12	8	9	9	10
Phoneme-Grapheme Knowledge	9	11	10	12	11	7	9	10	9	10	9	10	12	11	13	12	8	10	9	10
Brief Achievement	7	10	9	11	10	6	8	9	7	9	8	8	11	9	12	11	7	9	8	9
Broad Achievement	6	9	8	10	9	5	7	8	7	8	7	7	10	8	11	10	6	8	7	9

Appendix D

CAS2 AND FEIFER ASSESSMENT OF READING (FAR)

Table D.1 Values Needed for Significance When Comparing the CAS2 Extended and Core Battery PASS and Full Scale Scores to All Scores From the Feifer Assessment of Reading (FAR)

| | CAS2 12-Subtest Extended Battery | | | | | | | | | | CAS2 8-Subtest Core Battery | | | | | | | | | |
| | p = .05 | | | | | p = .10 | | | | | p = .05 | | | | | p = .10 | | | | |
	FS	Plan	Sim	Att	Suc	FS	Plan	Sim	Att	Suc	FS	Plan	Sim	Att	Suc	FS	Plan	Sim	Att	Suc
Subtests																				
Phonemic Awareness	9	11	10	12	11	7	9	9	10	9	10	12	11	13	12	8	10	9	11	10
Nonsense Word Decoding	11	13	12	13	13	9	11	10	11	11	12	13	13	15	14	10	11	11	12	12
Isolated Word Reading Fluency	10	12	11	13	12	9	10	10	11	10	11	13	12	14	13	9	11	10	12	11
Oral Reading Fluency	8	10	9	11	10	7	9	8	9	9	9	11	10	13	12	8	9	8	10	10
Positioning Sounds	10	12	11	13	12	8	10	9	11	10	11	13	12	14	13	9	11	10	12	11

(continued)

Table D.1 (continued)

| | CAS2 12-Subtest Extended Battery | | | | | | | | | | CAS2 8-Subtest Core Battery | | | | | | | | | |
| | $p = .05$ | | | | | $p = .10$ | | | | | $p = .05$ | | | | | $p = .10$ | | | | |
	FS	Plan	Sim	Att	Suc	FS	Plan	Sim	Att	Suc	FS	Plan	Sim	Att	Suc	FS	Plan	Sim	Att	Suc
Rapid Automatic Naming	11	13	12	13	13	9	11	10	11	11	12	13	12	15	14	10	11	10	12	11
Verbal Fluency	14	15	14	16	15	11	13	12	13	13	14	16	15	17	16	12	13	12	14	13
Visual Perception	12	13	13	14	13	10	11	11	12	11	12	14	13	15	14	10	12	11	13	12
Irregular Word Reading Fluency	10	12	11	12	12	8	10	9	10	10	11	12	11	14	13	9	10	10	11	11
Orthographical Processing	11	13	12	13	13	9	10	10	11	10	12	13	12	14	14	10	11	10	12	11
Semantic Concepts	11	13	12	14	13	9	11	10	11	11	12	14	13	15	14	10	11	11	12	12
Word Recall	17	18	17	18	18	14	15	15	15	15	17	18	18	19	19	14	15	15	16	16
Print Knowledge	9	11	10	12	11	8	9	9	10	9	10	12	11	13	12	8	10	9	11	10
Morphological Processing	10	12	12	13	12	9	10	10	11	10	11	13	12	14	13	9	11	10	12	11
Silent Reading Fluency	14	15	15	16	15	12	13	12	13	13	15	16	15	17	16	12	13	13	14	14
Indexes																				
Phonological	7	10	9	11	10	6	8	7	9	8	8	11	9	12	11	7	9	8	10	9
Fluency Index	9	11	11	12	11	8	9	9	10	9	10	12	11	13	12	8	10	9	11	10
Mixed Index	7	9	9	10	9	6	8	7	9	8	8	10	9	12	11	7	9	8	10	9
Comprehension Index	10	12	11	12	12	8	10	9	10	10	11	12	11	14	13	9	10	10	11	11
Total Index	7	9	9	10	9	6	8	7	9	8	8	10	9	12	11	7	9	8	10	9

CAS2 AND FEIFER ASSESSMENT OF MATH (FAM)

Table E.1 Values Needed for Significance When Comparing the CAS2 Extended and Core Battery PASS and Full Scale Scores to All Scores From the Feifer Assessment of Math (FAM)

	CAS2 12-Subtest Extended Battery										CAS2 8-Subtest Core Battery									
	$p = .05$					$p = .10$					$p = .05$					$p = .10$				
	FS	Plan	Sim	Att	Suc	FS	Plan	Sim	Att	Suc	FS	Plan	Sim	Att	Suc	FS	Plan	Sim	Att	Suc
Subtests																				
Forward Number Count	13	14	14	15	14	11	12	12	13	12	14	15	14	16	15	11	13	12	14	13
Backward Number Count	12	13	13	14	13	10	11	11	12	11	12	14	13	15	14	10	12	11	13	12
Numeric Capacity	16	18	17	18	18	14	15	14	15	15	17	18	17	19	18	14	15	15	16	15
Sequences	13	15	14	15	15	11	12	12	13	12	14	15	14	16	15	11	13	12	14	13
Object Counting	13	14	14	15	14	11	12	12	13	12	14	15	14	16	15	11	13	12	14	13
Rapid Number Naming	12	13	13	14	13	10	11	11	12	11	12	14	13	15	14	10	12	11	13	12
Addition Fluency	10	12	11	12	12	8	10	9	10	10	10	12	11	14	13	9	10	9	11	11

(*continued*)

Table E.1 (continued)

| | CAS2 12-Subtest Extended Battery | | | | | | | | | | CAS2 8-Subtest Core Battery | | | | | | | | | |
| | p = .05 | | | | | p = .10 | | | | | p = .05 | | | | | p = .10 | | | | |
	FS	Plan	Sim	Att	Suc	FS	Plan	Sim	Att	Suc	FS	Plan	Sim	Att	Suc	FS	Plan	Sim	Att	Suc
Subtraction Fluency	10	12	12	13	12	9	10	10	11	10	11	13	12	14	13	9	11	10	12	11
Multiplication Fluency	9	11	11	12	11	8	9	9	10	9	10	12	11	13	12	9	10	9	11	10
Division Fluency	10	12	11	12	12	8	10	9	10	10	11	12	11	14	13	9	10	9	11	11
Linguistic Math Concepts	13	14	14	15	14	11	12	12	12	12	14	15	14	16	15	11	12	12	13	13
Spatial Memory	14	15	15	16	15	12	13	12	13	13	14	16	15	17	16	12	13	13	14	14
Equation Building	12	13	13	14	13	10	11	11	12	11	13	14	13	15	14	11	12	11	13	12
Perceptual Estimation	17	18	18	19	18	14	15	15	15	15	17	19	18	19	19	15	15	15	16	16
Number Comparison	13	14	14	15	14	11	12	12	13	12	14	15	14	16	15	13	13	12	14	13
Addition Knowledge	11	13	12	13	13	9	11	10	11	11	12	13	12	15	14	10	11	10	12	11
Subtraction Knowledge	10	12	12	13	12	9	10	10	11	10	11	13	12	14	13	9	11	10	12	11
Multiplication Knowledge	10	12	11	12	12	8	10	9	10	10	11	12	12	14	13	9	10	10	12	11
Division Knowledge	10	12	11	13	12	8	10	9	11	10	11	13	12	14	13	9	11	10	12	11
Indexes																				
Procedural Index	9	11	11	12	11	8	9	9	10	9	10	12	11	13	13	9	10	9	11	10
Verbal Index	9	11	10	12	11	7	9	9	10	9	10	12	11	13	12	8	10	9	11	10
Semantic Index	9	11	11	12	11	8	10	9	10	10	10	12	11	14	13	9	10	9	11	11
Total Index	8	10	9	11	10	7	9	8	9	9	9	11	10	12	11	7	9	8	10	10

Appendix F

CAS2 AND BATERIA III

Table F.1 Values Needed for Significance When Comparing the CAS2 Extended and Core Battery PASS and Full Scale Scores to All Scores From the Bateria III

| | CAS2 12-Subtest Extended Battery | | | | | | | | | | CAS2 8-Subtest Core Battery | | | | | | | | | |
| | $p = .05$ | | | | | $p = .10$ | | | | | $p = .05$ | | | | | $p = .10$ | | | | |
	FS	Plan	Sim	Att	Suc	FS	Plan	Sim	Att	Suc	FS	Plan	Sim	Att	Suc	FS	Plan	Sim	Att	Suc
Subtests																				
Identificación de letras y palabras	8	11	10	11	11	7	9	8	9	9	9	11	10	13	12	8	9	9	11	10
Fluidez en la lectura	7	10	9	11	10	6	8	7	9	8	8	11	9	12	11	7	9	8	10	9
Rememoración de cuentos	15	16	16	17	16	13	14	13	14	14	16	17	16	18	17	13	14	13	15	14
Comprensión de indicaciones	7	9	8	10	9	6	8	7	8	8	8	10	9	12	11	7	8	7	10	9
Calculo	11	12	12	13	12	9	10	10	11	10	11	13	12	14	14	10	11	10	12	11
Ortografía	9	11	11	12	11	8	9	9	10	9	10	12	11	13	13	9	10	9	11	10

(continued)

Table F.1 (continued)

| | CAS2 12-Subtest Extended Battery | | | | | | | | | | CAS2 8-Subtest Core Battery | | | | | | | | | |
| | $p = .05$ | | | | | $p = .10$ | | | | | $p = .05$ | | | | | $p = .10$ | | | | |
	FS	Plan	Sim	Att	Suc	FS	Plan	Sim	Att	Suc	FS	Plan	Sim	Att	Suc	FS	Plan	Sim	Att	Suc
Fluidez en la escritura	11	13	12	13	13	9	11	10	11	11	12	13	13	15	14	10	11	10	12	12
Comprensión de textos	10	12	11	13	12	9	10	10	11	10	11	13	12	14	13	9	11	10	12	11
Problemas aplicados	10	12	11	12	12	8	10	9	10	10	11	12	11	14	13	9	10	10	12	11
Muestras de redacción	14	15	15	16	15	12	13	12	13	13	14	16	15	17	16	12	13	13	14	13
Memoria diferida— Rememoración de cuentos	11	13	13	14	13	10	11	10	11	11	12	14	13	15	14	10	11	11	13	12
Análisis de palabras	9	11	10	12	11	7	9	9	10	9	10	12	11	13	12	8	10	9	11	10
Vocabulario sobre dibujos	11	13	12	13	13	9	11	10	11	11	12	13	13	15	14	10	11	10	12	12
Comprensión oral	9	11	11	12	11	8	9	9	10	9	10	12	11	13	13	9	10	9	11	10
Corrección de textos	8	11	10	11	11	7	9	8	9	9	9	11	10	13	12	8	9	9	11	10
Vocabulario de lectura	8	11	10	11	11	7	9	8	9	9	9	11	10	13	12	8	9	9	11	10
Conceptos cuantitativos	11	12	12	13	12	9	10	10	11	10	11	13	12	14	14	10	11	10	12	11
Conocimientos académicos	10	12	11	12	12	8	10	9	10	10	11	12	11	14	13	9	10	10	12	11
Análisis de sonidos	13	14	14	15	14	11	12	12	13	12	14	15	14	16	15	11	12	12	13	13
Discernimiento de sonidos	7	9	8	10	9	6	8	7	8	8	8	10	9	12	11	7	8	7	10	9
Puntuación y mayúsculas	8	11	10	11	11	7	9	8	9	9	9	11	10	13	12	8	9	9	11	10

Clusters

Clusters																						
Amplia lectura	6	9	8	10	9	5	7	7	8	7	7	8	7	10	8	11	10	6	8	7	10	9
Destrezas básicas en lectura	7	10	9	11	10	6	8	7	9	8	8	9	8	11	9	12	11	7	9	8	10	9
Comprension de lectura	8	10	9	11	10	7	8	8	9	8	9	9	9	11	10	12	11	7	9	8	10	10
Lenguaje oral—Estandar	13	15	14	16	15	11	13	12	13	13	14	13	14	16	15	17	16	12	13	14	14	13
Lenguaje oral—Extendida	9	11	10	12	11	7	9	9	10	9	10	10	10	12	11	13	12	8	10	9	11	10
Comprension auditiva	10	12	11	13	12	9	10	10	11	10	11	11	11	13	12	14	13	9	11	10	12	11
Expresión oral	11	12	12	13	12	9	10	10	11	10	11	11	11	13	12	14	14	10	11	10	12	11
Razonamiento en matemáticas	7	10	9	11	10	6	8	7	9	8	8	9	8	11	9	12	11	7	9	8	10	9
Amplio lenguaje escrito	8	11	10	11	11	7	9	8	9	8	10	9	9	11	10	13	12	8	9	9	11	10
Destrezas básicas en escritura	8	10	9	11	10	7	8	8	9	8	9	9	9	11	10	12	11	7	8	8	10	10
Expresión escrita	11	12	12	13	12	9	10	10	11	10	13	12	13	14	12	14	14	10	11	10	12	11
Conocimientos académicos	8	11	10	11	11	7	8	9	9	8	11	10	11	13	10	13	12	8	9	9	11	10
Conocimiento de fonemas y grafemas	9	11	10	12	11	7	9	9	10	9	12	11	12	13	11	13	12	8	10	9	11	10
Destrezas académicas	7	10	9	10	10	6	8	7	9	8	8	9	8	11	9	12	11	7	8	8	10	9
Aplicaciones académicas	8	10	9	10	10	7	8	8	9	8	9	9	9	11	10	12	11	7	8	8	10	10
Aprovechamiento total	6	9	8	9	9	5	7	7	8	7	7	8	7	10	8	11	10	6	8	7	10	9

References

Alvarado, C. G., Ruef, M. L., & Schrank, F. A. (2005). *Woodcock-Munoz Language Survey–Revised*. Itasca, IL: Riverside.

American Association on Intellectual and Developmental Disabilities (AAIDD). (2010). *Intellectual disability: Definition, classification, and systems of support* (11th ed.). Washington, DC: Author.

American Psychiatric Association (APA). (2013). *Diagnostic and statistical manual of mental disorders* (5th ed.). Washington, DC: Author.

Anastasi, A., & Urbina, S. (1997). *Psychological testing* (7th ed.). New York, NY: Pearson Education.

Ashkenazi, S., Black, J. M., Abrams, D. A., Hoeft, F., & Menon, V. (2013). Neurobiological underpinnings of math and reading learning disabilities. *Journal of Learning Disabilities, 46,* 549–569.

Baddeley, A. D., & Hitch, G. (1974). Working memory. In G. A. Bower (Ed.), *The psychology of learning and motivation* (pp. 47–89). New York, NY: Academic Press.

Baldwin, A. Y. (2004). *Culturally diverse and underserved populations of gifted students.* Thousand Oaks, CA: Corwin Press.

Barkley, R. (1997). *ADHD and the nature of self-control.* New York, NY: Guilford Press.

Batalova, J., & McHugh, M. (2010). Number and growth of students in U.S. schools in need of English instruction (ELL Information Center Fact Sheet Series, Fact Sheet #1). Migration Policy Institute. Retrieved from http://www.migrationinformation.org/ellinfo/FactSheet_ELL2.pdf

Bialystok, E., Luk, G., Peets, K. F., & Yang, S. (2010). Receptive vocabulary differences in monolingual and bilingual children. *Bilingualism: Language and Cognition, 13,* 103–119.

Blais, C., Harris, M. B., Guerrero, J. V., & Bunge, S. A. (2010). Rethinking the role of automaticity in cognitive control. *The Quarterly Journal of Experiential Psychology, 65*(2), 265–276.

Blatchley, L. A., & Lau, M. Y. (2010). Culturally competent assessment of English language learners for special education services. *Communiqué Handout, 38,* 1–8.

Boden, C., & Kirby, J. R. (1995). Successive processing, phonological coding, and the remediation of reading. *Journal of Cognitive Education, 4,* 19–32.

Bracken, B. A., & McCallum, R. S. (2009). Universal nonverbal intelligence test. In J. A. Naglieri & S. Goldstein (Eds.), *Practitioner's guide to assessing intelligence and achievement* (pp. 291–314). New York, NY: Wiley.

Braden, J. P., & Athanasiou, M. S. (2005). A comparative review of nonverbal measures of intelligence. *Contemporary intellectual assessment: Theories, tests, and issues,* 557–577.

Brigham, C. C. (1923). *A study of American intelligence.* Princeton, NJ: Princeton University Press.

Brue, A. W., & Wilmshurst, L. (2016). *Essentials of intellectual disability assessment and identification.* Hoboken, NJ: Wiley.

Canivez, G. L. (2011). Hierarchical factor structure of the Cognitive Assessment System: Variance partitions from the Schmid-Leiman (1957) procedure. *School Psychology Quarterly, 26,* 305–317.

Carlson, J., & Das, J. P. (1997). A process approach to remediating word decoding deficiencies in chapter 1 children. *Learning Disabilities Quarterly, 20,* 93–102.

Casas, R., Guzmán-Vélez, E., Cardona-Rodriguez, J., et al. (2012). Interpreter-mediated neuropsychological testing of monolingual Spanish speakers. *The Clinical Neuropsychologist, 26*(1), 88–101.

Castellano, J. A., & Frazier, A. D. (2010). *Special populations in gifted education: Understanding our most able students from diverse backgrounds.* Waco, TX: Prufrock Press.

Catroppa, C., & Anderson, V. (2007). Recovery in memory function, and its relationship to academic success, at 24 months following pediatric TBI. *Child Neuropsychology, 13*(3), 240–261.

Catroppa, C., Anderson, V., Beauchamp, M., & Yeates, K. (2016). *New frontiers in pediatric traumatic brain injury: An evidence base for clinical practice.* Hove, UK: Routledge.

Christensen D. L., Baio J., Van Naarden Braun, K., Bilder, D., Charles, J., Constantino, J. N., ... Yeargin-Allsopp, M. (2016). Prevalence and characteristics of autism spectrum disorder among children aged 8 years—Autism and Developmental Disabilities Monitoring Network, 11 Sites, United States, 2012. *MMWR Surveillance Summaries, 65*(No. SS-3), 1–23.

Cormier, P., Carlson, J. S., & Das, J. P. (1990). Planning ability and cognitive performance: The compensatory effects of a dynamic assessment approach. *Learning and Individual Difference, 2,* 437–449.

Cormier, D. C., McGrew, K. S., & Ysseldyke, J. E. (2014). The influences of linguistic demand and cultural loading on cognitive test scores. *Journal of Psychoeducational Assessment, 32*(7), 610–623.

Cowan, R., & Powell, D. (2014). The contributions of domain-general and numerical factors to third-grade arithmetic skills and mathematical learning disability. *Journal of Educational Psychology, 106,* 214–229.

Crews, K. J., & D'Amato, R. C. (2009). Subtyping children's reading disabilities using a comprehensive neuropsychological measure. *International Journal of Neuroscience, 119,* 1615–1639.

Cummins, J. (1981). *Bilingualism and minority language children.* Ontario, Canada: Ontario Institute for Studies in Education.

Cummins, J. (1984). *Bilingualism and special education: Issues in assessment and pedagogy.* San Diego, CA: College-Hill Press.

Cummins, J., Alvarado, C. G., & Ruef, M. L. (1998). *Bilingual verbal ability tests: Comprehensive manual.* Itasca, IL: Riverside.

Cutting, L. E., Materek, A., Cole, C. A. S., Levine, T. M., & Mahone, E. M. (2009). Effects of fluency, oral language, and executive function on reading comprehension performance. *Annals of Dyslexia, 59,* 34–54.

Das, J. P. (1999). *PASS Reading Enhancement Program (PREP).* Edmonton, Alberta, Canada: Developmental Disabilities Centre, University of Alberta.

Das, J. P. (2000). PREP: A cognitive remediation program in theory and practice. *Developmental Disabilities Bulletin, 28*(2), 83–96.

Das, J. P. (2004). *The Cognitive Enhancement Training Program (COGENT).* Edmonton, Alberta, Canada: Developmental Disabilities Centre, University of Alberta.

Das, J. P. (2009). *Reading difficulties and dyslexia* (Rev. ed.). New Delhi, India: Sage.

Das, J. P., Hayward, V., Georgiou, G. K., Janzen, T., & Boora, N. (2008). Comparing the effectiveness of two reading intervention programs for children with reading disabilities. *Journal of Cognitive Education & Psychology, 7,* 199–222.

Das, J. P., Janzen, T., & Georgiou, G. K. (2007). Correlates of Canadian native children' reading performance: From cognitive styles to cognitive processes. *Journal of School Psychology, 45,* 589–602.

Das, J. P., Mishra, R. K., & Pool, J. E. (1995). An experiment on cognitive remediation or word-reading difficulty. *Journal of Learning Disabilities, 28,* 66–79.

Das, J. P., Naglieri, J. A., & Kirby, J. R. (1994). *Assessment of cognitive process: The PASS theory of intelligence.* Needham Heights, MA: Allyn & Bacon.

Dehaene, S. (2011). *The number sense: How the mind creates mathematics.* New York, NY: Oxford University Press.

Dehn, M. J. (2000). *Cognitive assessment system performance of ADHD children.* Paper presented at the annual NASP Convention, New Orleans, LA.

Department of Veterans Affairs. (2010). *Traumatic brain injury: Independent study course.* Washington, DC: Author.

Deprey, L., & Ozonoff, S. (2009). Assessment of comorbid psychiatric conditions in autism spectrum disorders. *Assessment of autism spectrum disorders,* 290–317.

Dombrowski, S. C., & Watkins, M. W. (2013). Exploratory and higher order factor analysis of the WJ-III full test battery: A school-aged analysis. *Psychological Assessment,* 25(2), 442–455.

Domenech, D., Sherman, M., & Brown, J. L. (2016). *Personalizing 21st century education: A framework for student success.* San Francisco, CA: Jossey-Bass.

Donders, J., & Janke, K. (2008). Criterion validity of the Wechsler Intelligence Scale for Children–Fourth Edition after pediatric traumatic brain injury. *Journal of the International Neuropsychological Society,* 14(04), 651–655.

Draper, K., & Ponsford, J. (2008). Cognitive functioning ten years following traumatic brain injury and rehabilitation. *Neuropsychology,* 22(5), 618.

DuPaul, G. J., & Stoner, G. (1994). *ADHD in the schools: Assessment and intervention strategies.* New York, NY: Guilford Press.

Dweck, C. (2006). *Mindset: The new psychology of success.* New York, NY: Random House.

Edwards, O. W., & Oakland, T. D. (2006). Factorial invariance of Woodcock-Johnson III scores for African Americans and Caucasians Americans. *Journal of Psychoeducational Assessment,* 24, 358–366.

Engle, R. W., & Conway, A. R. (1998). Working memory and comprehension. In R. H. Logie & K. J. Gilhooly (Eds.), *Working memory and thinking* (pp. 67–89). London, UK: Psychology Press.

Ewing-Cobbs, L., Barnes, M. A., & Fletcher, J. M. (2003). Early brain injury in children: Development and reorganization of cognitive function. *Developmental Neuropsychology,* 24(2–3), 669–704.

Fagan, J. R. (2000). A theory of intelligence as processing: Implications for society. *Psychology, Public Policy, and Law,* 6(1), 168–179.

Feifer, S. G. (2015). *Feifer assessment of reading.* Lutz, FL: PAR.

Feifer, S. G. (2016). *Feifer assessment of mathematics.* Lutz, FL: PAR.

Feifer, S. G., & Della Toffalo, D. A. (2007). *Integrating RTI with cognitive neuropsychology: A scientific approach to reading.* Middletown, CT: School Neuropsych Press.

Flanagan, D. P., & Ortiz, S. O. (2001). *Essentials of cross-battery assessment.* New York, NY: Wiley.

Flanagan, D. P., Ortiz, S. O., & Alfonso, V. C. (2007). *Essentials of cross-battery assessment with C/D ROM* (2nd ed.). New York, NY: Wiley.

Ford, D. Y. (2010). *Reversing underachievement among gifted Black students* (2nd ed.). Waco, TX: Prufrock Press.

Ford, D. Y. (2013). *Recruiting and retaining culturally different students in gifted education.* Waco, TX: Prufrock Press.

Ford, D. Y., Grantham, T. C., & Whiting, G. W. (2008). Culturally and linguistically diverse students in gifted education: Recruitment and retention issues. *Exceptional Children,* 74, 289–308.

Frasier, M. M., Garcia, J. H., & Passow, A. H. (1995). *A review of assessment issues in gifted education and their implications for identifying gifted minority students* (RM95204). Storrs, CT: University of Connecticut, National Research Center on the Gifted and Talented.

Fuchs, D., & Young, C. L. (2006). On the irrelevance of intelligence in predicting responsiveness to reading instruction. *Exceptional Children, 73*(1), 8–30.

Gagné, F. (1985). Giftedness and talent: Reexamining a reexamination of the definitions. *Gifted Child Quarterly, 29,* 103–112.

Georgiou, G. K., Das, J. P., & Hayward, D. V. (2008). Comparing the contribution of two tests of working memory to reading in relation to phonological awareness and rapid naming speed. *Journal of Research in Reading, 31,* 302–318.

Geva, E., & Wiener, J. (2015). *Psychological assessment of culturally and linguistically diverse children and adolescents: A practitioner's guide*. New York, NY: Springer.

Giessman, J. A., Gambrell, J. L., & Stebbins, M. S. (2013). Minority performance on the Naglieri Nonverbal Ability Test, Second Edition, versus the Cognitive Abilities Test, Form 6: One gifted program's experience. *Gifted Child Quarterly, 57,* 101–109.

Goldberg, E. (2009). *The new executive brain: Frontal lobes in a complex world*. New York, NY: Oxford University Press.

Goldstein, S., & Naglieri, J. A. (2009). *Austism Spectrum Rating Scale*. Toronto, Canada: Multi-Health Systems, Inc.

Goldstein, S., & Naglieri, J. A. (2010). *Autism Spectrum Rating Scales (ASRS): Technical manual*. Toronto, Canada: Multi-Health Systems, Inc.

Goldstein, S., & Naglieri, J. A. (2016). *Rating Scale of Impairment: Technical manual*. Toronto, Canada: Multi-Health Systems, Inc.

Goldstein, S., Naglieri, J. A., Princiotta, D., & Otero, T. M. (2014). Introduction: A history of executive functioning as a theoretical clinical construct. In S. Goldstein & J. A. Naglieri (Eds.), *Handbook of executive functioning* (pp. 3–12). New York, NY: Springer.

Gutentag, S., Naglieri, J. A., & Yeates, K. O. (1998). Performance of children with traumatic brain injury on the Cognitive Assessment System. *Assessment, 3,* 263–272.

Haddad, F. A., Garcia, Y. E., Naglieri, J. A., Grimditch, M., McAndrews, A., & Eubanks, J. (2003). Planning facilitation and reading comprehension: Instructional relevance of the PASS theory. *Journal of Psychoeducational Assessment, 21,* 282–289.

Hale, J. B., & Fiorello, C. A. (2004). *School neuropsychology: A practitioner's handbook*. New York, NY: Guilford Press.

Hale, J. B., Kaufman, A. S., Naglieri, J. A., & Kavale, K. A. (2006). Implementation of IDEA: Using RTI and cognitive assessment methods. *Psychology in the Schools,* 753–770.

Halstead, M. E., & Walter, K. D. (2010). Sport-related concussion in children and adolescents. *Pediatrics, 126*(3), 597–615.

Hayden, M. G., Jandial, R., Duenas, H. A., Mahajan, R., & Levy, M. (2007). Pediatric concussions in sports; a simple and rapid assessment tool for concussive injury in children and adults. *Child's Nervous System, 23*(4), 431–435.

Hayward, D., Das, J. P., & Janzen, T. (2007). Innovative programs for improvement in reading through cognitive enhancement: A remediation study of Canadian First Nations children. *Journal of Learning Disabilities, 40,* 443–457.

Hessen, E., Nestvold, K., & Anderson, V. (2007). Neuropsychological function 23 years after mild traumatic brain injury: A comparison of outcome after paediatric and adult head injuries. *Brain Injury, 21*(9), 963–979.

Huang, L. V., Bardos, A. N., & D'Amato, R. C. (2010). Identifying students with learning disabilities: Composite profile analysis using the Cognitive Assessment System. *Journal of Psychoeducational Assessment, 28,* 19–30.

Hynd, G. W., Voeller, K. K., Hern, K. L., & Marshall, R. M. (1991). Neurobiological basis of attention-deficit hyperactivity disorder (ADHD). *School Psychology Review, 20,* 174–186.

Iseman, J., & Naglieri, J. A. (2011). A cognitive strategy instruction to improve math calculation for children with ADHD: A randomized controlled study. *Journal of Learning Disabilities, 44,* 184–195.

Jaffe, K. M., Polissar, N. L., Fay, G. C., & Liao, S. (1995). Recovery trends over three years following pediatric traumatic brain injury. *Archives of physical medicine and rehabilitation, 76,* 17–26.

Jensen, A. R. (1976). Construct validity and test bias. *Phi Delta Kappan, 58,* 340–346.

Jensen, A. R. (1980). *Bias in mental testing.* New York, NY: Free Press.

Johnson, L., & Bhutani, V. K. (2011). The clinical syndrome of bilirubin-induced neurologic dysfunction. *Seminars in Perinatology, 35,* 101–113.

Kar, B. C., Dash, U. N., Das, J. P., & Carlson, J. S. (1992). Two experiments on the dynamic assessment of planning. *Learning and Individual Differences, 5,* 13–29.

Kasari, C., Gulsrud, A. C., Wong, C., Kwon, S., & Locke, J. (2010). Randomized controlled caregiver mediated joint engagement intervention for toddlers with autism. *Journal of Autism and Developmental Disorders, 40*(9), 1045–1056.

Kaufman, A. S. (1994). *Intelligent testing with the WISC-III*. New York, NY: Wiley.

Kaufman, A. S., & Kaufman, N. L. (1983). *Kaufman assessment battery for children.* Circle Pines, MN: American Guidance.

Kaufman, A. S., & Kaufman, N. L. (2004). *Kaufman assessment battery for children* (2nd ed.). Circle Pines, MN: American Guidance Service.

Kaufman, A. S., & Kaufman, N. L. (2015). *Kaufman Test of Educational Achievement* (3rd ed.). San Antonio, TX: Pearson.

Kaufman, A. S., & Lichtenberger, E. O. (2006). *Essentials of WAIS-III assessment* (3rd ed.). Hoboken, NJ: Wiley.

Kaufman, A. S., Lichtenberger, E. O., Fletcher-Janzen, E., & Kaufman, N. L. (2005). *Essentials of KABC-II assessment*. New York, NY: Wiley.

Kirby, J. R., & Williams, N. H. (1991). *Learning problems: A cognitive approach*. Toronto, Canada: Kagan and Woo.

Klingner, J. K., Artiles, A. J., & Mendez Barletta, L. (2006). English language learners who struggle with reading: Language acquisition or LD? *Journal of Learning Disabilities, 39,* 108–128.

Klinger, L., O'Kelley, S. E., & Mussey, J. L. (2009). Assessment of intellectual functioning in autism spectrum disorder. In S. Goldstein, J. A. Naglieri, & S. Ozonoff (Eds.), *The assessment of autism spectrum disorders* (pp. 209–252). New York, NY: Guilford Press.

Koziol, L. F., Beljan, P., John, M., & Barker, L. (2016). *Large-scale brain systems and neuropsychological testing: An effort to move forward*. New York, NY: Springer-Verlag.

Koziol, L., Budding, D., & Chidekel, D. (2010). Adaptation, expertise, and giftedness: Towards an understanding of cortical, subcortical, and cerebellar network contributions. *The Cerebellum, 9*(4), 499–529.

Kranzler, J. H., Flores, C. G., & Coady, M. (2010). Examination of the cross-battery approach for the cognitive assessment of children and youth from diverse linguistic and cultural backgrounds. *School Psychology Review, 39,* 431–446.

Lakin, J. M. (2012). Assessing the cognitive abilities of culturally and linguistically diverse students: Predictive validity of verbal, quantitative, and nonverbal tests. *Psychology in the Schools, 49*(8), 756–768.

Lau, M. Y., & Blatchley, L. A. (2009). A comprehensive, multidimensional approach to assessment of culturally and linguistically diverse students. In J. M. Jones (Ed.), *The psychology of multiculturalism in the schools: A primer for practice, training, and research* (pp. 139–171). Bethesda, MD: NASP.

Lewandowski, L., & Scott, D. (2008). Introduction to neuropathology and brain-behavior relationships. In R. C. D'Amato & L. C. Hartlage (Eds.), *Essentials of neuropsychological assessment: Treatment planning for rehabilitation* (2nd ed.). New York, NY: Springer.

Lezak, M. D. (1995). *Neuropsychological assessment* (3rd ed.). New York, NY: Oxford University Press.

Lichtenberger, E. O., Sotelo-Dynega, M., & Kaufman, A. S. (2009). The Kaufman assessment battery for children, second edition. In J. A. Naglieri & S. Goldstein (Eds.), *A practitioner's guide to assessment of intelligence and achievement*. New York, NY: Wiley.

Lohman, D. F., & Hagen, E. P. (2001). *Cognitive abilities test*. Itasca, IL: Riverside.

Luria, A. R. (1966). *Human brain and psychological processes*. New York, NY: Harper & Row.

Luria, A. R. (1973). *The working brain: An introduction to neuropsychology*. New York, NY: Basic Books.

Luria, A. R. (1980a). *Higher cortical functions in man* (2nd ed.). New York, NY: Basic Books.

Luria, A. R. (1980b). *Higher cortical functions in man* (2nd ed., rev. and exp.). New York, NY: Basic Books.

Luria, A. R. (1982). *Language and cognition*. New York, NY: Wiley.

Mahapatra, S., Das, J. P., Stack-Cutler, H., & Parrila, R. (2010). Remediating reading comprehension difficulties: A cognitive processing approach. *Reading Psychology, 30,* 428–453.

McCandliss, B. D., & Noble, K. G. (2003). The development of reading impairment: A cognitive neuroscience model. *Mental Retardation and Developmental Disabilities Research Reviews, 9,* 196–205.

McCrea, S. M. (2007). Measurement of recovery after traumatic brain injury: A cognitive-neuropsychological comparison of the WAIS-R with the Cognitive Assessment System (CAS) in a single case of atypical language lateralization. *Applied neuropsychology, 14*(4), 296–304.

McDermott, P., Fantuzzo, J., & Glutting, J. (1990). Just say no to subtest analysis: A critique on Wechsler theory and practice. *Journal of Psychoeducational Assessment, 8,* 280–302.

McGinley, A. D., Master, C. L., & Zonfrillo, M. R. (2015). Sports-related head injuries in adolescents: A comprehensive update. *Adolescent Medicine, 26*(3), 491–506.

McGrew, K. S., LaForte, E. M., & Schrank, F. A. (2014). Technical Manual. *Woodcock-Johnson IV*. Rolling Meadows, IL: Riverside.

McKenzie, K., Milton, M., Smith, G., & Ouellette-Kuntz, H. (2016). Systematic review of the prevalence and incidence of intellectual disabilities: Current trends and issues. *Current Developmental Disorders Reports, 2*(3), 104–115.

Meltzer, L. (2010). *Promoting executive function in the classroom*. New York, NY: Guilford Press.

Mercer, J. (1979). In defense of racially and culturally non-discriminatory assessment. *School Psychology Review, 8,* 89–115.

Mundy, P., Gwaltney, M., & Henderson, H. (2010). Self-referenced processing, neurodevelopment and joint attention in autism. *Autism, 14*(5), 408–429.

Mundy, P., Sigman, M., Ungerer, J., & Sherman, T. (1986). Defining the social deficits of autism: The contribution of non-verbal communication measures. *Journal of Child Psychology and Psychiatry, 27*(5), 657–669.

Muñoz-Sandoval, A. F., Woodcock, R. W., McGrew, K. S., & Mather, N. (2005). *Batería III Woodcock-Muñoz*. Itasca, IL: Riverside.

NAGC. (2010). *Redefining giftedness for a new century: Shifting the paradigm*. Retrieved from https://www.nagc.org/sites/default/files/Position%20Statement/Redefining %20Giftedness%20for%20a%20New%20Century.pdf

Naglieri, J. A. (1985). *Matrix Analogies Test*. San Antonio, TX: The Psychological Corporation.

Naglieri, J. A. (1986). WISC-R and K-ABC comparison for matched samples of Black and White children. *Journal of School Psychology, 24*, 81–88.

Naglieri, J. A. (1997). *Naglieri Nonverbal Ability Test*. San Antonio, TX: The Psychological Corporation.

Naglieri, J. A. (1999). *Essentials of CAS assessment*. Hoboken, NJ: John Wiley.

Naglieri, J. A. (2005). The Cognitive Assessment System. In D. P. Flanagan & P. L. Harrison (Eds.), *Contemporary intellectual assessment* (2nd ed., pp. 441–460). New York, NY: Guilford Press.

Naglieri, J. A. (2007). *Naglieri Nonverbal Ability Test, Second Edition*. San Antonio, TX: The Psychological Corporation.

Naglieri, J. A. (2008a). Traditional IQ: 100 years of misconception and its relationship to minority representation in gifted programs. In J. VanTassel-Baska (Ed.), *Critical issues in equity and excellence in gifted education series: Alternative assessment of gifted learners* (pp. 67–88). Waco, TX: Prufrock Press.

Naglieri, J. A. (2008b). *Naglieri Nonverbal Ability Test* (2nd ed.). San Antonio, TX: Pearson.

Naglieri, J. A. (2011a). The discrepancy/consistency approach to SLD identification using the PASS theory. In D. P. Flanagan & V. C. Alfonso (Eds.), *Essentials of specific learning disability identification* (pp. 145–172). Hoboken, NJ: Wiley.

Naglieri, J. A. (2011b). Using the PASS theory to uncover disorders in basic psychology processes: An example of specific learning disability. In N. Mather & L. E. Jafe (Eds.), *Comprehensive evaluations: Case reports for psychologists, diagnosticians, and special educators* (pp. 137–140). New York, NY: Wiley.

Naglieri, J. A. (2012). Psychological assessment by school psychologists: Opportunities and challenges of a changing landscape. In K. Geisinger & B. A. Bracken (Eds.), *APA handbook of testing and assessment in psychology*. Washington, DC: APA.

Naglieri, J. A. (2014). *CAS2 online scoring and report system*. Austin, TX: Pro-Ed.

Naglieri, J. A. (2015). One hundred years of intelligence testing: Moving from traditional IQ to second-generation intelligence tests. In S. Goldstein, D. Princiotta, & J. A. Naglieri (Eds.), *Handbook of intelligence: Evolutionary theory, historical perspective, and current concepts* (pp. 295–316). New York, NY: Springer.

Naglieri, J. A. (2016a). Theoretical and practical considerations of the WISC-V. In A. S. Kaufman, D. Coalson, & S. Engi Raiford (Eds.), *Intelligent testing with the WISC-V* (pp. 663–668). Hoboken, NJ: Wiley.

Naglieri, J. A. (2016b). *Naglieri Nonverbal Ability Test* (3rd ed.). San Antonio, TX: Pearson.

Naglieri, J. A., Booth, A. & Winsler, A. (2004). Comparison of Hispanic children with and without limited english proficiency on the Naglieri Nonverbal Ability Test. *Psychological Assessment, 16*, 81–84.

Naglieri, J. A., & Bornstein, B. T. (2003). Intelligence and achievement: Just how correlated are they? *Journal of Psycheducational Assessment, 21*, 244–260.

Naglieri, J. A., Brulles, D., & Lansdowne, K. (2008). *Helping all gifted children learn: A teacher's guide to using the NNAT2*. San Antonio, TX: Pearson.

Naglieri, J. A., & Brunnert, K. (2009). Wechsler nonverbal scale of ability. In J. A. Naglieri & S. Goldstein (Eds.), *Practitioner's guide to assessing intelligence and achievement* (pp. 291–314). New York, NY: Wiley.

Naglieri, J. A., & Conway, C. (2009). The Cognitive Assessment System. In J. A. Naglieri & S. Goldstein (Eds.), *A practitioner's guide to assessment of intelligence and achievement* (pp. 3–10). New York, NY: Wiley.

Naglieri, J. A., & Das, J. P. (1997). *Cognitive Assessment System*. Itasca, IL: Riverside.

Naglieri, J. A., Das, J. P., & Goldstein, S. (2014a). *Cognitive Assessment System* (2nd ed.). Austin, TX: Pro-Ed.

Naglieri, J. A., Das, J. P., & Goldstein, S. (2014b). *Cognitive Assessment System* (2nd ed.): *Brief.* Austin, TX: ProEd.

Naglieri, J. A., Das, J. P., & Goldstein, S. (2014c). *Cognitive Assessment System* (2nd ed.): *Rating Scale.* Austin, TX: ProEd.

Naglieri, J. A., & Ford, D. Y. (2003). Addressing under-representation of gifted minority children using the Naglieri Nonverbal Ability Test (NNAT). *Gifted Child Quarterly, 47,* 155–160.

Naglieri, J. A., & Goldstein, S. (2009). Understanding the strengths and weaknesses of intelligence and achievement tests. In J. A. Naglieri & S. Goldstein. *Assessment of intelligence and achievement: A practitioner's guide* (pp. 3–10). New York, NY: Wiley.

Naglieri, J. A., & Goldstein, S. (2013). *Comprehensive Executive Function Inventory.* Toronto, Canada: MHS.

Naglieri, J. A., Goldstein, S., Delauder, B. Y., & Schwebach, A. (2006). WISC-III and CAS: Which correlates higher with achievement for a clinical sample? *School Psychology Quarterly, 21,* 62–76.

Naglieri, J. A., Goldstein, S., Iseman, J. S., & Schwebach, A. (2003). Performance of children with attention-deficit/hyperactivity disorder and anxiety/depression on the WISC-III and Cognitive Assessment System (CAS). *Journal of Psychoeducational Assessment, 21,* 32–42.

Naglieri, J. A., & Gottling, S. H. (1995). A cognitive education approach to math instruction for the learning disabled: An individual study. *Psychological Report, 76,* 1343–1354.

Naglieri, J. A., & Gottling, S. H. (1997). Mathematics instruction and PASS cognitive processes: An intervention study. *Journal of Learning Disabilities, 30,* 513–520.

Naglieri, J. A., & Johnson, D. (2000). Effectiveness of a cognitive strategy intervention to improve math calculation based on the PASS theory. *Journal of Learning Disabilities, 33,* 591–597.

Naglieri, J. A., & Kryza, K. M. (2015). *Measure of mindset.* Retrieved from http://www.jacknaglieri.com/think-smart-.html

Naglieri, J. A., Moreno, M. A., & Otero, T. M. (2017). *Cognitive Assessment System–2: Español manual de administración y calificación.* Austin, TX: Pro-Ed.

Naglieri, J. A., & Otero, T. (2011). Cognitive Assessment System: Redefining intelligence from a neuropsychological perspective. In A. Davis (Ed.), *Handbook of pediatric neuropsychology* (pp. 320–333). New York, NY: Springer.

Naglieri, J. A., & Otero, T. M. (2012). The Cognitive Assessment System: From theory to practice. In D. P. Flanagan & P. L. Harrison (Eds.), *Contemporary intellectual assessment: Theories, tests, and issues* (3rd ed., pp. 376–399). New York, NY: Guilford Press.

Naglieri, J. A., & Otero, T. M. (2014). The assessment of executive function using the Cognitive Assessment System. In S. Goldstein & J. A. Naglieri (Eds.), *Handbook of executive functioning* (2nd ed., pp. 191–208). New York, NY: Springer.

Naglieri, J. A., Otero, T., DeLauder, B., & Matto, H. (2007). Bilingual Hispanic children's performance on the English and Spanish versions of the Cognitive Assessment System. *School Psychology Quarterly, 22,* 432–448.

Naglieri, J. A., & Pickering, E. (2010). *Helping children learn: Intervention handouts for use in school and at home* (2nd ed.). Baltimore, MD: Brookes.

Naglieri, J. A., & Rojahn, J. (2001). Evaluation of African-American and White children in special education programs for children with mental retardation using the WISC-III and Cognitive Assessment System. *American Journal of Mental Retardation, 106,* 359–367.

Naglieri, J. A., & Rojahn, J. R. (2004). Validity of the PASS theory and CAS: Correlations with achievement. *Journal of Educational Psychology, 96,* 174–181.

Naglieri, J. A., Rojahn, J., & Matto, H. (2007). Hispanic and Non-Hispanic children's performance on PASS cognitive processes and achievement. *Intelligence, 35,* 568–579.

Naglieri, J. A., Rojahn, J. R., Matto, H. C., & Aquilino, S. A. (2005). Black-White differences in intelligence: A study of the PASS theory and Cognitive Assessment System. *Journal of Psychoeducational Assessment, 23,* 146–160.

Naglieri, J. A., & Ronning, M. E. (2000). Comparison of White, African-American, Hispanic, and Asian children on the Naglieri Nonverbal Ability Test. *Psychological Assessment, 12,* 328–334.

Naglieri, J. A., Taddei, S., & Williams, K. (2013). US and Italian children's performance on the Cognitive Assessment System: A cross cultural equivalence study. *Psychological Assessment, 25,* 157–166.

National Center for Education Statistics. (2013). Table 204.50. Children 3 to 21 years old served under Individuals with Disabilities Education Act (IDEA), Part B, by race/ethnicity and type of disability: 2010–11 and 2011–12. Retrieved from https://nces.ed.gov/programs/digest/d13/tables/dt13_204.50.asp

National Clearinghouse for English Language Acquisition. (2011, February). The growing numbers of English learner students, 1998/99-2008/09.

Noble, K. G., & McCandliss, B. D. (2005). Reading development and impairment: behavioral, social, and neurobiological factors. *Journal of Developmental and Behavioral Pediatrics, 26,* 370–378.

O'Donnell, L. (2009). The Wechsler intelligence scale for children. In J. A. Naglieri & S. Goldstein (Eds.), *A practitioner's guide to assessment of intelligence and achievement* (4th ed., pp. 153–190). New York, NY: Wiley.

Ortiz, S. O., & Melo, K. E. (2015). Evaluation of intelligence and learning disability with Hispanics. In Geisinger, K. F. (Ed). (2015). *Psychological testing of Hispanics: Clinical, cultural, and intellectual issues* (2nd ed., pp. 109–133). Washington, DC: American Psychological Association.

Otero, T. M. (2015). Intelligence: Defined as neurocognitive processing. In S. Goldstein, D. Princiotta, & J. A. Naglieri (Eds.), *Handbook of intelligence: Evolutionary theory, historical perspective, and current concepts* (pp. 193–208). New York, NY: Springer.

Otero, T. M., Gonzales, L., & Naglieri, J. A. (2012). The neurocognitive assessment of Hispanic English-language learners with reading problems. *Archives of Clinical Neuropsychology,* 1–9.

Otero, T. M., Gonzales, L., & Naglieri, J. A. (2013). The neurocognitive assessment of Hispanic English-language learners with reading failure. *Applied Neuropsychology: Child, 2*(1), 24–32.

Parrila, R. K., Das, J. P., Kendrick, M., Papadopoulos, T., & Kirby, J. (1999). Efficacy of a cognitive reading remediation program for at-risk children in grade 1. *Developmental Disabilities Bulletin, 27,* 1–31.

Peña, A. M. (2012). Perceptions of Spanish/English bilingual school psychologists regarding competency in assessment and future training needs. Retrieved from http://hdl.handle.net/1903/12611

Pickard, K. E., & Ingersoll, B. R. (2015). Brief report: High and low level initiations of joint attention, and response to joint attention; Differential relationships with language and imitation. *Journal of Autism and Developmental Disorders, 45*(1), 262–268.

Pressley, M., Ed., & Woloshyn, V. (Ed.). (1995). *Cognitive strategy instruction that really improves children's academic performance.* Cambridge, MA: Brookline Books.

Redmond, M. R., Mumford, M. D., & Teach, R. (1993). Putting creativity to work: Effects of leader behavior on subordinate creativity. *Organizational Behavior and Human Decision Processes, 55,* 120–151.

Reiter, A., Tucha, O., & Lange, K. W. (2005). Executive functions in children with dyslexia. *Dyslexia, 11,* 116–131.

Renzulli, J. S. (1978). What makes giftedness? Re-examining a definition. *Phi Delta Kappa, 60*, 180–181.

Reynolds, C. R. (1990). Conceptual and technical problems in learning disability diagnosis. In C. R. Reynolds & R. W. Kamphaus (Eds.), *Handbook of psychological & educational assessment of children: Intelligence & achievement* (pp. 571–592). New York, NY: Guilford Press.

Roid, G. H. (2003). *Stanford-Binet intelligence scales* (5th ed.). Itasca, IL: Riverside.

Sakurai, Y., Asami, M., & Mannen, T. (2010). Alexia and agraphia with lesions of the angular and supramarginal gyri: Evidence for the disruption of sequential processing. *Journal of the Neurological Sciences, 288*, 25–33.

Sandak, R., Mencl, W. E., Frost, S., Rueckl, J. G., Katz, L., Moore, D. L., & Pugh, K. R. (2004). The neurobiology of adaptive learning in reading: A contrast of different training conditions. *Cognitive, Affective, & Behavioral Neuroscience, 4*, 67–88.

Sattler, J. M. (1988). *Assessment of children* (3rd ed.). San Diego, CA: Jerome M. Sattler.

Sattler, J. M. (2008). *Assessment of children: Cognitive foundations* (5th ed.). La Mesa, CA: Jerome M. Sattler.

Savage, R. C., & Wolcott, G. F. (1994). Overview of acquired brain injury. In R. C. Savage & G. F. Wolcott (Eds.), *Educational dimensions of acquired brain injury* (pp. 3–12). Austin, TX: Pro-Ed.

Schalock, R. L., Borthwick-Duffy, S. A., Bradley, V. J., Buntinx, W. H., Coulter, D. L., Craig, E. M., ... Shogren, K. A. (2010). *Intellectual disability: Definition, classification, and systems of supports*. Washington, DC: American Association on Intellectual and Developmental Disabilities.

Scheid, K. (1993). *Helping Students Become Strategic Learners*. Cambridge, MA: Brookline Books.

Schofield, N. J., & Ashman, A. F. (1987). The cognitive processing of gifted, high average, and low average ability students. *British Journal of Educational Psychology, 57*(1), 9–20.

Schrank, F. A., McGrew, K. S., & Mather, N. (2014). *Woodcock-Johnson IV*. Rolling Meadow, IL: Riverside.

Sesma, H. W., Slomine, B. S., Ding, R., & McCarthy, M. L. (2008). Executive functioning in the first year after pediatric traumatic brain injury. *Pediatrics, 121*(6), e1686–e1695.

Shadmehr, R., Smith, M. A., & Krakauer, J. W. (2010). Error correction, sensory prediction, and adaptation in motor control. *Annual Review Neuroscience, 33*, 89–108.

Shapiro, S. M. (2003). Bilirubin toxicity in the developing nervous system. *Pediatric Neurology, 29*(5), 410–421.

Shapiro, S. M., & Popelka, G. R. (2011). Auditory impairment in infants at risk for bilirubin-induced neurologic dysfunction. *Seminars in Perinatology, 35*, 162–170.

Shaywitz, S. (2003). *Overcoming dyslexia: A new and complete science-based program for reading problems at any level*. New York, NY: Random House.

Shifrer, D., Muller, C., & Callahan, R. (2011). Disproportionality and learning disabilities: Parsing apart race, socioeconomic status, and language. *Journal of Learning Disabilities, 44*(3), 246–257.

Sigman, M., Ruskin, E., Arbelle, S., Corona, R., Dissanayake, C., Espinosa, M., ... Robinson, B. (1999). Continuity and change in the social competence of children with autism, down syndrome, and developmental delays. *Monographs of the Society for Research in Child Development, 64*(1), 1–139.

Solso, R. L., & Hoffman, C. A. (1991). Influence of Soviet scholars. *American Psychologist, 46*, 251–253.

Soorani-Lunsing, I., Woltil, H. A., & Hadders-Algra, M. (2001). Are moderate degrees of hyperbilirubinemia in healthy term neonates really safe for the brain? *Pediatric Research, 50*, 701–705.

Sotelo-Dynega, M., Ortiz, S. O., Flanagan, D. P., & Chaplin, W. F. (2013). English language proficiency and test performance: An evaluation of bilingual students with the Woodcock-Johnson III tests of cognitive abilities. *Psychology in the Schools, 50,* 781–797.

Stanley, G. C., & Konstantareas, M. M. (2007). Symbolic play in children with autism spectrum disorder. *Journal of Autism and Developmental Disorders, 37*(7), 1215–1223.

Styck, K. M., & Watkins, M. W. (2013). Diagnostic utility of the Culture-Language Interpretive Matrix for the Wechsler Intelligence Scales for Children–Fourth Edition among referred students. *School Psychology Review, 42,* 367–382.

Suzuki, L. A., & Valencia, R. R. (1997). Race/ethnicity and measured intelligence. *American Psychologist, 52,* 1103–1114.

Taddei, S., & Venditti, F. (2010). The evaluation of cognitive processes in attention-deficit/hyperactivity disorder. *Psichiatria dell'infanzia e dell'adolescenza, 77,* 305–319.

The Center for Workforce Studies Report (July 2015). (2016, March). Retrieved September 24, 2016 from http://www.apa.org/workforce/index.aspx

US Census Bureau. (2012). American community survey. Retrieved from http://factfinder.census.gov/faces/tableservices/jsf/pages/productview.xhtml?pid=ACS_12_1YR_DP02&prodType=table

Valdés, G., & Figueroa, R. A. (1994). *Bilingualism and testing: A special case of bias.* Norwood, MA: Ablex.

Wasserman, J. D., & Becker, K. A. (2000 August). Racial and ethnic group mean score differences on intelligence tests. In J. A. Naglieri (Chair), Making assessment more fair: Taking verbal and achievement out of ability tests. Symposium conducted at the annual meeting of the American Psychological Association, Washington, DC.

Wechsler, D. (1991). *Wechsler intelligence scale for children* (3rd ed.). San Antonio, TX: The Psychological Corporation.

Wechsler, D. (2003). *Wechsler intelligence scale for children* (4th ed.). San Antonio, TX: The Psychological Corporation.

Wechsler, D. (2012). *Wechsler Preschool and Primary Scale of Intelligence* (4th ed.). San Antonio, TX: Pearson.

Wechsler, D. (2014). *Wechsler Intelligence Scale for Children* (5th ed.). San Antonio: Pearson.

Wechsler, D. (2015). *Wechsler Individual Achievement Test* (2nd ed.). San Antonio, TX: Pearson.

Wechsler, D., Coalson, D. L., & Raiford, S. E. (2008). *WAIS-IV: Wechsler Adult Intelligence scale.* San Antonio, TX: Pearson.

Wechsler, D., & Naglieri, J. A. (2006). *Wechsler Nonverbal Scale of Ability.* San Antonio, TX: Pearson.

Weiss, L. G., Muñoz, M. R., & Prifitera, A. (2015). Testing Hispanics with WISC-V and WISC-IV Spanish. WISC-V Assessment and Interpretation. *Scientist-Practitioner Perspectives, 215.*

Wendling, B. J., Mather, N., & Shrank, F. A. (2009). Woodcock-Johnson III tests of cognitive abilities. In J. A. Naglieri & S. Goldstein (Eds.), *A practitioner's guide to assessment of intelligence and achievement* (pp. 191–232). New York, NY: Wiley.

Weyandt, L. L., Willis, W. G., Swentosky, A., Wilson, K., Janusis, G. M., Chung, H. J., ... Marshall, S. (2014). A review of the use of executive function tasks in externalizing and internalizing disorders. In S. Goldstein & J. A. Naglieri (Eds.), *Handbook of Executive Functioning* (pp. 69–88). New York, NY: Springer.

Wong, T. T., Ho, C. S., & Tang, J. (2015). Defective number sense or impaired access? Differential impairments in different subgroups of children with mathematics difficulties. *Journal of Learning Disabilities, 8,* 1–13.

Woodcock, R. W., & Johnson, M. B. (1989). *Woodcock-Johnson psycho-educational battery–Revised*. Chicago, IL: Riverside.

Woodcock, R. W., McGrew, K. S., & Mather, N. (2001). *Woodcock-Johnson® III NU tests of achievement*. Boston, MA: Houghton Mifflin Harcourt.

World Health Organization (WHO). (2014, March). Comprehensive and coordinated efforts for the management of autism spectrum disorders. Paper presented at the Sixty-Seventh World Health Assembly. Provisional Agenda Item 13.4. Geneva, Switzerland: Author.

Yeates, K. O., Swift, E., Taylor, H. G., Wade, S. L., Drotar, D., Stancin, T., & Minich, N. (2004). Short- and long-term social outcomes following pediatric traumatic brain injury. *Journal of the international neuropsychological society, 10*, 412–426.

Yoakum, C. (1921). *Memoirs of the National Academy of Sciences, Vol. XV: Psychological examining in the United States Army*. Washington, DC: Goverment Printing Office.

Yoakum, C., & Yerkes, R. M. (1920). *Army mental tests*. New York, NY: Holt and Company.

Zirkel, P. A., & Thomas, L. B. (2010). State laws for RTI: An updated snapshot. *Teaching Exceptional Children, 42,* 56–63.

Zong, J., & Batalova, J. (2016, April 16). *Frequently Requested Statistics on Immigrants and Immigration in the United States*. Retrieved September 09, 2016, from http://www.migrationpolicy.org/article/frequently-requested-statistics-immigrants-and-immigration-united-states

About the Authors

Jack A. Naglieri, PhD, is a Research Professor at the Curry School of Education at the University of Virginia and Senior Research Scientist at the Devereux Center for Resilient Children. He holds a Diplomate in Assessment Psychology, was licensed as a School Psychologist in Virginia and Ohio, and had School Psychology certifications in New York, Georgia, Arizona, and Ohio. Dr. Naglieri has focused his efforts on theoretical and psychometric issues concerning intelligence, cognitive interventions, specific learning disabilities, ADHD, autism, emotional disorders, gifted identification, and fair assessment. Dr. Naglieri is the author of more than 300 scholarly papers, book chapters, books, and tests and has authored *Essentials of CAS Assessment, Assessment of Cognitive Processes: The PASS Theory, Helping Children Learn: Intervention Handouts, Essentials of WNV Assessment,* and *Helping All Gifted Children Learn.* Dr. Naglieri developed more than 30 tests and rating scales including the Cognitive Assessment System (1997), the Naglieri Nonverbal Ability Test, Second Edition (2008), and the Naglieri Nonverbal Ability Test (2016), Comprehensive Inventory of Executive Function (2012), and the Devereux Early Childhood Assessment for Preschoolers, Second Edition (2012). His most recent publications include the Cognitive Assessment System, Second Edition (2014), Cognitive Assessment System, Second Edition—Spanish (2017), CAS2: Brief (2014), and CAS2: Rating Scale (2014).

Tulio M. Otero, PhD, is an Associate Professor in the School and Clinical Psychology programs at the Chicago School of Professional Psychology. He received his postdoctoral diploma in Clinical Neuropsychology from Fielding University. He is also a practicing School Neuropsychologist working with a variety of age groups, concerns, and disabilities.

Dr. Otero has presented at national and international conferences on neurocognitive assessment and interventions based on PASS theory and the CAS2, the assessment of executive function and intervention, the fair assessment of Hispanics, cultural competency, and has published several papers and chapters on these topics. He has served as past president of the Hispanic Neuropsychological Society and is on the editorial review boards of the *Journal of Attention*

Disorders, Journal of Hispanics in Higher Education, and *Revista de Neuropsicología, Neuropsiquiatría y Neurociencias.* Dr. Otero is co-author of the Spanish edition of the *Cognitive Assessment System 2* and *Essentials of CAS2 Assessment.*

Additionally, Dr. Otero is a martial artist with a fourth-degree black belt ranking in Tae Kwon Do and hapkido. He uses the basic tenets of these martial art forms to motivate and change the mind-sets that limit his students and clients.

INDEX